M000190526

Your

Life's Plan

for

Abundance

A Course in Abundance, vol 3

Your

Life's Plan

for

Abundance

KIM MICHAELS

Copyright © 2014 Kim Michaels. All rights reserved. No part of this book may be used, reproduced, translated, electronically stored or transmitted by any means except by written permission from the publisher. A reviewer may quote brief passages in a review.

MORE TO LIFE PUBLISHING

www.morepublish.com

For foreign and translation rights,

contact info@ morepublish.com

ISBN: 978-9949-518-59-3

Series ISBN: 978-9949-518-53-1

The information and insights in this book should not be considered as a form of therapy, advice, direction, diagnosis, and/or treatment of any kind. This information is not a substitute for medical, psychological, or other professional advice, counseling and care. All matters pertaining to your individual health should be supervised by a physician or appropriate health-care practitioner. No guarantee is made by the author or the publisher that the practices described in this book will yield successful results for anyone at any time. They are presented for informational purposes only, as the practice and proof rests with the individual.

For more information:
www.ascendedmasterlight.com

www.transcendencetoolbox.com

CONTENTS

HOW TO USE THIS BOOK

The idea behind *A Course in Abundance* is to give you effective tools for shifting your consciousness. Many spiritual books give you understanding, and while this may be inspiring, it does not necessarily lead to practical change. The books in this course contain a unique combination of teachings and techniques for invoking spiritual light. The combination of teachings and exercises has the potential to help you go through a real transformation that will bring you to a higher level of your personal path.

The teachings and tools in this course are given by the universal spiritual teachers of humankind, also known as the ascended masters. The teachings in this course were given as direct, spoken dictations by an ascended master known as Mother Mary. She holds the Office of the Divine Mother for all people embodying on earth. The exercises invoke both Mother Mary and seven other representatives of the Divine Mother and eight representatives of the Divine Father. If you are not familiar with the ascended masters and their teachings, it is recommended that you read the book *The Power of Self,* which explains who the masters are, how they can help you and how you can follow the path to self-mastery offered by the masters. You can also find information on the website:

www.ascendedmasterlight.com. The invocations following each chapter are meant to be read aloud by you. You can read them in a slow, meditative way or you can give them faster and with more power in your voice. There is no one right way to give the invocations, but they obviously cannot work unless you read them aloud. If you desire more detailed instructions for how to give invocations, please visit the website: *www.transcendencetoolbox.com.* You might also find it helpful to give the invocations along with a recording. You can purchase and download sound files of the invocations from the website: *www.morepublish.com.*

It is suggested that you start using this book by studying the first chapter and then giving the first invocation at least once, but preferably once a day for nine consecutive days. You can then move on to the second chapter and so on until you have worked through all eight chapters and invocations. Once you are familiar with the teachings, you do not have to read the chapter before giving an invocation, yet you will probably find that reading at least part of a chapter helps you get more out of giving the invocation. You can also do a longer ritual of giving each invocation up to 33 times.

Depending on your speed, it takes 15-25 minutes to give one invocation. This means you can give all eight invocations (one after the other) in around two hours, which is a very powerful ritual. You do not have to give the opening prayer or the sealing with each invocation. You give an opening prayer when you start and the sealing after you finish the last invocation.

Feel free to be creative in the use of the tools included in this course. For example, you can give the matrix for another person or persons, even for the healing of the collective consciousness.

If you make the effort to overcome your initial resistance and build a momentum on giving the invocations, you will likely find that it is one of the most powerful and effective spiritual tools you have ever used. By combining this tool with a willingness to look into your own psyche and let go of limiting beliefs, you can turn your life into an upward spiral that will expand your ability to manifest spiritual and material abundance. Truly, as the masters say, everything revolves around your free will. If you can accept that transcendence is possible for you, then the results *will* be manifest for you. Invoke, and ye shall receive.

Please be aware that this course is a very special gift from the heart of the Divine Mother. The words in the course are given as direct dictation, meaning that they contain subtle keys to unlocking your understanding. You will not get the full benefit from the course by reading it with the intellectual, linear mind. The course is designed to unlock your intuition, your inner mystical knowing, and thereby reconnect you to what you already know deep within your being. Studying the course can be approached as a process of worshiping the Divine Mother. If you approach the course with reverence, you will attain greater benefits. You can use the course in a variety of ways, including using it as a meditative or contemplative tool. It is a powerful exercise to read the dictations aloud. It is perfectly valid to use it on your own, studying the dictations and giving the invocations. Yet it will give an accelerated benefit to use the course in a group setting. The course is not owned or controlled by any organization so it can be used freely by formal or informal groups. There is great benefit in a group of people meeting on a regular basis, studying and discussing one chapter and giving the corresponding invocation. Whenever two or three are gathered in the name of the Divine Mother, there she is in the midst of them.

Please note that for practical reasons, it has been necessary to publish this course in three separate books. In order to get maximum results, it is important that you follow the course in the order it was given. It is highly recommended that you start by working through Volume 1, then Volume 2 and finally Volume 3.

1 | YOUR HIGHEST
POTENTIAL

My beloved heart, in the previous chapter [See Volume 2] I explained to you the process whereby everything in the material universe has been brought into manifestation. I explained that everything starts as a general idea in the identity realm, is then lowered as a more specific idea in the mental realm, becomes even more specific and receives momentum and direction in the emotional realm and then manifests as an actual form or action in the material realm.

I promised to make this teaching more practical, and I will do so in this chapter by applying it to the question of how you can manifest the abundant life for yourself and for all life on this planet. Let us begin by talking about a topic that is an essential part of the manifestation of the abundant life, namely your creative power, your actual power to bring things into manifestation. If you have studied any of the prosperity teachings found on this planet, you will know that many of them stress the importance of having a goal, having a clear vision for what you want to accomplish. This is a very important part of manifesting the abundant life, for truly, as the Bible says: "Where there is no vision, the people perish" (Proverbs 29:18). If you have no idea what you want to manifest, how can you possibly bring it into manifestation, especially when you consider my teaching that everything is made from the Mother Light that has taken on a certain form because of an image that was imposed upon it by a self-aware mind. You might have heard about the concept of making a treasure map, which is simply a collage of pictures that illustrates what you want to see manifest in your life, such as greater material wealth, a nice house to live in or any other conditions. This is indeed one valid approach to manifesting abundance but it does have certain limitations. You can have the best possible vision without having the power to bring it into manifestation. The power aspect is what I will focus on in this chapter, and then we will later talk about how to purify your vision and have the highest vision for your creative potential.

***

The true key to manifesting the abundant life is to allow the pure light of God to flow through your four lower bodies. If the light can flow through unhindered and undiluted, God's abundant life *will* be manifest in your material circumstances. If your four lower bodies are indeed pure, the light of God will flow through them without being diluted in the process. As an example of a person who had this purity in his four lower bodies, look at the life of Jesus. Jesus had reached a level of attainment where he knew that he was not acting on his own power. He was not acting exclusively by using his physical body. He was not even acting exclusively by using psychic energy, energy that was brought into the identity, the mental or the emotional realm. Jesus knew that he of his own self could do nothing (John 5:30) because it was the Father within him who was doing the work (John 5:17). The Father within him was his I AM Presence and the light of God. He knew that without using the pure light of God, he could accomplish nothing of value, nothing of timeless significance.

By coming to this recognition, Jesus opened up and purified his four lower bodies whereby the light of God could flow through them and be directed by his outer mind. His mind, of course, was in perfect alignment with the divine plan for his mission in that incarnation. Jesus did indeed use all of his four lower bodies when he brought things into manifestation. Take for example the situation of Jesus raising Lazarus from the dead (John 11:1). Jesus does not even enter the tomb. He stays outside the tomb, he gathers all his concentration, and then he exclaims: "Lazarus, come forth!" (John 11:43). When Jesus said that, he did not speak softly. He was not speaking a prayer, he was not making a request. He was indeed taking dominion over his four lower bodies and with the full force of his total being, he was issuing a command. This command had all the power and intensity of his physical voice. His voice was infused with the intensity of his emotions, his unconditional love for Lazarus. His emotions were a perfect expression of the pure vision of Lazarus' awakening and healing that he held in his mental body. Jesus knew with absolute certainty that it was indeed possible for the power of God to re-infuse a dead body with life. His mental body was empowered by the sense of identity that came from knowing that he was a son of God, a co-creator with God, who was here to bring the abundant life into manifestation in the material universe. As Jesus said: "I am come that they might have life, and that they might have it more abundantly" (John 10:10).

Because Jesus' four lower bodies were pure, the power of God could flow through them and awaken the cells and atoms of the body of Lazarus, clear them of the imperfect thought-forms of disease and make it possible for his soul to reenter

his body, which was now purified of all infirmity. I am aware
that many people in today's world, even many Christians, ignore
Jesus' miracles or reject them as being superstition. They were
not the products of the imagination, nor were they the addi-
tions of the Gospel writers seeking to build Jesus up as a miracle
worker. They were indeed real, and they were the products of
the fact that Jesus had purified his four lower bodies so that the
power of God could flow through them in full force. Through
Jesus, the power of God could accomplish things that seemed
miraculous to people in a normal state of consciousness. They
were not miraculous, they were simply the higher spiritual law
brought into action in the material universe, thereby superseding
the material laws and their limitations.

Let me give you a sense of co-measurement of the power
of God that is possible for anyone who will walk the path of
Christhood that Jesus demonstrated. Again, consider Jesus'
statement: "He that believeth on me, the works that I do shall
he do also; and greater works than these shall he do" (John
14:12). Do you think Jesus was making an empty promise here?
So many Christians have ignored this statement. I can assure you
that this statement describes the fact that every human being on
earth has a Christ potential. If you are willing to follow the path
taken by Jesus, the path of overcoming the mortal self, of slaying
the dragon of the mortal self, you can indeed do the works that
Jesus did. God can do the same works through *you* that God did
through Jesus. When the power of God flows undiluted through
your four lower bodies, there is no limitation to what God can
do.

The dualistic mind springs from a sense of separation from
your source, from your own higher Being and God. Due to this
separation, you do not believe God can work through you, and
thus you are denying God the ability to work through you. The
dualistic beliefs that have accumulated in your four lower bodies

block the flow of God's light, and therefore your creative powers are reduced to a mere fraction of their true potential. You were designed to have the power of God flowing through your four lower bodies, and in their purified form, those bodies can hold the immense power demonstrated by Jesus. When you descend into the consciousness of separation and duality, the power can no longer flow. You now begin to believe that you are the doer, that you are acting on your own power and that you can act independently of God and God's light. Everything is made from the Ma-ter Light so you can do nothing without God's light. The only question is whether you are acting on the pure light of God or light that has been brought into a lower frequency spectrum.

This is a subtle distinction that has been overlooked by most people, even many spiritual gurus. When your sense of identity is centered around the physical body, you can act only by using the energies that vibrate within the material frequency spectrum. Because your consciousness cannot see beyond that spectrum, you can see no connection between material energy and God. You cannot see that even physical matter is made from the light of God that has been lowered in vibration and has taken on a specific form. You do not see God as the single cause behind the myriad manifestations. Due to the dualistic lies programmed into your mind by the mortal self and the prince of this world, you deny God's presence where you are. This denial forms a block so that God cannot work through you—because God never violates his own Law of Free Will. When you overcome the illusion of separation by letting the mind of Christ be in you, you realize that you – meaning the outer mind and mortal self – are not the doer. Everything is done with God's energy so God is always the ultimate cause. You can continue to maintain the illusion of separation whereby you confine yourself to a mere fraction of your true creative potential. Doing this is a choice and not some condition put upon you by an angry God. One might say that it *is* a condition put upon you by an angry god, namely the false god – the angry being in the sky – created by the prince of this world and the collective consciousness of humankind. When you begin to grasp the truth of Christ, you see that you have the potential to reclaim your original mission of being a co-creator with the real God, the inner God who longs to see you co-create the abundant life he envisions for you. Jesus came to set all people free from the limitations of their mortal selves and the dualistic reasoning that limits God's power and prevents God from working through them.

***

Everything is vibration, everything is energy. Your scientists measure the vibration of energy by counting the cycles per second of the energy wave, which is turned into a unit of measurement called Hertz. I am not saying that the numbers I give you here are necessarily the actual numbers that apply. I am simply giving you an example to show you the proportions and the differences between what is truly possible and what is the current reality for most people on earth. Everything in the four levels of the material universe is made of energy that vibrates at a certain frequency. Let us say that as the pure light of God enters the material frequency spectrum in the highest level of the identity realm, it vibrates at a frequency of 100,000 Hz, or cycles per second. It is a natural function of your identity body that it crystallizes the fluid energies of God into a more specific image of what you want to create in the material universe. As you do so, your identity body lowers the frequency of the energy. In an ideal scenario, the energies are lowered to the frequency of 75,000 Hz, after which they flow into the mental realm, the mental frequency spectrum. Your thoughts then take the overall blueprint created in your identity body and they make it even more specific whereby it is again lowered in frequency until it reaches the vibration of 50,000 Hz. At that frequency, it flows into the highest level of the emotional realm. Your emotions then make the plans of your thoughts even more specific and give them a clear direction. This lowers the energies to a frequency of 25,000 Hz, after which they enter the material realm, the material frequency spectrum.

The matter realm, the matter frequency spectrum, ranges in vibration from 1 to 25,000 Hz. This means that, in an ideal scenario, your conscious mind will be co-creating by directing light that vibrates at a frequency of 25,000 Hz or slightly below that mark. Everything in the material universe is created from the Ma-ter Light that is stirred into vibration by the creative force of the Father. That creative force was flowing through Jesus when he awakened Lazarus from the dead. It was the creative power of God that was streaming through his four lower bodies and therefore acted upon the Ma-ter Light that made up the cells and molecules of Lazarus' body. Because it could flow undiluted, the power of God entered the material realm at the maximum vibration of 25,000 Hz whereby it had the power to re-infuse light into the dead cells of Lazarus' body.

It is actually possible for a human being to have the power of directing light at a frequency of 25,000 Hz. This is the highest creative potential of a human being on earth. If you consider that the Ma-ter Light is like an ocean and the way you manifest things in the material universe is by stirring the ocean of the Ma-ter Light, then it becomes obvious that the more power you can put behind your efforts, the bigger the waves you can create and therefore the more power you have to bring things into manifestation.

For the sake of comparison, let us say that Jesus' power to bring things into manifestation came from the fact that his conscious mind could actually hold and direct light that vibrated at a frequency of 25,000 Hz. This is significant because if you can direct a light wave of a very high frequency at a light wave of a much lower frequency, you can raise the vibration of the low-frequency light. When Jesus awakened Lazarus, he directed a light wave of a very high frequency into the light waves that made up Lazarus' body. Even though these light waves had descended to a very low vibration, namely the vibration of inert matter, Jesus' power was so immense that it could change the vibration of those low-frequency waves. They again began vibrating at a level that would support conscious life, and this re-infused life into Lazarus' body, making it possible for his soul to reenter the body. If *you* had that power, you could re-infuse life into your current financial situation and overcome any limitation you face.

Jesus' creative power was at the level of 25,000 Hz. This was the level of his consciousness, caused by the fact that his four lower bodies were pure and could therefore serve as the conduits, as the transformers, for the maximum amount of power. In order to give you a sense of comparison, the average individual on planet earth today is not able, with his or her conscious mind, to direct light that vibrates at a frequency over 1,000 Hz. Many people cannot hold light in their minds that vibrates above 500 Hz. This illustrates the immense difference between the creative power of the average person and the creative power of Jesus. I am not trying to put Jesus on a pedestal. On the contrary, I am trying to help you accept your true potential by referring to Jesus as an example of a person who did not limit God's ability to work through him. You might look at the difference and think you could not possible bridge the gap between your present level of awareness and the consciousness of Jesus. This is an illusion because your four lower bodies were designed to hold light of the vibrations I have described. Even if you cannot yet conceive of wielding the power demonstrated by Jesus, consider what would happen if you doubled your current level of power. That goal should seem attainable to everyone, and it would provide an obvious boost to your efforts to bring the abundant life into manifestation. I am providing you with two goals. One is the highest potential, and the other is an intermediate goal. Strive to double your current power, and then use that as a springboard for even greater achievement.

Many scientists say that human beings are currently using five to ten percent of their brain capacity. If you take an appliance that is built for 220 Volt and plug it into a 110 Volt outlet, the appliance will not work because there simply is not enough power to run it. There are centers in your brain that are designed to work with energies of a higher frequency, meaning that your physical brain is designed to be a conduit for energies up to the 25,000 Hz. If there are no energies of that frequency entering your physical brain from your emotional body, those brain centers will lie dormant because there is not enough power to activate them. The higher brain functions are simply lying dormant in most human beings. If you are to truly manifest the abundant life, you need to purify your four lower bodies so that you can get back to the natural state, which is that the power of God can flow through your four lower bodies without being diluted and reduced below the natural level of vibration. As you purify your four lower bodies, more and more high-frequency energy will reach your conscious mind, and therefore you will increase your creative powers.

***

What is it that reduces the amount of power that reaches your conscious mind? The cause is that you have blocks in the four levels of your mind, in your etheric, mental and emotional bodies and in your physical mind—what some psychologists call your subconscious mind. These blocks will either stop the light from flowing through those bodies or reduce its vibration and thereby diminish its power. It is possible to have blocks in all levels of the lower mind, and this is indeed the case for most people on planet earth. For most people, the real problem is the blocks they have in their identity bodies. If a person believes that he or she is a mortal, human being, limited to the powers of the physical body, and if that belief is ingrained in the person's identity body, the light of God streaming through that person's identity body will be reduced in vibration far beyond the natural reduction from 100,000 to 75,000 Hz. Most people on earth have beliefs in their identity bodies that reduce the vibration of the light of God from 100,000 to below 2,000 Hz.

What keeps you alive, what keeps your four lower bodies functioning, is that the light of God is streaming through them. The pure light of God enters your identity body at a vibration of 100,000 Hz. If your identity body reduces that vibration to 2,000 Hz, your creative powers are reduced drastically right from the beginning. Before the energy even enters your mental body, it has been reduced to a very low level so your thoughts are already limited in their capacity. Your thoughts will reduce the vibration of the light further, and therefore it enters your emotional body at a much lower vibration than is natural. This reduces the power of your emotions, which are meant to give direction and momentum to the design of your thoughts. As I explained in the example of Jesus raising Lazarus, it takes energy of a certain frequency to re-infuse light into dead cells. If that frequency is not available to your emotional body and your conscious mind, is it any wonder that your goals are not being manifest? Is it any wonder that the cells of your physical body gradually become unable to hold the life force and therefore manifest disease or old age? Disease, old age and physical death are caused in part by a reduction in the power of the light that reaches the frequency spectrum of your physical body. The body eventually atrophies and can no longer function properly or even survive. Most people on this planet have reduced their creative powers so much that they only have enough light flowing through their four lower bodies to keep them alive. That is why so many people feel that their lives are a struggle, as if they are barely surviving. They are barely surviving because there is barely enough light flowing through their four lower bodies to keep their physical bodies and their conscious minds functioning.

It is like an appliance to which the electricity has been reduced to the point where the appliance is barely able to turn. Imagine a washing machine that turns so slowly that it takes two days to do a load of laundry. You would say that something has to be wrong with that washing machine, but because most people have never experienced their true potential, have never seen any human being function at their true potential, they think their state of reduced power is normal. They think this is unavoidable, they think this *is* their true potential. In reality, it is so far below their true potential that a spiritual teacher like myself sometimes feel like wringing my hands in despair, especially when I hear people talk as if their current state of struggle is normal, natural, unavoidable or perhaps even intended by God.

This is almost unbelievable, and it more than anything demonstrates what can happen when people descend into the duality consciousness and lose all sense of connection to the reality of the Christ mind. The reality of the Christ mind is that you have the capacity to work with light that vibrates at 25,000 Hz. Your current level of creative power might be that you cannot work with light above 1,000 Hz, which is only four percent of your full potential. If you knew and truly believed that it was possible for you to increase your creative power to the same level that Jesus demonstrated, you would obviously be making an effort to increase your creative power. When people deny their potential to exercise this creative power, it can only

be because they have become so entrapped in the duality consciousness that they have lost all sense of co-measurement. They
have lost the Christ standard, which demonstrates that there is
an alternative to their current struggle and misery. Consider the
irony that so many Christians revere Jesus yet see him as the
only son of God and thus the only person who could reach
that level of creative power. The main purpose of Jesus' mission
was to demonstrate the level of creative power that is normal
and natural for all human beings. This is a complete perversion
of the true intent behind Jesus' mission, and since it directly
opposes the mission of Christ, it can have come from only one
place, namely the mind of anti-christ. Only the mind of anti-
christ could have destroyed the example of Jesus by turning him
into an idol and putting him on a pedestal that sets him outside
the reach of any human being.

My beloved, can you sense my compassion and my passion
about this? I have so many human beings who pray to me daily
and give my rosaries. They pray to me as if I were a genie in a
bottle. When they give a rosary, I am supposed to jump out of
the bottle and solve their problems for them. God has given you
free will and I do not have the authority, nor do I have the desire,
to override it. I cannot uncreate what you have created because
it is *your* job to do so, which is the only way you can learn from
your past decisions and thus overcome your limited self-image.
How could you become a self-sufficient spiritual being by me
solving all of your problems for you? What I *can* do for you
is to show you the way to increase your creative power so that
you can – through the power of God within you – overcome
the sense of struggle. You can replace all your struggles with an
upward spiral that comes from multiplying the talents given to
you by God. This is what I *can* do for you, but it requires you
to get out of the passive approach of praying and then passively
waiting for me to do the work for you. You have to take the

active approach. Rather than praying for me to solve your problems *for* you, you have to pray to me and say: "Mother Mary, show me how to increase my creative powers so that the power of God within me can remove this limitation." *That* I can do; *that* I *will* do—if you will only open your mind and heart to my inner guidance and to the inner guidance of your Christ self. We are ready to show you how you take the next step that leads you up the spiral staircase until you once again get to the top of the staircase and can see the light of your I AM Presence shining through your four lower bodies. That light can stream through your lower bodies and create, in the material realm, what seems like miracles to the dualistic mind. *This* is my desire, *this* is my passion.

***

How do we begin this process of purifying your four lower bodies? Let me start by giving you a more detailed understanding of how the four lower bodies serve to transform light into physical appearances. Let us say that you have come to the conclusion that you want to manifest more abundance in your life and you have decided to take an active approach. You have studied certain teachings on how to use the power of your mind to attract more abundance. You have adopted a positive mental attitude, defined a clear vision and have created a treasure map of what you want. You are now daily engaging in a ritual of focusing your attention on the vision of what you want to accomplish, using affirmations or prayers to create a wave of energy that is supposed to manifest for you, or attract to you, what you envision. Many people have taken this approach to bringing abundance into their lives, although the specific steps they have taken might be different than what I describe here. I am not saying that this is not a valid approach; I am only saying that I want you to understand what needs to happen for this approach to work. The universe is a mirror so if you send out a wave of positive energy, crystallized around a specific vision, that vision should eventually be reflected back to you by the cosmic mirror as physical circumstances. While this is true, we can now gain a more in-depth picture of the process. Before the energy can be returned to you as physical circumstances, it must pass through the four levels of the material universe, including your own lower bodies. If there is anything – at any of those levels – that will neutralize your positive energy or counteract your abundant vision, the power of your effort might be reduced or entirely blocked. If you are a house divided against yourself, you have certain beliefs or misqualified energies in your identity, mental, emotional or subconscious mind that counteract the vision you have formed with your conscious mind. Unless you remove those blocks, your efforts simply will not be successful. You can keep sending out positive energy from the level of the conscious mind, but it is all neutralized at the higher levels of your own mind. It never cycles back down to the matter realm in the form of the circumstances you desire.

I have so far given you a fairly linear image of your four lower bodies. I have said that the light of God first streams into your identity body and is gradually reduced in vibration, after which it flows into the mental, then the emotional and then finally into the physical body. I am sure that many who read this teaching will see this as a linear process with the light flowing along a straight line. This means that there would be a gap between your conscious mind and your identity body. In reality, life is not linear but far more spherical and interdependent. In order to give you a different image – yet still a linear image – let me ask you to consider the face of a clock. The 12 o'clock line represents the highest level of your identity body. The light first enters your four lower bodies at the 12 o'clock line. If you draw a line from the 12 to the 6, you divide the face of the clock into two halves. If you draw another line from the 3 to the 9, you divide the circle of the clock into four quadrants. Now imagine that each of these quadrants of the circle represents one of your four lower bodies. The first quadrant, between the 12 and the 3 o'clock line, represents your identity body, and the light first flows to the 1 and then on to the 3. It then enters your mental body, flows from the 3 to the 6, enters your emotional body and flows beyond the 9 where it enters your physical body, or rather your physical mind. As the light flows from the 10 to the 11 and then beyond, what happens? You close the circle and you are now back at the 12, which means that your conscious mind is not separated from your identity body by some chasm or gap. Your four lower bodies are interconnected, and a more correct image than even the face of the clock would be that your identity body forms a sphere, your mental body forms a smaller sphere that exists inside the larger sphere of your identity body, and so on to your physical mind. Your conscious mind is a smaller sphere inside the greater spheres of the other levels of the mind.

Imagine that you start at the level of your conscious mind and create a vision for the abundance you want to manifest in your life. You then use affirmations and prayers to infuse that vision with energy. In order for the energy that you send out to be reflected back to you by the cosmic mirror as the physical circumstances you envision, it has to first flow through the four levels of the material universe. For each level it flows through, your vision must pass through the filter of the beliefs you hold in that level of your mind. It can potentially be blocked or distorted by those beliefs, and the power of the energy can be reduced by any imperfect energies stored in your higher mind. For example, if your etheric body holds the image that you are a miserable sinner who does not deserve God's abundance, your conscious vision can be completely neutralized by this belief before it even starts to descend towards physical manifestation. The beliefs at each level serve as a frame of reference for deciding whether the impulse should be acted upon, whether it should be sent on to the next level. As you send a vision from the conscious mind, it first passes through your identity body. If you have a belief in that body which says your vision cannot be manifest, it will obviously go no further.

***

When you create a vision of abundance, that vision will not become manifest unless it goes beyond the physical level. If your sense of identity is completely confined to the physical mind and the physical body, you can only work with the energies in the matter realm. Your vision of what you want to accomplish cannot go beyond the level of energy that you can manipulate with your physical body and outer mind. How can your efforts to visualize abundance accomplish anything beyond what you are already capable of doing with your physical body?

When you open yourself to using the power of vision, you are sending an energy impulse that goes beyond the physical body. You are now believing that there must be more to life than the matter realm, there must be a higher way to manifest abundance than what you can do with the body. You generate an energy impulse that goes from your conscious mind into your identity body. If that energy impulse could flow through your identity, mental, emotional and physical minds without being blocked or diluted, your vision of what you want to attain would be instantly manifest in your physical reality. This is what you saw in the life of Jesus. Jesus actually made a physical command to turn the water into wine, and it was instantly manifest, just as Lazarus instantly awoke from the dead when Jesus made the command. As you start an effort to manifest abundance, you generate an energy impulse that flows into your identity body. In your identity body, one of two things will happen. If your identity body is pure – and if your conscious vision is in alignment with the Christ vision for your life – your energy impulse will be infused with the strength of the undiluted power of God that is present in your identity body. The energy impulse will become much stronger than what you were able to generate with your conscious mind.

If your identity body is polluted by an imperfect self-image, your energy impulse will be weakened. It might be entirely blocked by a sense that you are a mortal human being who does not have the power to manifest abundance. Perhaps you have the sense that you are a miserable sinner who does not deserve what your conscious mind desires. It is entirely possible that your efforts to manifest abundance, all of your heartfelt and well-meant efforts to use affirmations, prayers and the power of vision, are blocked at the level of your identity body.

It is also possible that some of the energy you generate with the conscious mind will be sent into your mental body after passing through your identity body. It might be diluted, it might be reinforced, but it passes into the mental realm. What happens if you have imperfect thoughts in your mental body? These thoughts can also completely block the energy or they can reduce its power or change the vision. Likewise, if the energy manages to make its way into your emotional body, imperfect feelings, such as fear, guilt or shame, can block or further diminish the energy impulse. Even your physical mind, namely the subconscious layers of that mind, can block or distort the energy. If some of the energy makes it through all levels of your mind, it will enter the material realm, but will it be a more powerful impulse than what you sent out?

Many people have come to the conclusion that they need and want to manifest more abundance and that they can use the power of their minds to bring it about. Most of these people are somewhat spiritual so they are at a higher level of awareness than the norm. Let us say that a person is able to use the conscious mind to send out an energy impulse that vibrates at the level of 2,000 Hz. This is fairly high compared to the average person who rarely goes beyond 1,000 Hz. That energy impulse now enters the person's identity body, and because the person is more spiritual, let us say that the energy impulse is multiplied and doubled in strength, as Jesus promised in his parable about the multiplication of the talents. The energy is now at 4,000 Hz and enters the person's mental body. The natural state of affairs is that energy from the identity body would enter the mental body at a frequency of 75,000 Hz so we still have a drastic difference compared to the person's true potential. Let us now say that the person has certain imperfect beliefs in the mental body that reduce the impulse. It is not blocked but reduced in strength to 3,000 Hz and then enters the emotional body. There are certain emotional wounds that reduce the energy impulse further, plus there are some unresolved issues in the subconscious mind. By the time the energy impulse reenters the matter realm, it is back down to 2,000 Hz. The person has not multiplied the creative power of the energy impulse, and therefore the person is literally treading water without getting anywhere.

***

I have watched millions of sincere people who have studied some kind of abundance technique and who have applied it by using visualizations, affirmations and prayers, thinking they would bring about abundance as they were promised by their prosperity guru. For a time they have, with great enthusiasm, practiced their visualizations and affirmations, having the great hope that any minute the desired abundance would manifest.

So many of them have been disappointed, and it pains my heart to see how their enthusiasm one day dissipates and they end up being discouraged and disillusioned. They end up accepting what their mortal selves and the prince of this world have been telling them all along, namely that they are ordinary human beings who do not have the power to manifest abundance out of thin air.

This is such a pain to my heart, and it is one of the main motivations for my bringing forth this course. If these people would make a determined effort to purify their four lower bodies, their efforts to manifest abundance would no longer be blocked by their own minds. They would increase their creative powers, and although it might take time to do this, they would eventually begin to see actual results of this process.

Many people begin the process of manifesting abundance because they are desperate, because they feel like they have their backs against the wall and they need to do something different to get themselves out of debt or get themselves out of this or that crisis. I ask you to consider the psychology that is at play here. Many people have accepted that their present level of abundance is all they deserve or all they are capable of having. They have reached a certain level of resignation concerning their present state of abundance, or rather lack of it. They accept their lot in life and think they can have nothing better. These people will do nothing to manifest abundance and, obviously, they have no chance of increasing their creative powers. Then you have a group of people who reach the point where they decide they have to do something different. If they reach that decision out of desperation, out of facing a crisis, they want instant and immediate results. If they do not get instant gratification, they often get discouraged.

Desperate people often fall for the promises made by the prosperity gurus who have discovered that they can sell their wares by manipulating people's emotional bodies. Some gurus have realized that when people are desperate, they are grasping for a quick way out. The prosperity guru who makes the most elaborate promises, will attract people with the greatest desperation. The prosperity guru's techniques will not work so people's desperation is likely to be increased, but at least the guru has made his cut, has extracted his pound of flesh. He has even proven his own claim that his system works—*for him*.

It is not my intention in this course to offer you a quick fix. I cannot offer you a quick fix because there is no quick fix. If you are to have true abundance manifest in your life, you can do this, but you can do it in only one way. That is by systematically purifying your four lower bodies from the imperfect beliefs and impure energies that block the flow of God's abundance in your life. If you are willing to go through this process, I *can* and *will* help you. I will give you the tools you need in order to purify your four lower bodies, as I have already done with my previous invocations.

It will take time to purify your four lower bodies, and the reason is that the blocks that exist in those bodies were not created overnight. Some of them were created in childhood and have been reinforced throughout your lifespan. Others were created in past lives, perhaps many lifetimes ago, and have therefore been reinforced over the centuries and the millennia of your sojourn on earth. Some of your blocks were created at the moment you began the descent into the duality consciousness, and some have been with you from the moment your mortal self was created.

No tool can burn them away in an instant. Even if such a tool existed, burning away your imperfect beliefs in an instant would only shatter your sense of identity and leave you in an identity crisis, not knowing who you are any more. This has indeed happened to people who have attempted to force their spiritual growth by unbalanced means. The tools I am giving you are very balanced and thus very safe. I give you techniques that are so powerful that you can consume blocks that have been in your four lower bodies for thousands of years, and you can do so within a matter of months or a few years.

There is no technique on earth that is so powerful that it can instantly turn you into a perfect human being. That is why I have talked to you about a spiritual path. That is why I have said that for each step you have descended the spiral staircase, and gone into the depths of the duality consciousness, you must take one step in the opposite direction and gradually climb higher. There is no shortcut because the energies that have been misqualified by your imperfect beliefs must be transformed back into their original purity before you can be free of them, before they will no longer block the manifestation of God's abundance in your life. This is a perfectly scientific, even a somewhat mechanical, process that anyone can complete by having the proper tools. It will take time, and therefore it will not produce instant results for most people. It will require a commitment, and for most people it will require a lifetime commitment. I am not saying that it will take the rest of your life to see results. Many people will indeed experience results within a matter of weeks or months. What I am saying is that the process of ascending back up the spiral staircase should be approached as a lifetime labor of love. For the rest of your life on earth, you will continue to climb one step at a time.

It may be that you have already started this process in past lives and you are much closer to the top than you might think. It is possible that before you leave this earth, you can manifest a high degree of Christ consciousness, perhaps even the full Christ consciousness demonstrated by Jesus. You can therefore walk the earth in true spiritual freedom, meaning that you have no more blocks in your four lower bodies. In your present state of mind you cannot know how close you are to reaching the top of the spiral staircase, and that is why I bring to your attention one of the most important statements made by Jesus: "In your patience possess ye your souls" (Luke 21:19).

I have seen so many people who started walking the spiritual path, who started using a spiritual technique, with great enthusiasm and hope. When they did not have the instant gratification they expected, they became discouraged. Some even became disappointed, angry or bitter. This, of course, did nothing to accelerate their spiritual growth but only took them even further down the spiral staircase, into the depth of duality and despair. I do not desire anyone who uses this course to run into this wall of disappointment, which is truly one of the most powerful traps set by the prince of this world and the mortal self. They will first try to prevent you from discovering or accepting the spiritual path. If they cannot prevent you from taking the first steps up the spiral staircase, they will – for every step you take – try to make you feel that it is not moving fast enough, that you are not getting the results you were promised compared to the unrealistic expectations they have programmed into your mind. They will try to make you snap into disappointment, despair, doubt and anger so that you stop your progress and tumble back down the staircase to the level where they feel they have you under control. This is their plan, this is their design. There is only one way to avoid falling into this trap, and that is by fixing your mind firmly on the fact that you are deliberately and consciously engaging in a long-term process. It is long-term because you understand that what needs to be done is the hard work of clearing your four lower bodies from the debris that has accumulated over thousands of years. You realize that this will take time and it will take effort on your part. You also realize that if you do the work, the results *will* manifest. This is not a matter of wishful thinking, of hopes or daydreams. It is a very scientific process. Unfortunately, most people don't understand the need to take an energy impulse through all four levels, and this causes many sincere people to give up just before their energy impulse is ready to descend into the matter realm.

Imagine that you are suddenly awakened from a long sleep and you realize you are in a dark building. There is very little light coming into that building, but you notice that there is a skylight in the roof. As you take a closer look, you realize that the skylight is covered with dirt so that it hardly lets any light through. There is nothing mystical about this. The glass in the skylight is perfectly capable of allowing light to pass through it; the light is simply being blocked by dirt on the surface of the glass. If you start in one corner and systematically clear off the dirt, you can clean the entire skylight and the light will inevitably flow through it and enlighten the room in which you abide. If you systematically clear the panes of glass represented by the four levels of your mind, the light of God *will* inevitably shine through your mind. This will manifest God's abundance in your physical experience and it will give you a vastly expanded experience of life, including your own spiritual nature and your true purpose for coming to earth.

***

What will it take to purify your four lower bodies? What are the practical steps you need to take in order to accomplish this task? I have earlier hinted at what blocks the light from flowing through your mind. I have said that everything revolves around your free will and the choices you make. Every choice you make is based on your current level of awareness, your current level of understanding and knowledge—which is determined by the beliefs you hold in the four levels of your mind. At the level of your identity body, every belief you have is determined by how you see yourself, how you see the world and how you see your

potential to manifest what you desire. At the level of your identity body we find certain beliefs that you have come to accept
and that you have allowed to enter the sphere of self. If you
have a belief in your identity body that is limited compared to
the pure vision of Christ for your potential, this belief will have
several effects:

• The belief will limit your ability to bring light from
your I AM Presence into your identity body. For example, if you believe you are a mortal human being, how
could you possibly accept an unlimited stream of light
from your spiritual self? You will inevitably reduce the
amount of light flowing into your identity body.

• The belief will form a filter. As the light of God
passes through that filter, it is reduced in vibration
beyond the natural reduction that is supposed to take
place in your identity body. Many people have a sense
of identity that reduces the light from 100,000 Hz to
under 2,000 Hz. This will reduce the amount of light
and the intensity of the light that flows into your mental body, thus diminishing the power of your thoughts.
The strength at which the light enters the mental body
determines the potential power of your thoughts. Your
thoughts cannot be more powerful than the strength of
the light coming from your identity body.

• The belief will misqualify a certain amount of light
that will accumulate in your identity body. As it accumulates, it will form a barrier that will clog up your identity
body. This level of your mind can eventually become
so filled with debris that there is no room for a higher
sense of identity, that there is little room for light to

pass through from Above and that there is no opening through which your conscious mind can see beyond the material realm and have a spiritual experience.

You now see the effects of having imperfect beliefs in your identity body. A person can have certain imperfect beliefs in the mental body, which will have similar effects. Of course, the pane of glass between the mental and emotional bodies can also be obstructed, and the same holds true for your emotional body. By the time the light reaches your conscious mind, which is the level where you direct that light into conscious action, there is very little light coming through. The effect of this is twofold. One effect is that it reduces the creative power you have at the level of the physical brain and body. It also reduces your vision, your ability to see beyond the matter realm. This happens because you normally attempt to get a higher vision by looking through your four lower bodies so if the panes of glass are polluted, you cannot see through them with your conscious mind.

In order to clear your four lower bodies, you will have to do two things. You will have to consciously discover the imperfect beliefs that you have come to accept at each level of your mind. You will then have to consciously replace those imperfect beliefs, those dualistic beliefs, by making decisions based on the truth of Christ. When you do replace an imperfect belief, you remove the filter that causes the light of God to be reduced in strength and to form debris that prevents the light from flowing freely. You have not thereby removed the ashes, the debris, that has already accumulated in your four lower bodies. The second task you need to accomplish is to remove the misqualified energy in your four lower bodies. This, of course, is a process of which most people are completely unaware because neither orthodox religion nor materialistic science can explain to them the need to do this or the way to do this. I hope that what I have given you so far has explained the need to purify the misqualified energy that has accumulated in your four lower bodies. I hope you can also see the way to do this. It is really quite simple, and your scientists have already discovered this process in their laboratories.

The energy that has accumulated in your four lower bodies takes the form of energy waves that vibrate at very low frequencies. The only way to remove such energy is to raise its frequency, its vibration, back to its original purity. This is very simple to do because your mind has a built-in capacity to let high-frequency light flow through it from the spiritual realm. Your task is to find a systematic method whereby you can invoke high-frequency light from the spiritual realm, draw it down into your four lower bodies and direct it into the misqualified energy that has accumulated there. If you will go through this process, you can and will clear your four lower bodies.

***

I hope you have been using my invocations as you have been following the course. I now want to give you a deeper understanding so that you can be fully aware of what it takes to purify your four lower bodies. I also want you to know what it takes to overcome another major block to the manifestation of God's abundance in your life, namely the causes you have set in motion in the past, the causes that will inevitably cycle through the four levels of the material universe and therefore be reflected back to you by the cosmic mirror.

I know this course is very long, and I know it takes you far beyond what you were taught in kindergarten or Sunday school. I trust that if you have endured with me to this point, you will want to go all the way and gain a full understanding of how the material universe works and how you can use that understanding to remove not only the inner blocks in your own mind but also the outer blocks of your former actions, the causes you have set in motion in past lives and that have manifested as the physical circumstances you experience in this lifetime.

Follow me as I explain to you what you should have been taught in kindergarten and Sunday school but what neither the orthodox churches nor materialistic science wanted to teach you. They failed to teach you this because they have become so infiltrated by the dualistic reasoning of the mind of anti-christ that they can no longer bring you the true teachings of Christ that Jesus wanted you to have and still wants you to have in this age. That is indeed why both Jesus, myself and many other of the spiritual teachers who serve humankind have found it necessary to speak to people in this age and to bring forth the progressive revelation that people deserve to have because they have risen to a higher level of awareness. They can now ask more specific questions than could be asked in the past. If you ask, you shall receive. Because so many people have sincerely wondered about the deeper mysteries of life and why their situation is the way it is, I have come to give you the answers. You will find that at some level of your being, you too have had those questions.

2 | I INVOKE LIGHT INTO MY FOUR LOWER BODIES

In the name I AM THAT I AM, Jesus Christ, I call to all representatives of the Divine Mother and the Divine Father, especially Maraytaii, Archangel Michael and Mother Mary, to help me clear my identity, mental, emotional and physical bodies from all lower energies and limiting beliefs. Help me accept my creative powers and see the factors that block the flow of my God-given creativity, including...

[Make personal calls.]

1. I surrender the passive approach

1. I have a sense of co-measurement of the power of God and I know it is possible for me to walk the path of Christhood that Jesus demonstrated.

Archangel Michael, light so blue,
my heart has room for only you.
My mind is one, no longer two,
your love for me is ever true.

Archangel Michael, you are here,
your light consumes all doubt and fear.
Your Presence is forever near,
you are to me so very dear.

2. I know Jesus made a true promise when he said that if I truly
follow him, I shall do the works that he did and greater works.

Archangel Michael, I will be,
all one with your reality.
No fear can hold me as I see,
this world no power has o'er me.

Archangel Michael, you are here,
your light consumes all doubt and fear.
Your Presence is forever near,
you are to me so very dear.

3. I am following the path taken by Jesus, the path of overcoming the mortal self, of slaying the dragon of the mortal self. God
can do the same works through me that God did through Jesus.

Archangel Michael, hold me tight,
shatter now the darkest night.
Clear my chakras with your light,
restore to me my inner sight.

Archangel Michael, you are here,
your light consumes all doubt and fear.
Your Presence is forever near,
you are to me so very dear.

4. When the power of God flows undiluted through my four lower bodies, there is no limitation to what God can do.

Archangel Michael, now I stand,
with you the light I do command.
My heart I ever will expand,
till highest truth I understand.

Archangel Michael, you are here,
your light consumes all doubt and fear.
Your Presence is forever near,
you are to me so very dear.

5. I am reclaiming my original mission of being a co-creator with the real God, the inner God who longs to see me co-create the abundant life he envisions for me.

Archangel Michael, in my heart,
from me you never will depart.
Of hierarchy I am a part,
I now accept a fresh new start.

Archangel Michael, you are here,
your light consumes all doubt and fear.
Your Presence is forever near,
you are to me so very dear.

6. I am purifying my four lower bodies and returning to the natural state. The power of God is flowing through my four lower bodies without being diluted and reduced below the natural level of vibration.

> Archangel Michael, sword of blue,
> all darkness you are cutting through.
> My Christhood I do now pursue,
> discernment shows me what is true.

> **Archangel Michael, you are here,**
> **your light consumes all doubt and fear.**
> **Your Presence is forever near,**
> **you are to me so very dear.**

7. I am purifying my four lower bodies whereby more high-frequency energy reaches my conscious mind. I am restoring my higher brain functions and increasing my creative powers.

> Archangel Michael, in your wings,
> I now let go of lesser things.
> God's homing call in my heart rings,
> my heart with yours forever sings.

> **Archangel Michael, you are here,**
> **your light consumes all doubt and fear.**
> **Your Presence is forever near,**
> **you are to me so very dear.**

8. Mother Mary is showing me the way to increase my creative power. Through the power of God within me, I am overcoming the sense of struggle and replacing all my struggles with an upward spiral that comes from multiplying the talents given to me by God.

Archangel Michael, take me home,
in higher spheres I want to roam.
I am reborn from cosmic foam,
my life is now a sacred poem.

Archangel Michael, you are here,
your light consumes all doubt and fear.
Your Presence is forever near,
you are to me so very dear.

9. I surrender the passive approach of praying and then waiting for Mother Mary to do the work for me. I am taking the active approach and I say: "Mother Mary, show me how to increase my creative powers so that the power of God within me can remove this limitation."

Archangel Michael, light you are,
shining like the bluest star.
You are a cosmic avatar,
with you I will go very far.

Archangel Michael, you are here,
your light consumes all doubt and fear.
Your Presence is forever near,
you are to me so very dear.

2. I transcend discouragement

1. I open myself to the power of vision. I am sending an energy impulse that goes beyond the physical body. I know there is more to life than the matter realm, there is a higher way to manifest abundance than what I can do with the body.

> O Cosmic Mother, sound the gong,
> that calls me home where I belong.
> I know you love me tenderly,
> and in that knowing I am free.

> **Maraytaii, I resonate**
> **with song that opens cosmic gate.**
> **Your melody makes me vibrate**
> **my sense of self I recreate.**

2. I am generating an energy impulse that goes from my conscious mind into my identity body. The energy impulse is flowing through my identity, mental, emotional and physical minds without being blocked or diluted.

> O Cosmic Mother, hold me tight,
> I resonate with your own light.
> Your music purifies my heart,
> your love to all I do impart.

> **Maraytaii, I resonate**
> **with song that opens cosmic gate.**
> **Your melody makes me vibrate**
> **my sense of self I recreate.**

3. My identity body is pure and my conscious vision is in alignment with the Christ vision for my life. My energy impulse is infused with the strength of the undiluted power of God that is present in my identity body. The energy impulse becomes stronger than what I was able to generate with my conscious mind.

> O Cosmic Mother, we are one,
> your heart is like a blazing sun.
> My being can but amplify,
> the sacred sound you magnify.

> **Maraytaii, I resonate
> with song that opens cosmic gate.
> Your melody makes me vibrate
> my sense of self I recreate.**

4. The stronger energy impulse now flows into my mental body where it is again reinforced by the power of God. My vision of how to accomplish my goal becomes clearer.

> O Cosmic Mother, I now hear,
> the subtle sound of Sacred Sphere.
> As I attune to Cosmic Hum,
> the lesser self I overcome.

> **Maraytaii, I resonate
> with song that opens cosmic gate.
> Your melody makes me vibrate
> my sense of self I recreate.**

5. The energy impulse now flows into my emotional body where it is again reinforced by the power of God. My desires are aligned with the vision of Christ.

O Cosmic Mother, take me home,
I am in sync with Sacred OM,
The sound of sounds will raise me up,
so only light is in my cup.

**Maraytaii, I resonate
with song that opens cosmic gate.
Your melody makes me vibrate
my sense of self I recreate.**

6. The energy impulse flows into the material level where the Christ vision for my life is effortlessly manifest.

O Cosmic Mother, I will be,
a part of cosmic symphony.
All that I AM, an instrument,
for sound that is from heaven sent.

**Maraytaii, I resonate
with song that opens cosmic gate.
Your melody makes me vibrate
my sense of self I recreate.**

7. I know this is a scientific process that cannot fail. If my vision is not manifest, I know the return current is being blocked by limiting beliefs and low-frequency energies in my four lower bodies.

O Cosmic Mother, I now call,
to enter sacred music hall.
I will be part of life's ascent,
towards the starry firmament.

Maraytaii, I resonate
with song that opens cosmic gate.
Your melody makes me vibrate
my sense of self I recreate.

8. I am transcending all discouragement and disillusionment. I know I am more than a human being and that I have the power to manifest abundance in my life.

O Cosmic Mother, tune my strings,
my total being with you sings.
Your song I now reverberate,
as cosmic love I celebrate.

Maraytaii, I resonate
with song that opens cosmic gate.
Your melody makes me vibrate
my sense of self I recreate.

9. I am fully determined to continue my efforts to purify my four lower bodies. I will continue my efforts to manifest abundance until they are no longer blocked by my own mind.

O Cosmic Mother, I love you,
your love song keeps me ever true.
You fill me with your sacred tone,
and thus I never feel alone.

Maraytaii, I resonate
with song that opens cosmic gate.
Your melody makes me vibrate
my sense of self I recreate.

3. I am committed to the process

1. I am increasing my creative powers, and I am starting to see actual results of this process.

> Archangel Michael, light so blue,
> my heart has room for only you.
> My mind is one, no longer two,
> your love for me is ever true.
>
> **Archangel Michael, you are here,**
> **your light consumes all doubt and fear.**
> **Your Presence is forever near,**
> **you are to me so very dear.**

2. I surrender all sense of desperation, all sense of wanting immediate results, instant gratification.

> Archangel Michael, I will be,
> all one with your reality.
> No fear can hold me as I see,
> this world no power has o'er me.
>
> **Archangel Michael, you are here,**
> **your light consumes all doubt and fear.**
> **Your Presence is forever near,**
> **you are to me so very dear.**

3. I accept that there is no quick fix. I know I can manifest true abundance in my life, but I can do it in only one way. I am systematically purifying my four lower bodies from the imperfect beliefs and impure energies that block the flow of God's abundance in my life.

Archangel Michael, hold me tight,
shatter now the darkest night.
Clear my chakras with your light,
restore to me my inner sight.

Archangel Michael, you are here,
your light consumes all doubt and fear.
Your Presence is forever near,
you are to me so very dear.

4. The process of manifesting abundance is a perfectly scientific, even a somewhat mechanical process. I am fully committed to this process, and it is a lifetime commitment.

Archangel Michael, now I stand,
with you the light I do command.
My heart I ever will expand,
till highest truth I understand.

Archangel Michael, you are here,
your light consumes all doubt and fear.
Your Presence is forever near,
you are to me so very dear.

5. I am approaching the process of ascending back up the spiral staircase as a lifetime labor of love. For the rest of my life on earth, I will continue to climb one step at a time.

Archangel Michael, in my heart,
from me you never will depart.
Of hierarchy I am a part,
I now accept a fresh new start.

**Archangel Michael, you are here,
your light consumes all doubt and fear.
Your Presence is forever near,
you are to me so very dear.**

6. I know that before I leave this earth I will manifest a high degree of Christ consciousness as demonstrated by Jesus. I will walk the earth in true spiritual freedom, meaning that I have no more blocks in my four lower bodies.

Archangel Michael, sword of blue,
all darkness you are cutting through.
My Christhood I do now pursue,
discernment shows me what is true.

**Archangel Michael, you are here,
your light consumes all doubt and fear.
Your Presence is forever near,
you are to me so very dear.**

7. I surrender the sense that I am not moving fast enough, that I am not getting the results I was promised. I surrender the unrealistic expectations programmed into my mind.

Archangel Michael, in your wings,
I now let go of lesser things.
God's homing call in my heart rings,
my heart with yours forever sings.

**Archangel Michael, you are here,
your light consumes all doubt and fear.
Your Presence is forever near,
you are to me so very dear.**

8. I am transcending all attempts by my ego and dark forces to get me to snap into disappointment, despair, doubt and anger. I will continue my progress and ascend the staircase to the level where I am free from all control by lower forces.

Archangel Michael, take me home,
in higher spheres I want to roam.
I am reborn from cosmic foam,
my life is now a sacred poem.

**Archangel Michael, you are here,
your light consumes all doubt and fear.
Your Presence is forever near,
you are to me so very dear.**

9. I am fixing my mind firmly on the fact that I am deliberately and consciously engaging in a long-term process. I understand that what needs to be done is the hard work of clearing my four lower bodies from the debris that has accumulated over thousands of years.

Archangel Michael, light you are,
shining like the bluest star.
You are a cosmic avatar,
with you I will go very far.

Archangel Michael, you are here,
your light consumes all doubt and fear.
Your Presence is forever near,
you are to me so very dear.

4. I am anchored on the upward path

1. I realize that the process will take time, and it will take effort on my part. I also realize that when I do the work, the results *will* manifest. This is not a matter of wishful thinking, of hopes or daydreams. It is a very scientific process.

O Cosmic Mother, sound the gong,
that calls me home where I belong.
I know you love me tenderly,
and in that knowing I am free.

Maraytaii, I resonate
with song that opens cosmic gate.
Your melody makes me vibrate
my sense of self I recreate.

2. When I systematically clear the panes of glass represented by the four levels of my mind, the light of God will inevitably shine through my mind. This will manifest God's abundance in my physical experience and it will give me a vastly expanded experience of life, including my own spiritual nature and my true purpose for coming to earth.

O Cosmic Mother, hold me tight,
I resonate with your own light.
Your music purifies my heart,
your love to all I do impart.

**Maraytaii, I resonate
with song that opens cosmic gate.
Your melody makes me vibrate
my sense of self I recreate.**

3. I invoke the light of God to consume all energies in my identity, mental and emotional bodies that prevent me from seeing the limitations in the way I see myself, how I see the world and how I see my potential to manifest what I desire.

O Cosmic Mother, we are one,
your heart is like a blazing sun.
My being can but amplify,
the sacred sound you magnify.

**Maraytaii, I resonate
with song that opens cosmic gate.
Your melody makes me vibrate
my sense of self I recreate.**

4. Mother Mary, help me see all limiting beliefs at the level of my identity body. Help me reconnect to the pure vision of Christ for my true identity as a co-creator with God.

O Cosmic Mother, I now hear,
the subtle sound of Sacred Sphere.
As I attune to Cosmic Hum,
the lesser self I overcome.

Maraytaii, I resonate
with song that opens cosmic gate.
Your melody makes me vibrate
my sense of self I recreate.

5. Mother Mary, help me see all limiting beliefs at the level of my mental body. Help me reconnect to the pure vision of Christ for how I can manifest my divine plan.

O Cosmic Mother, take me home,
I am in sync with Sacred OM,
The sound of sounds will raise me up,
so only light is in my cup.

Maraytaii, I resonate
with song that opens cosmic gate.
Your melody makes me vibrate
my sense of self I recreate.

6. Mother Mary, help me see all limiting beliefs at the level of my emotional body. Help me reconnect to the pure vision of Christ for my higher desires.

O Cosmic Mother, I will be,
a part of cosmic symphony.
All that I AM, an instrument,
for sound that is from heaven sent.

Maraytaii, I resonate
with song that opens cosmic gate.
Your melody makes me vibrate
my sense of self I recreate.

7. Mother Mary, help me consciously discover the imperfect beliefs that I have come to accept at each level of my mind. I will consciously replace those imperfect beliefs, those dualistic beliefs, by making decisions based on the truth of Christ.

> O Cosmic Mother, I now call,
> to enter sacred music hall.
> I will be part of life's ascent,
> towards the starry firmament.

> **Maraytaii, I resonate
> with song that opens cosmic gate.
> Your melody makes me vibrate
> my sense of self I recreate.**

8. I am anchoring myself firmly on the upward path. I have the inner knowing – which is beyond mere belief – that no power on this earth, neither my mortal self nor the prince of this world, can take me off the spiritual path.

> O Cosmic Mother, tune my strings,
> my total being with you sings.
> Your song I now reverberate,
> as cosmic love I celebrate.

> **Maraytaii, I resonate
> with song that opens cosmic gate.
> Your melody makes me vibrate
> my sense of self I recreate.**

9. I am transcending the sense of struggle and suffering. I have anchored myself on the upward path of self-transcendence and I am coming home to my Cosmic Mother and my I AM Presence.

O Cosmic Mother, I love you,
your love song keeps me ever true.
You fill me with your sacred tone,
and thus I never feel alone.

**Maraytaii, I resonate
with song that opens cosmic gate.
Your melody makes me vibrate
my sense of self I recreate.**

Sealing

In the name of the Divine Mother, I call to Maraytaii, Archangel Michael and Mother Mary for the sealing of myself and all people in my circle of influence in the creative flow of the Divine Mother, the River of Life. I call for the multiplication of my calls by all representatives of the Divine Mother, so that we form the perfect figure-eight flow of "As Above, so below." Thus, I accept that this is fully manifest, because the mouth of the Lord, the Divine Mother that I AM, has spoken it. Amen.

3 | MIND OVER BRAIN

My beloved heart, I would like to build upon the teachings I have given you in the previous chapter. I first of all want to tell you more about the physical part of your mind, which I have so far mentioned but not truly described. Medical scientists have conducted various experiments on the brain in their attempts to understand the brain and discover its higher functions. For example, they have found that by inducing certain chemicals, they can stimulate experiences that are very similar to what people report during spiritual or near-death experiences. This has led some scientists to conclude that all spiritual experiences, and all religion, spring from certain chemical or electromagnetic processes in the brain. They conclude that there is nothing beyond the brain but that all religion is produced within the brain. Some surgeons have performed open brain surgery and have found that they can stimulate areas of the brain and trigger certain experiences. Again, this has led the materialistic scientists to conclude that all spiritual experiences are produced by the brain—that God is the product of a misfiring of neurons in the brain.

It is understandable that a person who has decided that there is nothing beyond the material realm will come to this conclusion. This lack of vision is a product of the fact that the person has chosen to confine his or her mind to the matter realm. The conscious mind of that person simply cannot see beyond the matter realm and will not accept the possibility that there could be a deeper explanation. The reason most people use only 5-10 percent of their brain capacity is that the higher brain centers require a higher form of energy in order to be activated. Those brain centers can be artificially activated by certain chemicals or by an outer stimulation. This does not mean that the stimulation of the brain centers produces a spiritual experience. It only means that the brain centers are designed to facilitate an experience so that the conscious mind can grasp such an experience while you are still in a physical body. The purpose is to allow you to experience that there is more to life than the material universe—while you are abiding in, one might say trapped in, the matter realm.

A genuine spiritual experience takes place when the Conscious You separates itself from the physical mind and the physical body and therefore reaches beyond the matter realm. The Conscious You reaches into the identity realm or even beyond it into the spiritual realm. This is completely natural, and the Conscious You has the capacity to identify itself with anything, anywhere. The Conscious You has the potential to separate itself from the body, even on a temporary basis, and reach up to the higher parts of your identity, your true identity as a spiritual being. When you reconnect to that identity, high-frequency light streams through your four lower bodies and you can have a variety of spiritual experiences.

It is quite possible for the Conscious You to have spiritual experiences that cannot filter through to your conscious mind. This can be caused by blocks in the higher levels of your mind, but there is also a certain class of spiritual experiences that cannot be consciously known while you are in a physical body. The simple reason is that the human brain does not have centers that are capable of facilitating such experiences. When you do have a spiritual experience that filters through to your conscious awareness, it is because the physical brain is capable of facilitating such an experience. The Conscious You has reached into a higher realm and has released a stream of light that filters down to the physical brain and activates one of the higher brain centers. It is this activation of the brain center that gives you a conscious experience. It is quite possible that the Conscious You can have spiritual experiences that cannot be translated by the brain and thus cannot be known to the conscious mind. Many spiritual people disentangle themselves from the body while they sleep and travel to the spiritual realm where they receive instructions from their spiritual teachers. That is why you sometimes wake up with a new sense of clarity and with the answer to a question you have been pondering. This is also why you can have certain dreams just before you wake up that are very lucid and seem to carry a profound message. Sometimes this might be a greater understanding of a problem or it might be a premonition concerning a future event. It might also be a sense of flying, a sense of being free or the sense of being part of something greater than your physical body. It might be a sense of being outside your physical body, looking down upon it.

All of these experiences are real experiences, yet it is true, as scientists have discovered, that it is possible to generate such experiences by stimulating the physical brain in various ways. This does not mean that the brain produces the experience. Reasoning this way is the same as reasoning that the film screen produces the images that appear on the screen. It is true that the brain can influence the exact form and content of a spiritual experience, which is one reason two people can have different experiences.

***

Having explained this characteristic of the physical brain, I would like to move on and talk more about what I have called the physical part of your mind. You are an immortal spiritual being, and you have taken on this particular physical body only for a time. In the past, you have been embodied in other bodies in different circumstances. This fact is the only way to explain one of the major blocks to your efforts to manifest God's abundance in your life. The blocks that appear in your four lower bodies can be divided into two categories. There are long-term blocks and short-term blocks. There are certain blocks in the four levels of your mind that were produced in this particular lifetime, and there are other blocks that were produced in past lives.

If you truly want to clear your four lower bodies, you need to go beyond what you have experienced in this lifetime. In order to go beyond, you need to understand that there are levels of the mind. There is more than one valid way to explain what I will give you next. For the sake of simplicity, I will give you a model which describes your mind as having two major components. There is the larger, higher or long-term component of your four lower bodies. This is the component that you carry with you from lifetime to lifetime. You also have a component that is attached to this particular physical body in this lifetime, yet this component also has an identity level, a mental realm, an emotional realm and a mind that is enmeshed with, and to some degree produced by, the physical brain. You have a larger energy field that is beyond your present body, and within it is a smaller field that is centered around the physical body and interwoven with the body and the brain.

As you grew up in this lifetime, you built a certain sense of identity based on your particular circumstances, such as your family background, nationality, race, ethnic group, sex and other aspects of your physical situation. This put contents into the container of the short-term identity body. This sense of identity was to a large degree affected by your heredity and your environment, yet it was not exclusively produced by these external factors, as psychologists claim. What influences your short-term sense of identity is your *reactions* to external circumstances in this lifetime, and those reactions are largely determined by the contents of your long-term mind, the mind that was created during previous lifetimes.

The long-term identity body is not affected by the specific characteristics related to this lifetime. It stores the larger sense of identity based on beliefs about yourself. For example, it might store the belief that you are a human being or a miserable sinner, a belief that might have been reinforced in this lifetime but was likely created many lifetimes ago. The long-term identity body stores more general beliefs whereas the short-term identity body stores the identity relating to your current embodiment. The deeper part of your being, which is what most psychologists and spiritual teachers call the soul, is beyond this particular lifetime. It does not see itself as a person with your name, sex, nationality, race and so on. It does not identify itself as being a nurse, a teacher or whatever your occupation might be.

The identity body that is specific to your present lifetime will be wiped clean after the death of this body, and that is why most people do not remember their past lives. The records of those lives are stored elsewhere and you can uncover them, but they are not stored in your short-term identity body. This is actually a grace, in the sense that you receive an opportunity to start over without remembering the mistakes you might have made in your previous lifetimes. The downside is that many people are born without a strong sense of continuity. This gives rise to the fear of death that comes from believing that your identity will be lost when your body dies. Your most precious possession is your individuality, your sense of identity, so your greatest fear is to lose it. That is why it is actually very cruel that children are brought up without an understanding of reincarnation. Knowing that your long-term identity will not die with the physical body can completely relieve you of the fear of death, a fear that is paralyzing to many people and gives them a sense that life is pointless. Why strive to improve yourself and become a better person when all is lost at the end of this life? The improvements you make are not lost but become your "treasures laid up in heaven" (Matthew 6:20), meaning that they are stored in your long-term identity body (even in your causal body in the spiritual realm) and will therefore serve as a foundation that you can build upon in your next lifetime (and after you permanently graduate from earth's schoolroom).

It is possible that what you experience in this lifetime, and the decisions you make based on those experiences, can have an effect on your long-term sense of identity. Your long-term sense of identity has a profound effect on the sense of identity you build in this lifetime. The contents of your long-term mental and emotional bodies have a major effect on how you respond to the situations you encounter in this lifetime. For better or worse, you are building upon the foundation laid in past lives, yet you do have the potential to improve upon that foundation, which, of course, is your only hope of being free of the past.

As an example, let us say that your long-term identity body contains the belief that you are a miserable sinner and that everything you do is a sin. This will carry over into your present lifetime and give you a tendency to gravitate towards a religion that reinforces this belief. You will find it easy to accept such a religion and you will find it difficult to break free from it, which is why many people simply will not look beyond the religion in which they grew up. The contents of your long-term mind will form the parameters for how you respond to life in this particular lifetime. The Conscious You still has the potential to go beyond the programming from the past. In many cases, the conscious mind builds a sense of identity in the current lifetime that is somewhat in conflict with the person's long-term identity. This is important because it opens the possibility that you can reinforce the internal contradictions that make you a house divided against itself.

For example, many people have a belief in their long-term identity bodies that they are not worthy to receive God's abundance. Some people have used a specific teaching on abundance and a set of affirmations to create the short-term sense of identity as being worthy of having abundance. If they have not fully understood what I explained in the previous chapter, this new sense of identity may not go beyond the short-term identity body. It can clash with, and easily be overruled by, the more powerful long-term sense of identity. The person's attempt to use a genuine technique to raise his or her spiritual awareness has not truly helped. It has only created a greater internal conflict, and this is one of the ways in which your mortal self and the prince of this world can put you in a spiritual catch-22. They do this by seeking to make you accept a belief in your short-term mind that conflicts a belief you already hold in your long-term mind. This temporary belief will prevent you from resolving the limiting belief you have in the long-term mind. If you have built a firm belief in this lifetime that you are worthy to receive God's abundance, you might not think that you need to go deeper into your psychology and resolve the long-term belief that you are not worthy. This can prevent you from making long-term progress, which can only be attained by purifying your long-term mind. You are, so to speak, creating a temporary movie that is projected onto the screen of your consciousness, and although it might obscure some of the images projected by your long-term mind, it does nothing to actually clean the filmstrip in the long-term mind. It should be obvious that if you want true freedom, you need to go beyond the short-term mind and clear your long-term mind.

There are prosperity gurus, psychologists and holistic healers who have a valid technique for purifying your emotions, your thoughts and even your sense of identity. If a technique works only on the short-term mind, it cannot have the maximum effect on your growth. There are also some gurus who are not seeking to help you resolve the blocks in your short-term mind. Instead, they present you with techniques aimed at creating a new program in the short-term mind, a program that will supposedly bring you great abundance by simply overriding preexisting programs. Without the resolution of the limitations from the past, this will inevitably add to your internal conflicts by creating a new program that conflicts already existing programs in both your short-term and long-term minds. On a computer two programs can be in conflict with each other, and it can cause the computer to crash. The subconscious part of your mind is in some ways similar to a computer. If you put conflicting beliefs or patterns into it, you will experience a form of mental or emotional paralysis.

This also applies to many forms of therapy, especially the therapy developed by mainstream psychology, which is based on a largely materialistic paradigm. You might have been exposed to certain traumatic experiences in this lifetime that have given you emotional scars and have caused you to form certain imperfect beliefs in your short-term mental body and even build an imperfect self-image. It is quite possible that you can use a form of therapy to resolve these blocks in your short-term mind, and truly this can have a beneficial effect. If you do not go beyond the short-term mind, you are not actually making progress in this lifetime. You are simply turning back the clock to the starting point, and thus you are, so to speak, back to square one. In order to truly progress, you need to go beyond the short-term mind, and you can use your experiences in this lifetime as a springboard for this effort. The way you react to situations in this lifetime is determined by the patterns in your long-term mind. By examining your reactions, you can uncover the deeper patterns and work on resolving them. This requires a greater commitment and a clear vision that you are more than your short-term mind. In order to be completely free, you need to go all the way back to the beliefs that originated with your decision to turn away from God, to turn away from your spiritual teacher, and go it alone. This was when you allowed your mortal self and the prince of this world to be your teachers.

***

My beloved, in order to attain the truly abundant life and be permanently free from the limitations that block God's abundance, you need to take a long-term view. The conditions you face in this life are a product of a very complex picture, namely the beliefs that you have accepted in past lives and that still reside in your four lower bodies, in the long-term part of your mind. Once you have this long-term view, it will be much easier for you to recognize that what I have told you so far is only one side of the coin of life.

What I have described so far is the internal component to your life, namely what is happening in your own psychology, what is happening inside your four lower bodies. The price you pay for taking physical embodiment is that you are ultimately responsible for what you do with God's energy through your physical body, or rather through your four lower bodies. What I have explained up until now is that whatever you do will have a direct effect upon yourself because it puts beliefs in your four

lower bodies, and they form a filter that causes you to misqualify energy. This energy accumulates in your four lower bodies
and reduces your creative power. It also reduces your vision
and your ability to see beyond your immediate situation and the
material universe. We might apply the old saying that you are
only hurting yourself.

We now need to take this one step further and recognize
that not everything you do while you are in a physical body hurts
yourself only. When you take a physical action, you potentially
affect other people, and because you are responsible for your
use of energy, any action will be mirrored back to you by the
cosmic mirror. This return of your past actions can block the
manifestation of God's abundance in this lifetime, which makes
it necessary for you to know how to dissolve the return of your
past actions before they manifest as material circumstances.

It is not only your physical actions that affect other people. Everything on planet earth is made of energy. As there is
an energy field around your physical body, there is an energy
field around the entire planet. Part of this planetary energy field
serves as a storehouse for the imperfect energies generated by
humankind throughout the ages. This is what the psychologist
Carl Jung called the "collective unconscious," and this is indeed
an important discovery. When you descend into a physical body,
your four lower bodies exist within the greater energy field of the
collective consciousness of humankind. You can be affected by
the collective consciousness, and you affect the consciousness
of the whole. For example, many people are so overwhelmed
by the energies of the collective consciousness that they have
very little individuality. They find it difficult to think for themselves and make their own decisions. They want society to think
for them and to tell them what to do. You see this in the people who blindly follow the latest fashion trend or whatever fad
happens to be popular in their society. If you had been among

these people, you would not be studying this course. Most people who are spiritually aware have a stronger sense of individuality. They have, to some degree, separated themselves from what we might call the mass consciousness. If you are to have any hope of attaining real spiritual growth, you need to separate yourself from the mass consciousness. You need to protect your personal energy field from being overrun by the energies in the mass consciousness.

The contents in your four lower bodies will contribute, for better or for worse, to the mass consciousness. You cannot simply look at the mass consciousness as something that was created independently of you and for which you have no responsibility. If you raise your personal consciousness, you will raise the consciousness of the whole. This is what Jesus described when he said: "And I, if I be lifted up from the earth, will draw all men unto me" (John 12:32). The inner meaning is that the only reason humankind has progressed beyond the level of the caveman is that in every generation there have been a few individuals who discovered the power of their minds and used that discovery to raise their individual consciousness. They pulled everyone else up a little bit, and it is the raising of the collective consciousness that has opened the way for all of the progress seen in known history. Since the incarnation of Jesus, humankind has progressed immensely. The last 2,000 years have seen more progress than the previous 10,000 years. This is not all caused by the victory of Jesus but also by the fact that many people have attained a higher degree of Christ consciousness and have therefore raised the collective consciousness. Nevertheless, Jesus deserves to be recognized as the forerunner who initiated this latest cycle of progress.

If you allow imperfect beliefs and misqualified energies to remain in your four lower bodies, you are contributing to dragging down the collective consciousness. While you are in a

physical body, the contents of your four lower bodies are contributing to the situation found on the planet as a whole. You are
either helping to make things worse or you are helping to make
things better. As the popular saying goes: "If you are not part of
the solution, you are part of the problem."

***

Your thoughts and feelings have a profound impact on the
planet as a whole so you cannot reason that only your actions
affect other people. There is a dividing line between your
thoughts and feelings and your physical actions. The contents
of your identity, mental and emotional bodies do affect the collective consciousness, but when you take a physical action, you
have generated a different kind of energy impulse, an impulse
that has a more direct affect on other people.

There is a subtle distinction. Jesus made a very profound
statement when he said: "Whosoever looketh on a woman to
lust after her hath committed adultery with her already in his
heart" (Matthew 5:28). Your thoughts and feelings are very
powerful and can send out strong energy impulses that can enter
the minds of other people and affect their thoughts and feelings, which can then lead them to take certain actions. A distinction needs to be made between your thoughts and feelings
and your physical actions. For example, the laws of society say
that if you are thinking about committing a crime, you cannot
be prosecuted by the law. The moment you commit a physical
action, you will be subject to the law. When you take a physical
action, you have brought your thoughts and feelings into the
lowest level of the material realm, namely the matter realm. This
realm is the most dense of the four levels of the material universe, which means that what is brought into the matter realm is
more difficult to change than what still exists only as a thought

or feeling. You might be having an imperfect thought, and you might even infuse that thought with intense emotions that cause you to desire something which the law says you cannot have. As long as you have not taken physical action, your thoughts and desires are not irreversible. Your feelings are very fluid and can easily be changed or given a new direction. Your thoughts are even more fluid and are even easier to change. At the level of your thoughts, you can instantly change your plans by receiving a higher understanding that makes you realize you were going in the wrong direction. At this level you can learn a lesson without having created irreversible physical consequences.

Even though your thoughts and feelings have an effect on other people, it is quite easy for you to change your thoughts and feelings. The moment you have taken a physical action, nothing can make that action undone. Once you take a physical action, you have brought your thoughts and feelings into the realm of time and space, and as the popular saying goes: "You cannot turn back the clock." You cannot undo what has been brought to the level of physical action.

The existence of the four levels of the material universe is actually a form of protection that allows people who are trapped in the duality consciousness to exercise their free will without instantly destroying themselves or each other. A physical action begins in your identity body, takes a more distinct shape in your mental body and receives direction and momentum in your emotional body. As long as it has not crossed the line to the matter realm, it can still be reversed by you coming to a higher understanding. If the material universe had only one level, any impulse you had would instantly be precipitated as a physical action and you would have no opportunity to stop it. Any imperfect thought would inevitably have physical consequences that you could not escape. Because the universe has four levels, you can have many imperfect thoughts and feelings, but as long as you don't allow them to become physical actions, you will not suffer physical consequences. How many times in your life have you had imperfect thoughts and feelings, but because you did not take action, you avoided the unpleasant consequences? How difficult would your life have been if every imperfect thought resulted in a physical consequence?

Knowing about your four lower bodies gives you an incredible opportunity to take dominion over your life by purifying them of all imperfect thoughts and feelings. The more pure your four lower bodies are, the more you will be in control of your reactions to life's trials. Instead of feeling like you have no choice, like you are unable to choose between several ways to respond to a given situation, you can now choose to respond in the way that is best for you from a long-term perspective. You can choose to follow Jesus' advice to turn the other cheek instead of seeking revenge (Matthew 5:39).

The Law of Free Will has an important impact on what we are talking about here. Let us say that you think another person has done something wrong and you are very angry about it. In your mind, you go over the other person's actions again and again, and you are therefore sending out a powerful impulse of psychic energy. As that energy enters the other person's mind, it is likely to stir up the person's emotional body and make him or her more agitated. You have affected the other person and made him or her more prone to act in anger. The energy you send is still at the mental and emotional level, meaning that the person has a choice concerning whether to act upon it. *You* are responsible for what you send out, but you are *not* responsible for what the other person does with that energy. He or she is responsible for the actions taken. At this point you have influenced the other person's free will, but you have not directly violated the person's free will.

The moment you take a physical action, such as seeking revenge, the equation is fundamentally changed. By committing an act of violence against the other person, you have directly violated the person's free will. You have taken your thoughts and feelings out of the psychic realm and have brought them into the matter realm where they have become irreversible. Before you did this, the other person might have ignored the energy impulse you sent, but after you take action, it is no longer possible for the other person to ignore what you did. You are still not responsible for how the other person responds to your actions (as he or she is not responsible for your reaction), but you have crossed a line and your actions are now irreversible. You have moved beyond the fluid level of thought and feeling, beyond the level of experimentation, and into the level of irreversible consequences. For every action, there is an opposite reaction. When you take physical action, you create an inevitable consequence for yourself and others. This is one more reason to purify your four lower bodies. You can then remove imperfect thoughts and desires before they take the form of physical actions and therefore have consequences that are far more difficult to overcome.

There is a reality that many people have been programmed to reject. They might have been programmed by an orthodox religion or by materialistic science, but behind these outer belief systems is the prince of this world. He is trying to prevent you from accepting ultimate responsibility for your situation and your future. The prince of this world is trying to make you believe that you can escape accountability for your past actions by denying that you have lived before this lifetime. When you recognize the fact that you have lived before, you realize that you cannot escape anything by denying its existence. The only true escape is through self-transcendence.

One of the main reasons that the teachings on reincarnation were removed from Christianity was that many people were trapped in the duality consciousness. They were not willing to accept accountability for what they had done in past lifetimes. With the illogical logic of the dualistic mind, they reasoned that if they ignored or denied the concept of reincarnation, they would somehow escape accountability. They would then be able to live their lives in the illusion that their present actions could not come back to haunt them in a future lifetime. As the Bible says: "Vengeance is mine; I *will* repay, saith the Lord." (Romans 12:19) and "God is not mocked: for whatsoever a man soweth, that shall he also reap" (Galatians 6:7).

These simple quotes reveal that the Bible has an underlying recognition of the reality of reincarnation. The law of God says that you are responsible for whatever you do with God's energy. This energy will be reflected back to you by the cosmic mirror, and you will inevitably experience conditions that outpicture the actions you have taken in the past. Whatever you do onto others, you will inevitably experience yourself.

What happens if a person commits murder and is never caught by society? Seemingly, the person has escaped punishment for the deed that took the life of another human being and thus interfered with that person's free will. God's law is inescapable, and therefore when you commit a physical action, you are setting in motion a cause, an energy impulse. This impulse will cycle through the four levels of the material realm, and it will be returned to you as a physical circumstance. This will take time, and the reaction from the universe occurs in a future lifetime.

The Bible says God will visit the inequity of the fathers onto the third and forth generation (Exodus 34:7). To the dualistic mind, this sounds like an angry being in the sky, but when you recognize the reality of reincarnation, you can gain a deeper understanding. The third and fourth generation might not simply be the physical children but could be your own soul reincarnated three or four lifetimes later. Do you see a possible connection between the third and fourth generation mentioned in the Bible and the existence of four levels of the material universe? Do you think this is just a coincidence or could it possibly have a deeper meaning?

***

If you have not grown up with an understanding of reincarnation, this can be a somewhat uncomfortable, perhaps even a fearful, topic. It is my goal to give you everything you need in order to understand what could be blocking the manifestation of God's abundance in your life. In order to fully understand this, you need to recognize that in a past life you could have set in motion causes that are now manifesting as physical circumstances. These circumstances are blocking the manifestation of God's abundance in your life. When you accept this, you will be able to see beyond the ominous, fearful belief that you are being punished by an angry God and that there is no escape. You will be able to see that the law of God is actually set up to give you the best possible opportunity for growth.

The material universe has a built-in delay factor. The cosmic mirror does not instantly reflect back to you what you do onto others. This is a grace period and let me now explain how this works. There are many people who have had a very difficult childhood and a very difficult life. They have grown up in circumstances that made it almost inevitable that they would develop a short-term sense of identity that was very low compared to their Christ potential. Because of the current imperfect conditions on earth, many people have been predisposed to commit actions that can only limit themselves and harm others. If those actions were immediately reflected back by the cosmic mirror, many people would destroy themselves and therefore lose the opportunity for further growth in this embodiment.

It is entirely possible that humankind could collectively create a downward spiral that would, in a very short period of time,
destroy the entire planet as a platform for spiritual growth. In
order to avoid such a scenario, God has set up the material universe with four levels. When you commit a physical action, you
are generating an energy impulse that is sent out into the material realm. This impulse will cycle through the four levels of the
material realm, and only after passing through the three higher
levels will it come back to you in the form of actual, physical
circumstances. The outworking of this law of cause and effect,
what Eastern religions call the law of karma, is very complex
so what I give you here is a simplified image. For the sake of
simplicity, let us say that you kill another human being. By committing this physical action, you generate a cause, and the effect
of it is that you take away that person's opportunity for growth
for the remainder of what would have been the natural life span.
Obviously, this interferes directly with the other person's free
will. What effect will this have on you?

Before we take this further, I want to make it very clear to
you that even though you have violated God's law, God has
absolutely no desire to punish you. The entire concept of an
angry and punishing God is a product of the dualistic mind,
the mind of anti-christ. If you have committed the act of killing
another human being, your act is the product of a grave imbal-
ance in your three higher bodies. You can kill someone only if
you have severely imbalanced emotions, and they must spring
from a set of self-centered thoughts that again spring from a
warped sense of identity. God has given you free will but God
desires to see you be free of any imperfect sense of identity. If
you kill another human being, God has no desire to punish you,
but God does have a desire to see you free yourself from the
beliefs that caused you to commit that act. How can you best
free yourself from those selfish beliefs? The ultimate way to free

yourself from the desire to kill other people would be that you were killed yourself so that you experience what it is like to lose an opportunity to be in embodiment. There are many people who are only set free from their imperfect desires and beliefs when they experience tragedy in their own lives. Only then are they awakened to reflect on and reexamine some of their deeply held beliefs. Ultimately, it might be necessary for you to experience actually being killed before you can free yourself from the imperfect beliefs that caused you to kill another.

Because God is not an angry God, but a merciful God, he has set up a universe that does not instantly kill you when you kill another. Instead, the energy impulse generated when you killed the other person cycles through the four levels of the material realm. This gives you an opportunity to resolve your dualistic beliefs before the energy impulse, the karma, comes back to you as a physical circumstance that results in you being killed. The universe is set up to present you with the best possible opportunity to learn your lessons and rise above your limited beliefs. As the energy from your past actions comes back to you, it first enters your identity body. It will activate the beliefs that caused you to kill another person in a past life, and this gives you an opportunity to examine those beliefs. For example, you might have thoughts about why it is wrong to kill. If you do not take the first opportunity, the energy impulse will cycle through your mental and emotional bodies where you get further opportunities to examine and resolve your thoughts and feelings. If you still ignore the opportunity, the energy cycles into the matter realm where it will be manifest as a circumstance that you cannot ignore.

You can choose how you want to learn your lessons in life. Do you want to learn them the easy way or the hard way? Do you want to attend the inner school of seeking spiritual understanding (with all thy getting, get understanding), or do you want to attend the School of Hard Knocks? This gives you an immense opportunity. There are some spiritual teachings that talk about the descent of karma. The reality is that an imperfect action committed by you in the past will come back to you by descending through the four levels of the material realm. Because your four lower bodies are a part of the material realm, as an action from the past descends, it passes through your four lower bodies. It passes through the four levels of your mind before it manifests as a physical circumstance. You can consume that energy impulse, you can consume that descending karma, in the identity, the mental or the emotional realm. You can prevent it from becoming a physical reality.

I fully understand why many people in the West tend to reject the concept of karma and reincarnation. They do this because for 1,500 years the Christian religion has denied the reality of reincarnation. Many people in the West are presented with the concept of reincarnation through Eastern teachings, and some of these teachings present a very fatalistic view of reincarnation. Such teachings say that everything that happens to you in this life is a product of causes you have set in motion in past lives, and therefore there is nothing you can do to escape these events. This is an outright lie promoted by the prince of this world. It is an attempt to get people to give up without even trying to change their destiny and their future. The reality is that reincarnation and karma is set up to give you the maximum amount of opportunity to change your situation, to change your past or at least the effect your past has on your present and your future. You cannot change the actions you committed in a past life, but you *can* change the energy impulses you set in motion in the past. You can requalify the misqualified energy as it descends through the identity, mental and emotional realms and thereby prevent it from manifesting as a physical circumstance.

It is quite possible that in a past life you set in motion a karma that prevents you from having abundance in this life. If you cannot change that karma, how could you possibly change your physical circumstances? You can decide with your conscious mind that you are going to pray or give affirmations all day long, but if your efforts are not powerful enough to consume the descending karma, you have literally no way to change your physical circumstances. If you are sincere about manifesting the abundant life, you need to discover how you can consume your karma from past lifetimes before it becomes physical and is therefore much more difficult to overcome. A thought and a feeling can easily be reversed, but once you cross the line into the matter realm, you cannot turn back the clock. Likewise, your karma from past lives can easily be consumed before it reaches the matter realm, but once it crosses the line and takes on a dense physical form, it is much more difficult to free yourself from it.

In order to give you a visual image of this, let me ask you to consider a volcano that spews out a stream of lava that is flowing down the mountainside. The lava is liquid and fluid, and it is easy to change its course. The lava finally hits the ocean and is cooled down so quickly that it instantly solidifies. Now the lava is solid, and it is very difficult to remove. If you had a tool that could handle the fluid lava, it would be easy to remove. The hardened lava must be broken into smaller pieces before you can remove it. This is comparable to the difference between karma that is still descending and karma that has entered the matter realm and become physical.

***

How can you prevent your past actions from manifesting as undesirable physical circumstances? God has no desire to

punish you; God simply wants you to be free from your imperfect beliefs. Because God gave you free will, you can be free only
through your own choosing. The ultimate way to prevent your
karma from manifesting is to purify your four lower bodies. If
you clear all levels of your mind from the imperfect beliefs and
energies that caused you to commit murder in a past life, there is
absolutely no point in having you experience the physical karma
of that action. If you have already learned the lesson you are
meant to learn, why would you need to experience the physical
circumstances? It is quite possible that God or your spiritual
teachers can set aside the descent of this karma. The imperfect
energies created in the past still have to be balanced, and it is
your responsibility to do so. You can do so by invoking spiritual light that re-qualifies the imperfect energies by raising their
vibration. You can be free of your past actions without experiencing the physical consequences. This can happen only when
you consume the karma being reflected back by the cosmic mirror before it descends to the matter realm.

When you clear your four lower bodies, your descending karma will be consumed almost automatically. In order to
explain the mechanics of this, let me go back to the image of
an imperfect belief in your identity body. As an example, consider the belief that you are a separate individual and that you
can hurt other people without affecting yourself, a belief that is
very common on this planet and springs from the duality consciousness. This belief has the effect of reducing the amount of
energy and the vibration of the energy flowing into your identity
body. Because you are not multiplying your talents, the energy
flow from the spiritual realm is reduced. There simply is not
much high-frequency light flowing into your identity body. The
imperfect belief in your identity body is what resulted in you
taking a selfish physical action, and this physical action created
an energy impulse, namely your karma. As this energy impulse

filters through your identity body, there is no light of a higher vibration to raise the vibration of the karma, there is no light to consume that karma and prevent it from descending further. The misqualified energies in your identity body will not block the karma because it has the same vibration as the accumulated energy. The karma can flow unhindered into your mental body and is now one step closer to becoming manifest as a physical circumstance.

What happens when you remove the imperfect beliefs and the misqualified energies in your identity body? Your identity body now becomes filled with light. This is described in one of Jesus' more esoteric statements when he said that if your eye is single, your whole body is full of light (Matthew 6:22). One meaning of this is that if your identity body is "single" – it is not a house divided against itself by dualistic beliefs so you see yourself as one with God – your identity body will be full of light. The light that can be held in your identity body has a very high vibration, which means that it has the potential to consume the lower vibration of the returning karma. If the karma has a vibration of 800 Hz and your identity body can hold light that vibrates at 90,000 Hz, the more powerful light can easily consume the karma and prevent it from descending further.

What about karma that has already descended into the mental or the emotional realm? You can consume this karma by clearing those two lower bodies the same way you clear your identity body. When your identity body is already cleared, it becomes much easier to clear the two lower bodies. What about a karma that is ready to cross over into the matter realm? What can you do to prevent that from manifesting? The way to do this is to invoke high-frequency spiritual energy through a proper technique and direct it into consuming that karma. In order to do so effectively, you must also engage in a sincere process to purify your higher bodies, and this is precisely what my invocations are designed to do.

***

What I have given you up until this point is a much more complex picture of life than what you have been given by orthodox religions or by materialistic science. In the beginning, this can seem somewhat overwhelming. I am actually presenting you with a unique opportunity to escape the limitations that you experience every single day of your life. The question becomes whether you would rather continue to experience those limitations for the rest of your life, or whether you are willing to make a determined effort to raise yourself above those limitations once and for all?

Many people are so overwhelmed by the energies they carry, the misqualified energies in their four lower bodies and the descending karma, that they cannot pull themselves out of their present frame of mind. They cannot step off the treadmill of their daily lives to do something different that will free them permanently. If you had been one of those people, you would not have had the attention or the desire to follow this course. You do indeed have the potential to use the teachings and the tools I give you in this course. You can reverse the downward spiral in which you might be trapped. Instead, you can create a permanent upward spiral that will gradually lead you from where you are right now to where you truly want to be in life, namely as a being who has peace of mind and who is in the flow of God's abundance. By making a determined effort, you can indeed turn your life around, you can turn it into an upward spiral. This will not happen overnight, but I remind you of the saying that a journey of a thousand miles begins with one step. What you need to add is that if you keep taking one small step at a time, you *will* inevitably arrive at the destination.

The real key to breaking the downward spiral is to find an efficient way to purify your four lower bodies of the imperfect beliefs and the misqualified energies that have accumulated there over many lifetimes. This is indeed what I present to you in this course: a systematic approach to purifying your four lower bodies. Everything I have given you in this course is designed to challenge some of the dualistic beliefs stored in your four lower bodies. By following the course to this point, you are already well on your way to exposing those beliefs. You have also been using the practical techniques for invoking high-frequency spiritual energy and directing it into the blocks in your four lower bodies.

In the following chapter, I will expose one of the traps set by your mortal self and by the prince of this world, namely the trap of pride in its many disguises. This is the trap of thinking you know everything, and therefore you do not need to follow any authority figure that is beyond your mortal self and the authority figures of this world. You might recall the old saying that pride goes before the fall. While this is true, the bigger problem is that pride prevents you from getting up after the fall. It truly is no longer significant that you have fallen—because this is a fact that you *cannot* reverse. What you *can* change is what happens after the fall, namely that instead of remaining stuck in the duality consciousness, you can start an upward spiral that frees you from the mind of anti-christ and takes you back up the spiral staircase until you are, once again, united with your higher being. Allow me to expose to you the subtle plot of pride that is designed to keep you trapped in a spiritual catch-22 from which there seems to be no escape. There *is* no escape, except to follow the true teacher who is sent by God to set you free.

4 | I INVOKE FREEDOM FROM KARMA

In the name I AM THAT I AM, Jesus Christ, I call to all representatives of the Divine Mother and the Divine Father, especially Nada, Jesus and Mother Mary, to help me transform all past karma before it enters the physical level. Help me accept my creative powers and see the factors that block the flow of my God-given creativity, including...

[Make personal calls.]

1. I neutralize my past actions

1. I am the Conscious You reaching up to my I AM Presence and releasing a stream of light that filters down to the physical brain and activates my higher brain centers.

O Jesus, blessed brother mine,
I walk the path that you outline,
a great example to us all,
I follow now your inner call.

**O Jesus, let the Fire of Joy,
consume the devil's subtle ploy,
transfigured is our planet earth,
the golden age is given birth.**

2. I am transcending any limiting beliefs in both my long-term and short-term identity bodies. I am healing any conflict between these two aspects of my identity body.

O Jesus, open inner sight,
the ego wants to prove it's right,
but this I will no longer do,
I want to be all one with you.

**O Jesus, let the Fire of Joy,
consume the devil's subtle ploy,
transfigured is our planet earth,
the golden age is given birth.**

3. I am transcending any internal conflict and the attempts of my mortal self and the prince of this world to put me in a spiritual catch-22. I am no longer a house divided against itself.

O Jesus, I now clearly see,
the Key of Knowledge given me,
my Christ self I hereby embrace,
as you fill up my inner space.

O Jesus, let the Fire of Joy,
consume the devil's subtle ploy,
transfigured is our planet earth,
the golden age is given birth.

4. I am going deeper into my psychology and resolving both long-term and short-term beliefs that say I am not worthy. I am indeed worthy to receive God's abundance.

O Jesus, show me serpent's lie,
expose the beam in my own eye,
as Christ discernment you me give,
in oneness I forever live.

O Jesus, let the Fire of Joy,
consume the devil's subtle ploy,
transfigured is our planet earth,
the golden age is given birth.

5. I am examining my reactions to life and uncovering the deeper patterns. I am going all the way back to my decision to turn away from God, to turn away from my spiritual teacher, allowing my mortal self and the prince of this world to be my teachers.

O Jesus, I am truly meek,
and thus I turn the other cheek,
when the accuser attacks me,
I go within and merge with thee.

O Jesus, let the Fire of Joy,
consume the devil's subtle ploy,
transfigured is our planet earth,
the golden age is given birth.

6. I realize that the conditions I face in this life are a product of a very complex picture, namely the beliefs that I have accepted in past lives and that still reside in my four lower bodies.

> O Jesus, ego I let die,
> surrender ev'ry earthly tie,
> the dead can bury what is dead,
> I choose to walk with you instead.

> **O Jesus, let the Fire of Joy,**
> **consume the devil's subtle ploy,**
> **transfigured is our planet earth,**
> **the golden age is given birth.**

7. I realize that in the past I have taken actions that have generated karma. This returning karma can block the manifestation of God's abundance in this lifetime. I am dissolving the return of my past actions before they manifest as material circumstances.

> O Jesus, help me rise above,
> the devil's test through higher love,
> show me separate self unreal,
> my formless self you do reveal.

> **O Jesus, let the Fire of Joy,**
> **consume the devil's subtle ploy,**
> **transfigured is our planet earth,**
> **the golden age is given birth.**

8. I recognize that there is a dividing line between my thoughts and feelings and my physical actions. When I take a physical action, I have brought my thoughts and feelings into the lowest level of the material realm where it is more difficult to change.

O Jesus, what is that to me,
I just let go and follow thee,
with this I do pass ev'ry test,
to find with you eternal rest.

**O Jesus, let the Fire of Joy,
consume the devil's subtle ploy,
transfigured is our planet earth,
the golden age is given birth.**

9. A physical action begins in my identity body, takes a more distinct shape in my mental body and receives direction and momentum in my emotional body. I am coming to a higher understanding that allows me to reverse my mental impulses before they become physical.

O Jesus, fiery master mine,
my heart now melting into thine,
I love with heart and mind and soul,
the God who is my highest goal.

**O Jesus, let the Fire of Joy,
consume the devil's subtle ploy,
transfigured is our planet earth,
the golden age is given birth.**

2. I am consuming my karma

1. I am taking dominion over my life by purifying my four lower bodies of all imperfect thoughts and feelings.

O Nada, blessed cosmic grace,
filling up my inner space.
Your song is like a sacred balm,
my mind a sea of perfect calm.

With Nada's secret melody,
my mind remains forever free.
Conducting Nada's symphony,
eternal peace I do decree.

2. I am in control of my reactions to life's trials. Instead of feeling like I have no choice, I can now choose to respond in the way that is best for me from a long-term perspective. I choose to follow Jesus' call to turn the other cheek.

O Nada, in your Buddhic mind,
my inner peace I truly find.
As I your song reverberate,
your love I do assimilate.

With Nada's secret melody,
my mind remains forever free.
Conducting Nada's symphony,
eternal peace I do decree.

3. I am removing imperfect thoughts and desires before they take the form of physical actions and therefore have consequences that are far more difficult to overcome.

O Nada, beauty so sublime,
I follow you beyond all time.
In soundless sound we do immerse,
to recreate the universe.

With Nada's secret melody,
my mind remains forever free.
Conducting Nada's symphony,
eternal peace I do decree.

4. I recognize the fact that I have lived before. I cannot escape anything by denying its existence. The only true escape is through self-transcendence.

O Nada, future we predict
where nothing Christhood can restrict.
With Buddhic mind we do perceive,
a better future we conceive.

With Nada's secret melody,
my mind remains forever free.
Conducting Nada's symphony,
eternal peace I do decree.

5. I recognize that in a past life I could have set in motion causes that are now manifesting as physical circumstances. These circumstances may be blocking the manifestation of God's abundance in my life.

O Nada, future we rewrite,
where might is never, ever right.
Instead, the mind of Christ is king,
we see the Christ in every thing.

With Nada's secret melody,
my mind remains forever free.
Conducting Nada's symphony,
eternal peace I do decree.

6. God has set up a universe that does not give me an instant return of karma. The energy impulses I generate cycle through the four levels of the material realm. I am resolving my dualistic beliefs before the energy impulse, the karma, comes back to me as a physical circumstance.

> O Nada, peace is now the norm,
> my Spirit is beyond all form.
> To form I will no more adapt,
> I use potential yet untapped.

> **With Nada's secret melody,**
> **my mind remains forever free.**
> **Conducting Nada's symphony,**
> **eternal peace I do decree.**

7. I am learning my lessons and rising above my limited beliefs. I am examining and resolving all limiting beliefs in my identity, mental, emotional and physical bodies.

> O Nada, such resplendent joy,
> my life I truly can enjoy.
> I am allowed to have some fun,
> my solar plexus like a sun.

> **With Nada's secret melody,**
> **my mind remains forever free.**
> **Conducting Nada's symphony,**
> **eternal peace I do decree.**

8. When an action from the past descends, it passes through my four lower bodies before it manifests as a physical circumstance. I am consuming the descending karma in the identity, the mental and the emotional realm, even at the physical level.

O Nada, service is the key,
to living in reality.
For I see now that life is one,
my highest service has begun.

**With Nada's secret melody,
my mind remains forever free.
Conducting Nada's symphony,
eternal peace I do decree.**

9. I cannot change the actions I committed in a past life, but I am changing the energy impulses I set in motion in the past. I am requalifying the misqualified energy as it descends through the identity, mental and emotional realms and thereby preventing it from manifesting as a physical circumstance.

O Nada, we do now decree,
that life on earth shall be carefree.
With Jesus we complete the quest,
God's kingdom is now manifest.

**With Nada's secret melody,
my mind remains forever free.
Conducting Nada's symphony,
eternal peace I do decree.**

3. I am filled with light

1. I am consuming any karma created in a past life that prevents me from having abundance in this life. I am changing the karma and my physical circumstances.

> O Jesus, blessed brother mine,
> I walk the path that you outline,
> a great example to us all,
> I follow now your inner call.

> **O Jesus, let the Fire of Joy,**
> **consume the devil's subtle ploy,**
> **transfigured is our planet earth,**
> **the golden age is given birth.**

2. I am discovering and consuming my karma from past lifetimes before it crosses the line and takes on a dense physical form.

> O Jesus, open inner sight,
> the ego wants to prove it's right,
> but this I will no longer do,
> I want to be all one with you.

> **O Jesus, let the Fire of Joy,**
> **consume the devil's subtle ploy,**
> **transfigured is our planet earth,**
> **the golden age is given birth.**

3. I am clearing all levels of my mind from the imperfect beliefs and energies that caused me to make karma in a past life, thereby neutralizing the need for having me experience the physical karma of my actions.

> O Jesus, I now clearly see,
> the Key of Knowledge given me,
> my Christ self I hereby embrace,
> as you fill up my inner space.

> **O Jesus, let the Fire of Joy,**
> **consume the devil's subtle ploy,**
> **transfigured is our planet earth,**
> **the golden age is given birth.**

4. I am learning the lesson I am meant to learn, and thus there is no need to experience the physical circumstances.

> O Jesus, show me serpent's lie,
> expose the beam in my own eye,
> as Christ discernment you me give,
> in oneness I forever live.

> **O Jesus, let the Fire of Joy,**
> **consume the devil's subtle ploy,**
> **transfigured is our planet earth,**
> **the golden age is given birth.**

5. I am asking God and my spiritual teachers to set aside the descent of my physical karma. I am fully accepting my responsibility to balance the imperfect energies created in the past.

O Jesus, I am truly meek,
and thus I turn the other cheek,
when the accuser attacks me,
I go within and merge with thee.

O Jesus, let the Fire of Joy,
consume the devil's subtle ploy,
transfigured is our planet earth,
the golden age is given birth.

6. I am balancing my karma by invoking spiritual light that requalifies the imperfect energies by raising their vibration.

O Jesus, ego I let die,
surrender ev'ry earthly tie,
the dead can bury what is dead,
I choose to walk with you instead.

O Jesus, let the Fire of Joy,
consume the devil's subtle ploy,
transfigured is our planet earth,
the golden age is given birth.

7. I am free of my past actions without experiencing the physical consequences. I am consuming the karma being reflected back by the cosmic mirror before it descends to the matter realm.

O Jesus, help me rise above,
the devil's test through higher love,
show me separate self unreal,
my formless self you do reveal.

O Jesus, let the Fire of Joy,
consume the devil's subtle ploy,
transfigured is our planet earth,
the golden age is given birth.

8. I completely surrender the belief that I am a separate individual and that I can hurt other people without affecting myself.

O Jesus, what is that to me,
I just let go and follow thee,
with this I do pass ev'ry test,
to find with you eternal rest.

O Jesus, let the Fire of Joy,
consume the devil's subtle ploy,
transfigured is our planet earth,
the golden age is given birth.

9. I am removing the imperfect beliefs and the misqualified energies in my four lower bodies and they are now filled with light.

O Jesus, fiery master mine,
my heart now melting into thine,
I love with heart and mind and soul,
the God who is my highest goal.

O Jesus, let the Fire of Joy,
consume the devil's subtle ploy,
transfigured is our planet earth,
the golden age is given birth.

4. I am in an upward spiral

1. Because my four lower bodies are purified, my vision is single, it is undivided. Mine eye is single and my whole body is full of light.

> O Nada, blessed cosmic grace,
> filling up my inner space.
> Your song is like a sacred balm,
> my mind a sea of perfect calm.
>
> **With Nada's secret melody,**
> **my mind remains forever free.**
> **Conducting Nada's symphony,**
> **eternal peace I do decree.**

2. I am taking the opportunity to escape the limitations that I experience every single day of my life.

> O Nada, in your Buddhic mind,
> my inner peace I truly find.
> As I your song reverberate,
> your love I do assimilate.
>
> **With Nada's secret melody,**
> **my mind remains forever free.**
> **Conducting Nada's symphony,**
> **eternal peace I do decree.**

3. I am making a determined effort to raise myself above those limitations once and for all.

O Nada, beauty so sublime,
I follow you beyond all time.
In soundless sound we do immerse,
to recreate the universe.

**With Nada's secret melody,
my mind remains forever free.
Conducting Nada's symphony,
eternal peace I do decree.**

4. I am pulling myself above my present frame of mind.

O Nada, future we predict
where nothing Christhood can restrict.
With Buddhic mind we do perceive,
a better future we conceive.

**With Nada's secret melody,
my mind remains forever free.
Conducting Nada's symphony,
eternal peace I do decree.**

5. I am stepping off the treadmill of my daily life and doing
something different that will free me permanently.

O Nada, future we rewrite,
where might is never, ever right.
Instead, the mind of Christ is king,
we see the Christ in every thing.

With Nada's secret melody,
my mind remains forever free.
Conducting Nada's symphony,
eternal peace I do decree.

6. I am reversing the downward spiral in which I have been trapped.

O Nada, peace is now the norm,
my Spirit is beyond all form.
To form I will no more adapt,
I use potential yet untapped.

With Nada's secret melody,
my mind remains forever free.
Conducting Nada's symphony,
eternal peace I do decree.

7. I am creating a permanent upward spiral that will gradually lead me from where I am right now to where I truly want to be in life.

O Nada, such resplendent joy,
my life I truly can enjoy.
I am allowed to have some fun,
my solar plexus like a sun.

With Nada's secret melody,
my mind remains forever free.
Conducting Nada's symphony,
eternal peace I do decree.

8. I am a being who has peace of mind and who is in the flow of God's abundance.

> O Nada, service is the key,
> to living in reality.
> For I see now that life is one,
> my highest service has begun.

> **With Nada's secret melody,**
> **my mind remains forever free.**
> **Conducting Nada's symphony,**
> **eternal peace I do decree.**

9. I am free from the mind of anti-christ. I am ascending back up the spiral staircase and I am, once again, united with my higher being.

> O Nada, we do now decree,
> that life on earth shall be carefree.
> With Jesus we complete the quest,
> God's kingdom is now manifest.

> **With Nada's secret melody,**
> **my mind remains forever free.**
> **Conducting Nada's symphony,**
> **eternal peace I do decree.**

Sealing

In the name of the Divine Mother, I call to Nada, Jesus and Mother Mary for the sealing of myself and all people in my circle of influence in the creative flow of the Divine Mother, the River of Life. I call for the multiplication of my calls by all representatives of the Divine Mother, so that we form the perfect figure-eight flow of "As Above, so below." Thus, I accept that this is fully manifest, because the mouth of the Lord, the Divine Mother that I AM, has spoken it. Amen.

5 | DEALING WITH EMOTIONAL PAIN

My beloved heart, let me bring together some of the things we have discussed in the last several chapters to present you with an overall view of what you need to accomplish in order to purify your four lower bodies, overcome the consequences of your past actions and manifest the abundant life. Let us begin by talking about the resistance to your efforts to purify your four lower bodies.

Many people have experienced highly traumatic situations in this lifetime, and such situations can be associated with great emotional pain. When I say that in order to be free of the blocks in your emotional body you need to take a look at the beliefs behind those blocks, I know many people will immediately resist doing so. They know that thinking back to the situations from their past will plunge them into a state of emotional pain and discomfort. I am in no way blaming people for such reactions, for it is quite understandable that they want to avoid the emotional pain. What if I could show you a method whereby you could reduce the intensity of the emotional pain before you actually start looking at the painful situations from the past? If the intensity of the pain is reduced, it would only be a temporary and bearable discomfort to take a look at the past. In that case, it would be well worth the effort to go through a temporary discomfort in order to permanently free yourself from an imperfect belief that is affecting you 24 hours a day. This would be a very good investment, just as it would be a good investment to buy stocks if you could double your money.

The other major form of opposition that people run into as they begin to purify their four lower bodies is what we might call the force of habit. As a visual image, imagine water that is running down a hillside. The water tends to carve little grooves in the hillside, and once a groove has started to form, it will funnel more water. The groove will become deeper until it eventually becomes a gully containing a river. This is how habits form in your four lower bodies. As the light flows through your four lower bodies, it follows the path of least resistance.

If you have an imperfect belief in your mental body, the belief, and the misqualified energy resulting from the belief, will form a barrier that will make it harder for the light to flow. The light will tend to flow around it, and thereby your thoughts are steered into a certain pattern, causing your feelings to follow suit. This has the effect of limiting the options you can see, and thus it limits your creative expression. This causes you to set up a mental and emotional habit that, so to speak, programs you to respond to certain situations in a specific way. At the level of the conscious mind, you do not have control over your reactions to specific situations. Your reactions are predetermined by the habits that exist in your emotional, mental and identity bodies as well as in your physical mind.

If you look at people you know, and perhaps look at your own life, you will see that this is a very common problem. Many people literally do not have the option to choose their reaction to a specific situation. Due to habits that were set up in the past, they will inevitably respond with anger to certain situations.

They simply cannot stop themselves from doing so, and the effect is often that a relationship between two people is locked into a destructive or dysfunctional pattern. One person says something that the other person doesn't like. The second person responds with anger, and then the first person also responds with anger. The two people are now angry with each other, and none of them have the power to break free from the anger and choose a more loving reaction to the situation.

The extreme form of a habit is an addiction to a physical substance, such as drugs or alcohol. There are many more subtle habits and, in fact, any pattern of behavior starts in the higher bodies as a mental and emotional habit. The main problem with breaking a habit is that there is quite a resistance to doing so. Tracks have been carved in the levels of your mind, and the energy will tend to flow in those tracks. It takes great effort to change the patterns at the higher levels of the mind. Many people have tried to change a particular habit but have been unsuccessful. They find that they can change the habit for a while, but doing so is an uphill battle. As soon as they relax just a little bit, they snap back into the old patterns.

Others manage to change the outer behavior, but they have to fight an ongoing battle, possibly for the rest of their lives, to keep themselves from snapping back into the old pattern of behavior. This is not the abundant life, for how can you enjoy life when you are constantly fighting this battle with yourself? I understand that many people are reluctant to tackle habits because they know from experience that it is very difficult to remove an old habit. What if I could show you a way to diminish the resistance to breaking a habit, to diminish the magnetic force that pulls you into certain patterns of thoughts, feelings and behavior?

***

What causes you to feel emotional pain when you think about a traumatic situation from your past is the accumulated energy in your higher bodies, especially the emotional body. What makes it so difficult to break a habit is likewise the accumulated energy in your emotional body, in your mental body and even in your identity body. This energy literally forms an energy field that has much the same effect as a magnetic field. The field around a magnet will pull on a metal object that comes within the range of the field. If you have such "magnetic" fields in your four lower bodies, they will pull on your thoughts and emotions. They will literally pull your thoughts and emotions into a certain pattern, and that is why your reactions to certain situations are predetermined—preprogrammed.

When you use a powerful technique for purifying the misqualified energy and thereby raise its vibration, the intensity of the emotional pain associated with past situations is reduced. You can now think about these situations without being overwhelmed by pain. You can look at them objectively, almost as if you were dealing with another person. It is always easy for you to solve other people's problems, and the reason is that you are not emotionally involved. You can look at the situation more objectively and see the solution that for the other person is hidden behind a veil of emotional energy.

When you reduce the magnetic pull that causes you to follow certain patterns of behavior, you can break a habit much easier and often without the normal "withdrawal symptoms." By removing the energy, you will make it far easier for yourself to reexamine painful situations from your past. You can uncover the decisions you made while you were in those situations. You can consciously replace those decisions by making better decisions based on the clearer vision you now have. When you remove the magnetic pull of an old habit, it becomes much easier for you to uncover the decisions behind that habit. You

can change those decisions and carve a new and more productive trail in your subconscious mind. You can build a positive
habit rather than a limiting one. What I am showing you here is
that there are three main components to freeing yourself from
your past:

• One is the internal component of overcoming the
imperfect decisions and beliefs that are stored in your
identity, mental, emotional and physical minds. This
involves both decisions in your long-term mind, the
mind that you carry with you from lifetime to lifetime,
and in your short-term mind, the mind that is attached
to your current physical body.

• The second component is that you must transform
the misqualified energy stored in your four lower bodies.
This will make it easier for you to break limiting habits
and it will make it easier for you to heal the scars from
past trauma.

• The third component is that you must consume the
energy impulse, the karma, that is reflected back to you
by the cosmic mirror according to your past actions.

When you find and apply a powerful technique for accom-
plishing these three goals (such as my invocations), your life
will immediately take a turn for the better and you can quickly
establish an upward spiral. By putting forth a determined
effort for a while, you can make this spiral self-sustaining and
self-reinforcing.

Consider how easy it is for people to create a downward
spiral for themselves. They have accepted a number of negative
beliefs that cause them to misqualify energy. These beliefs and

the misqualified energy pull their thoughts and feelings into certain patterns that lead to actions that are not in their own best interest. These actions have consequences, and as people experience the negative consequences, the patterns in their higher bodies cause them to respond with negative thoughts and emotions. This misqualifies even more energy and reinforces their negative beliefs, which obviously solidifies the mental and emotional patterns. This, of course, misqualifies even more energy, and a downward spiral can form very quickly. This spiral becomes self-reinforcing, self-perpetuating, and it can literally take people down to a point where they feel they are mentally and emotionally paralyzed. They have nowhere to go, they cannot move, they feel boxed in from every side and feel like they have no options left in life. This is not because they actually have no options but because the imperfect beliefs and the misqualified energy in their four lower bodies prevent them from seeing the options or prevent them from acting upon their vision. They think they cannot change themselves, and therefore they cannot see how to change their outer situations. This is, of course, what psychologists call depression, and it can easily develop into a more severe mental illness.

Most people on this planet have grown up in circumstances that caused them to create such a downward spiral, and you should not expect that breaking such a spiral will happen overnight or without putting forth a determined effort. If you are determined, and if you are willing to do the work, you can break this spiral and create an upward, self-perpetuating spiral instead. Once you have turned things around, your life will literally take on an entirely new dimension. You will then begin to experience the abundant life, not only in the form of material abundance but also in the form of spiritual abundance. With spiritual abundance I mean greater happiness, greater peace of mind, an expanded vision of life's opportunities and a sense of purpose and fulfillment, which all adds up to what I talked about earlier, namely wholeness. It is well worth the effort to break the downward spiral and create an upward one. I have now given you the understanding you need for how you can accomplish this task, and I hope I have also given you the motivation you need to make the decision that you will indeed do the work. If you have given the invocations along with this course, you have already transmuted a great deal of energy and you have challenged many subconscious beliefs. If you have read to this point without giving the invocations, it is not too late to go back and start giving them.

***

I want to talk about a topic that many people in the self-help field, even many people engaged in spiritual growth, tend to overlook. Because they do not understand this concept, they make their personal growth much more difficult than it needs to be. There came a point when you, meaning the Conscious You, decided to turn your back upon your spiritual teacher. There came a point when you decided that because you had made certain wrong decisions, you no longer wanted to make decisions. This gave birth to your mortal self, and since that point, your mortal self has made many of the decisions in your life. It is the very fact that you have allowed your mortal self to make decisions for you that has created the downward spiral. Your mortal self is born of duality and can only make decisions based on duality. Such decisions will inevitably limit your creative powers and will generate imperfect consequences that will be reflected back to you by the cosmic mirror.

What is it going to take to break the stranglehold that the mortal self has on the Conscious You and your sphere of self? There is only one way for this to happen, namely that the

Conscious You must separate itself from the mortal self. It must come apart and be God's chosen "people," meaning that you have chosen to reach for the higher reality of Christ instead of the dualistic so-called reality – the idol – presented by your mortal self and the prince of this world. You must literally stop identifying yourself with – or as – the mortal self.

For this to happen, you must do several things. You must first make the overall decision that you are willing to take back full responsibility for your life, for your destiny and for your salvation. After you make that overall decision, you must decide that you are willing to take a look at each of the decisions that caused you to take a step down the spiral staircase. You must be willing to understand why those were dualistic decisions that limited your creative powers. Finally, you must replace those decisions by reaching for the higher understanding of the Christ mind that empowers you to make a better decision.

Let me introduce a subtle distinction here. After you decided not to make decisions, you allowed your mortal self to make many of the decisions in your life. All of the decisions made by your mortal self were dualistic decisions. I am not saying that you have to consciously uncover, see through and replace each of the dualistic decisions made by your mortal self in all of your embodiments. Each time you took a step down the spiral staircase, you made a decision that took you further away from God. Who made that decision? The Conscious You did! The decision was always influenced by one or more lies presented by your mortal self and the prince of this world, but you allowed yourself to be affected by these lies because you were not truly willing to take responsibility for yourself and get a clear vision of what the decision entailed.

Imagine that instead of walking down an unbroken staircase, you are walking down the stairs in a building with many floors. You make the decision to walk down the first flight of stairs until you reach the next floor down. Once you reach that floor, you can walk around and explore each of the rooms on that floor. No matter what you do on that floor, you will not descend any further. In order to descend further, you must go back to the staircase and walk down the next flight of stairs. In order to go down to a lower floor, you – meaning the Conscious You – must make a decision. By making this decision, you accept a new sense of identity that outpictures yourself as being further separated from God than you were on the higher floor. Once you have descended to that level, your mortal self will take over, and it will make numerous decisions based on the new sense of identity you have built. None of those decisions will take you further down, although they will build stronger habits that will make it harder for you to climb back up and easier for you to make the decision to descend further.

Your mortal self is much like a computer. It is programmed to make certain decisions, but it cannot by itself change its programming. In order to change the programming, the Conscious You must be involved, as a programmer is needed in order to change the programming of a computer. While your mortal self cannot accept a new sense of identity on its own, it can be easily influenced by outside forces, be it other people, certain belief systems or even direct influence from the prince of this world. Your mortal self can indeed urge you to accept a lower sense of identity, but it is always up to you to make the decision to descend to the next floor. As an example, consider that as a child you draw a picture and then show it to an adult. You get a negative reaction from the adult, and you lose interest in drawing. What really happened is that because of the unpleasant reaction, the Conscious You made the decision: "I am not a creative person." In order to avoid future pain, you decided never to express your creativity again. Although this might seem like a relatively minor decision, it can have a profound impact on your life. You might have cut off any chance of ever having a job that requires creative expression, which might have prevented you from fulfilling your life's plan and experiencing the joy of being creative. Your mortal self might have made many decisions based on the belief that you can't draw, such as what occupation to pursue or what to study – or not to study – in college. The one decision you need to consciously undo is the original one that caused you to build the sense of identity as a person who has no creative ability. Consider the even deeper decisions, such as the idea that you are a mortal human being and not a spiritual being, or that you are a separate individual who can do anything you want because you are more important than other people. Imagine how such decisions – made many lifetimes ago – could have affected every aspect of your current sense of identity, causing you to deny your true potential as a co-creator with God.

The good news is that you do not have to consciously replace each decision ever made by your mortal self. You only have to undo the decisions that took you down another step, or another floor, on the cosmic staircase. Once you undo one of those decisions, all of the decisions that sprang from that bigger decision will easily be left behind. You must still purify the misqualified energy resulting from those decisions, but the decisions themselves are gone. The bad news is that you will have to consciously undo each decision that took you down another step, and in order to do that you will have to overcome what we might call the original habit, the master habit.

***

There is a subtle mechanism at play here. The simple fact is that when your mortal self was created, and when you allowed it to take at least partial control over your life, you established a pattern of denial, a pattern of running away from situations or decisions that seemed unpleasant or overwhelming. In essence, the Conscious You decided that it did not want to experience certain situations, that it did not want to experience the consequences of its past choices and that it did not want to experience the agony of making new choices in a situation that was already deeply affected by imperfect choices from the past—making it seem like there were no good options left. That is why the Conscious You withdrew from such situations and allowed the mortal self to make the decision concerning how to respond to an unpleasant situation. This behavior has established a very deep-seated and very subtle pattern of running away from decisions that are unpleasant or seem too difficult. This is a pattern of thinking that by ignoring or denying something, you can avoid experiencing that something. If you are to undo the dualistic choices that make up your mortal self and keep it alive and in control, you will have to break this habit, to break this pattern, of turning your back upon anything that seems unpleasant or overwhelming. You must stop running away from decisions. You must be willing to turn around and face what you have not been willing to face up until now.

I have observed many, many spiritual seekers who were awakened to the spiritual side of life through discovering a particular religion, spiritual philosophy or guru. They became very enthusiastic and immediately threw themselves into an intense period of studying the new teaching and practicing its techniques for growth. This did indeed cause them to open their minds to a new and higher understanding, and they did make progress by doing so. After a while, many people get to a point where they can make no further progress unless they break the pattern of running away from difficult decisions. This is a very critical point on your spiritual path, and I can assure you that the mortal self and the prince of this world know exactly what is at stake. If you manage to break the pattern of running away, they will lose their power over you. They might still be able to influence you for a while and slow down your progress, but once you pass the critical point of taking full responsibility for yourself, they will no longer be able to control you fully. It is only a matter of time before they lose all influence over you. Once you pass the critical point, you will have generated an upward spiral that the mortal self and the forces of this world cannot reverse.

Your mortal self and the prince of this world will do everything they possibly can to prevent you from breaking the pattern of running away. They will do this by setting up the false path, the path that seems right onto a man, but the ends thereof are the ways of death. What they say is that you don't really need to face what is unpleasant, you don't really need to make the difficult decisions. Instead, all you need to do is to follow an outer teacher, an outer authority. You need to believe in the doctrines of a particular religion, you need to follow its practices, you need to do the things they tell you to do and to avoid doing the things they tell you not to do. You need to follow an outer leader, an outer guru, rather than to go within and wrestle with the task of seeing through the dualistic lies of your mortal self and reaching for the higher understanding of your Christ self. What they are saying is that even though you have found a spiritual teaching and started a spiritual practice, you can still maintain the habit of running away. By doing all the outer things just right, you can be saved without actually changing yourself and your approach to life, without actually undoing your past decisions.

This promise is a completely false promise. You simply cannot manifest your eternal life until you have set yourself free from all identification with the mortal self. Jesus gave an important parable where he talks about a wedding feast to which all are invited (Matthew 22:2). He describes how one person had entered without wearing a wedding garment, and that person was then bound hand and foot and cast into outer darkness where there was weeping and gnashing of teeth. This is a dramatic way of telling the story, but the reality behind it is that in order to enter the spiritual realm, you have to wear the wedding garment. This means you must have purified your four lower bodies from all elements of duality, all elements of anti-christ. You must have put on the wedding garment of the Christ consciousness. If you have not put on this higher state of consciousness, you cannot enter the consciousness of the abundant life, and therefore you will be bound hand and foot by your own dualistic beliefs. You will remain in the outer darkness of the dualistic state of mind, in which life is a continuous struggle. This is not the punishment of an angry God, this is simply the consequence of your own choices—or lack of choices. You simply cannot win your salvation, your eternal life, and you cannot manifest the abundant life, unless you break the habit of running away from what is unpleasant.

***

What will it take for you to break that habit? Let me give you an understanding that might help you. Everything is subject to your free will. In order for you to be free of an imperfect belief in one of your four lower bodies, you must make the choice to let go of, to dismiss, that belief. You must overcome the illusion that the belief is true or that it is somehow necessary or unavoidable. You must overcome any emotional attachment to it so that you are willing to let it go. You must literally be willing to let that aspect of your mortal self die.

You have to give away the imperfect belief, yet the problem is that you simply cannot give away what you do not own. This is logical from your everyday experience. If you do not have a toy, you cannot give that toy to a child. If you do not have the money, you cannot give them away in order to pay your bills.

Before you can give away an imperfect belief, you must take ownership of that belief and the fact that it entered your sphere of self. How can you take ownership of a belief as long as you maintain the habit that causes you to run away from anything that is unpleasant or complicated? This habit will literally prevent you from taking ownership of, from taking responsibility for, your past choices, and thus it prevents you from doing the one thing that is the master key to freeing yourself from those choices.

As long as you maintain the habit of running away, of not wanting to take responsibility for the beliefs and decisions stored in your four lower bodies, you will keep yourself in a catch-22. There is literally no escape from this as long as you keep running away. The false path presented by the prince of this world and your mortal self is based on the claim that there is an escape, that there is an automatic or guaranteed salvation. Some religions claim that if only you keep following them, you will one day wake up in heaven. Others claim that an outer savior, such as Jesus, will solve your problems for you and you will one day wake up in heaven. This simply is not possible. How could you ever wake up anywhere else but where you are? You will not wake up until you decide that you are willing to wake up right *here,* right *now.*

What we are talking about here is the perfect trap, set by the prince of this world. He first lies to you in order to get you to make a mistake. He then tricks you into establishing a pattern of running away from your past decisions. Finally, he presents you with the false path which justifies the tendency to run away by saying that you can be saved by following an outer authority. All in all, this adds up to the perfect storm, and the Conscious You is literally like a ship without rudder and compass, a ship that is "driven with the wind and tossed" (James 1:6). In order to overcome this lie, you only need to see that true salvation is oneness with your source. How can you ever get back to oneness with your source as long as you are running away from God? How can running away from home bring you back home? It is the Father's good pleasure to give you the kingdom, but in order to receive it you have to accept what God offers you freely. You have come to accept a completely false image of God, an idol that was carefully engineered by the prince of this world in order to prevent you from freely accepting God's gift of the abundant life. You have been programmed by your mortal self to look at God as an angry God who wants to punish you for your mistakes. This has given rise to the subtle belief – which many religions are based on, even though none of the leaders and followers realize what is happening – that you can *buy* your salvation, that you can make a bargain with God. This belief gives people the impression that they have to do something to compensate God for their sins, as if an infinite and all-powerful God needed some sacrifice from human beings. This is what caused so many past religions to perform blood sacrifices, even human sacrifices, to please their gods. This is an attempt to buy your way into heaven.

This dualistic thinking is born out of the sense of separation from God. It portrays God as an external, remote God and his kingdom as being somewhere else. Jesus said that the kingdom of God is within you, meaning that nothing can prevent you from entering it, except the inner conditions in your own mind. Imagine that you are walking down the street and you see a person with a booth full of beautiful garments. You find one you like and ask: "How much?" The person says: "It's free, you can have it!" You refuse to believe this and hand him some money. He, on the other hand, refuses to take your money for they have no value to him. You only become more persistent and think he is rejecting your offering, but the more you insist on giving him money, the more persistent he becomes in pushing it away. The person absolutely refuses to take your money so the only way you can have the garment is to accept it as a gift. If you will not let go of the sense that you have to pay for it, how could you possibly receive it?

Now imagine that you have a person who has lived all his life in a dark cave. You tell him about the wonderful properties of the sun and encourage him to go outside the cave to see the sun. He seems willing to follow you, but on the doorstep he says: "How much does it cost?" You answer: "It costs nothing, it is free to look at the sun!" He immediately begins to look suspicious and refuses to believe that the sun is free. If the sun is as wonderful as you say it is, there must be a price to pay for looking at it. You, on the other hand, can see how ridiculous it is for a person to insist on having to pay for looking at the sun. My beloved, humankind is like that person. Most people have lived their entire lives, and even many lifetimes, inside the cave of the mortal self, and they have never seen the sun of their own higher selves. God sends them teachers and messengers to tell them about the sun outside the cave, but when they try to follow such a teacher, the doorkeeper – the prince of this world in disguise – insists that they have to pay before they can leave the cave. Instead of simply walking through the door, people frantically attempt to pay up, thus keeping themselves inside the cave indefinitely, for how could they ever pay a price that is not required?

There is a subtle distinction here. There *is* a price to pay because you are responsible for the choices you have made and the energy you have misqualified. You must undo those choices and raise the vibration of the energy. This is not something that can be done *automatically* by blindly following an outer leader. It cannot be done by running away from your past, it cannot be done without looking at the beam in your own eye. If you keep thinking that as long as you do outer things to please God you can pay your way into heaven, you will never enter the wedding feast. How could you, when the doorway is located inside your own mind and when you are constantly looking for it outside yourself? You are trying to buy your way through an external, non-existing doorway. In reality, the doorway to heaven is inside yourself, and all that is required is for you to remove the debris in your four lower bodies that prevents you from seeing the doorway. You must remove the magnetic pull that keeps you bound to an earthly sense of identity and thereby prevents you from leaving the mortal sense of life behind. You cannot take your dualistic beliefs with you into heaven. There is literally nothing you could possibly do with the dualistic mind that would force or obligate God to let you enter heaven. Your mortal self and the prince of this world – including many religious leaders – will vehemently deny this truth. They are the victims of their own dualistic beliefs, and they are engaged in the impossible quest of using the mind of anti-christ to free themselves from the mind of anti-christ. It is easier for a camel to go through the eye of the needle (Matthew 19:24) than it is for a rich man – a person who is "rich" because he thinks he owns the path to salvation and is attached to his "possessions" – to enter heaven.

No one can free *you* from an imperfect belief against your free will. *You* must make the choice to let go of that imperfect belief, and you cannot do so until you are willing to accept responsibility for having allowed that belief to enter your four lower bodies in the first place. If you will not take that responsibility, you simply cannot have the power to set yourself free. By not accepting responsibility, by maintaining the habit of running away, you are literally keeping yourself imprisoned by the imperfect beliefs in your four lower bodies. This is a very simple equation, and I hope you can see the immense impact it has on your life. If you can break the habit of running away, you can permanently turn your life around and put it on a positive track.

What makes it difficult to break any habit, including the habit of running away from what is unpleasant, is that the misqualified energy stored in your four lower bodies causes you to feel pain or causes you to remain stuck in certain patterns. Once again, by removing that misqualified energy, you will make it so much easier for yourself to let go of your imperfect beliefs.

***

    Let me summarize these ideas. The problem we are facing is that you have built a very deep habit of running away from making difficult decisions. The core of this habit is your inability to see what is the best possible decision, and this is due to the fact that you have descended into the duality consciousness and no longer have the unified vision of the Christ mind. In the duality consciousness there are always many options and there are arguments to support each option. It becomes difficult to choose which is the best one. In reality, all of the options you see are defined by the duality consciousness and they will all lead to unpleasant consequences. You are in a situation described by the old saying: "You are damned if you *do* and damned if you *don't*." Once you have experienced that all of your choices lead to unpleasant consequences, is it any wonder you no longer want to make decisions?

    What is the key to breaking this deadlock? If you had a clear vision that allowed you to see what is the best possible choice in every situation, it suddenly would not be so hard to make decisions. Even though you have chosen to descend into the jungle of the duality consciousness, God has not left you comfortless. As Jesus said, God has sent you a comforter (John 14:26) in the form of your Christ self. This is your internal teacher who is here to guide you back up the spiral staircase. For each step you need to take, your Christ self can present you with the guidance you need in order to make the best possible decision. In order for you to receive this inner direction, you must ask in the right frame of mind. You must take full responsibility for your life. You must be willing to change yourself, which means you must be willing to see each dualistic belief that you need to overcome. You must allow the true teacher to expose to you all false beliefs you hold, even if it causes you some discomfort. I have seen many people who discovered the spiritual side of life and became aware of the concept of higher guidance. Some pray to Jesus or myself, some pray to other spiritual figures and some pray to their own higher selves. As long as people have not seen beyond the habit of running away, they simply *cannot* or *will not* receive the answers we give them. It is a law of God that when you ask, you *will* receive an answer. The problem is that so many people ask for help, but they do not truly want help to help themselves. They do not want the guidance that will help them make the right decisions, they want some kind of magical solution so they do not have to make decisions. They do not want help to become self-sufficient co-creators who take full responsibility for their lives. They want *us* to solve their problems for them so they can continue to run away.

Let me give you an absolute standard. A false teacher will gladly help you maintain the habit of running away from making your own decisions. A true teacher will never do anything to reinforce that habit and will, in fact, do everything possible to shake you out of that habit. When you ask from a state of mind that is still running away from making decisions, you cannot hear your true teacher. Instead, you hear the false teachers of your mortal self or an outer guru who wants you to follow him instead of making your own decisions.

Jesus outlined your responsibility as a co-creator with God when he said: "My Father works hitherto and I work" (John 5:17). God has worked by creating you with a unique individuality, by giving you free will and by creating an entire universe in which you can exercise your free will. It is *your* responsibility to build upon that foundation by making choices concerning what you will co-create. You can never run away from making choices; this is simply an impossible dream created by and upheld by your mortal self who wants to make decisions for you. If you can see the fallacy of running away, and if you can make the decision that you are willing to work on breaking this habit, you will find that your inner guidance will become much clearer. As you follow this guidance to the best of your ability, you will increase your ability to hear your inner teacher. You will gradually find that you can now make decisions that help you grow instead of creating consequences that limit your growth. This is the only way your life can be turned into an upward spiral— by you making decisions based on the true guidance of a true teacher. As long as you keep searching for a teacher who will make decisions for you, you will remain in the downward spiral and your life will be an ongoing struggle.

***

You can make it easier for yourself to take responsibility for your life by building on what I have told you in previous chapters, namely that God has no desire to blame you for your past choices. Many people have a problem with shame, guilt or low self-esteem. They feel that if they were to acknowledge the fact that they have made wrong choices in the past, they will be plunged into such an intense feeling of guilt or shame that it will destroy whatever self-esteem they have. Once again, the intensity of any emotion is caused by an accumulation of misqualified energy in your emotional body. By removing that energy, you reduce the intensity. You can also do much by adopting the attitude that God never required you to be perfect. God gave you free will and the right to experiment with that free will. God does not blame you for having made certain choices; God simply wants you to learn from those choices and free yourself from the decisions and their effects. You do not need to feel shame or guilt over your past mistakes. Such feelings can only prevent you from learning the lessons and becoming free of those mistakes. What you need to do is to openly admit the mistakes, learn the lessons that need to be learned and then let go of the dualistic beliefs that caused you to make the mistakes.

There is another subtle distinction here. Every mistake you ever made was influenced by or entirely based on the duality consciousness, the mind of anti-christ. This consciousness is not part of your true being, it is not an integral part of your sphere of self. The real you, the immortal spiritual being that you truly are, did not make those mistakes. The mistakes were made because you had built a temporary sense of identity based on the duality consciousness, and this sense of identity is ultimately unreal. You cannot take this to the extreme and say that the Conscious You had no responsibility for those decisions. If you do so, you are also saying that the Conscious You does not have the power to free itself from the past. The Conscious You *did* make the decisions but it did so because it was no longer identifying itself as a co-creator with God. The Conscious You made those mistakes based on a specific view of the world, a view influenced by the duality consciousness. The Conscious You was looking through the filter of a lesser sense of identity. This filter, this sense of identity based on separation from God, is ultimately unreal and not a part of you. The Conscious You can separate itself from that sense of identity by reaching up and reconnecting with its immortal identity. Doing so must involve an act of conscious will. You must be willing to stop running away from making decisions, and you must be willing to let the mortal sense of identity die.

You cannot bear the thought of having no identity. You cannot let the mortal sense of identity die if you have nothing to put in its stead. That is why I have stressed the importance of starting with a clearing of your identity body. Only by uncovering your highest sense of identity, will you have something to replace the mortal sense of identity. Only when you know and fully accept that you are a co-creator with God, can you truly let the mortal sense of identity die. This is the only way to build a true sense of self-esteem, a self-esteem built on the rock of Christ whereby you know who you are. You know you are a co-creator with your God and you know your Creator gave you the right to take dominion over the earth and bring his kingdom into manifestation.

Every human being has been brought up with certain expectations of what life should be. Every human being has built certain expectations over many lifetimes. If you can change your expectations of what life should be like, you can make things much easier for yourself. One of the most subtle expectations is precisely the idea that God requires you to be perfect. This is the belief that you have to live up to some otherworldly, superhuman standard in order to be acceptable in the eyes of God. It is *not* the people who never made mistakes that have ascended to heaven. The beings you find in the spiritual realm, the beings who have passed the final exam on planet earth, are not beings who were perfect while they walked the earth, beings who never made mistakes. On the contrary, many of the beings who today are ascended made many mistakes while they were on earth. This is even true of Jesus, whom so many Christians consider to have been perfect.

The beings who have ascended are not those who never made mistakes but those who were most willing to recognize their mistakes, to learn from them and then to let them go. The one thing which more than anything else will keep you out of heaven, will keep you outside the abundant life, is that you hold on to things, that you hold on to your past. The one thing which more than anything else will plunge you into the abundant life and catapult you into heaven is that you are willing to let go of all imperfections, let go of your past. Your mortal self and the prince of this world want you to believe that you can never be free of your past. This is an insidious lie, and the reality is that you *can* be free of any imperfection from your past. In order to be free of such imperfections, you must be willing to let go of them. My beloved, keep this simple statement in mind: "It is not how much you hold on to that will get you into heaven; it is how much you let go of that will get you into heaven." This is indeed why Jesus said that he who seeks to save his life shall lose it whereas he who is willing to lose his life – lose his dualistic sense of identity for the sake of coming up higher – shall find immortal life (Matthew 16:25).

***

I have now explained to you one of the factors that causes so many people to hold on to the past. It is simply the pattern of avoidance, of running away from the past. This is the fear of pain. People avoid looking at their imperfect decisions from the past because they fear the pain of the shame, guilt and regret associated with self-examination. There is another reason which influences all human beings, although some people are more trapped by it than others. This is the sense that you do not need to change, that you do not need to let go of the past, that you do not need to admit you have made mistakes and that you do not need to understand why you made those mistakes. This condition can be summed up in one word, and that word is "pride."

Pride does indeed go before the fall, but what I am concerned about is the pride that prevents you from rising again after you have fallen. That kind of pride is the pride which says that you do not need to reach for the higher truth of the Christ mind because you already know what you need to know in order to be saved. You already have the truth, which is given to you by some outer religion, by some outer doctrine or belief system. You do not need to humble yourself and ask for guidance from a true spiritual teacher, in fact you need no teacher.

There are millions of people who are trapped in this form of pride, even though they completely fail to see that it is pride. They are so convinced that they belong to the only true religion or the only true belief system, such as materialistic science or orthodox Christianity. They are completely unwilling to consider that their belief system, or their entire approach to life, might indeed be limited, incomplete or in error because it is based on the consciousness of anti-christ. This, of course, is exactly what these people's mortal selves and the prince of this world want them to think. The devil loves nothing better than when he can make people believe in a lie and then make them believe the double lie that the first lie is the absolute, infallible truth that – as long as they don't question it – is guaranteed to bring them to heaven.

The forces of this world want people to feel that they already know everything, that they have life all figured out. They do not need to reach for the true teacher who is a representative of the universal Christ mind. The real turning point that took you down the spiral staircase was not the fact that you experimented with the duality consciousness. The real problem was that after becoming entangled with the duality consciousness, you decided that you did not want to return to the true teacher who was your personal representative of the universal Christ mind. Since then, you have been following false teachers, namely your mortal self and various representatives of the prince of this world, the mind of anti-christ. These are people who are trapped in the consciousness of duality, but as Jesus said, such people often appear in disguise. They are the wolves who appear in sheep's clothing (Matthew 7:15). They even appear as the devil who is transformed into an angel of light (2Corinthians 11:14), they appear as the false prophets who claim to be representing God or representing Christ, but in reality they will take you onto the false path of anti-christ. They are truly the blind leaders, and if you would have the abundant life, you must open your eyes and stop following them (Matthew 15:14).

People who are trapped in this state of consciousness have one overriding characteristic, namely that they believe they could not possibly be wrong. This ties in with the tendency to run away from taking responsibility for your salvation. If you are to free yourself from an imperfect decision made in the past, you will have to admit that the decision was wrong, that it was not the best possible decision and that it needs to be replaced by a better decision. If you are trapped by pride, you are going to be unwilling to make that admission, you are going to be unwilling to humble yourself and say: "I do not have the understanding I need in order to make the best possible decision, or I would not have made mistakes in the past. I need to reach for that understanding, and the way to get understanding is to seek the help of a qualified teacher who truly represents the Christ mind and can see what I cannot see."

***

The only real problem on planet earth is that people have turned their backs on the true teacher and have followed the false teacher instead. The only real solution is that people recognize this error, separate themselves from their entanglement with the false teachers and once again accept the loving guidance of a true teacher. Consider Jesus' parable of the tares among the wheat (Matthew 13:24). It is an illustration of the fact that so many people on earth have allowed themselves to become so entangled with the consciousness of anti-christ, and the people who have embodied that consciousness, that God cannot remove the representatives of anti-christ from the earth without also pulling up the wheat, namely the people who still have some commitment to true spirituality. You need to separate yourself from the consciousness of anti-christ and the pride that is the hallmark of this consciousness. The consciousness of anti-christ literally believes that it knows better than God how to run the universe, and therefore this state of mind accepts no authority above and beyond itself. It will not accept God as the ultimate authority, and it will not accept the universal Christ mind, and a person who embodies that mind, as the true representative of God in this world. It will not accept any spiritual being or any embodied being as a representative of the universal Christ mind, and that is indeed why you saw certain people who completely rejected Jesus when he walked this earth in the flesh. Such people want the embodied Christ out of this world so that he or she cannot set the people free from their imprisonment.

Some of these people claim to be very religious or very spiritual. They often claim to be the representatives of the only true religion. When the Living Christ stood before them in the flesh, they rejected him, plotted against him and eventually caused his death. This shows you what those who embody the consciousness of anti-christ will do in order to prevent Christ truth from being preached on earth. Their arrogance, their pride, is so deep that they have little chance of freeing themselves from it. *You* can quickly free yourself from that pride, if only you are willing to see it for what it is and realize how it imprisons you in a very narrow mental box.

How do you free yourself from the pride of anti-christ? It is a universal principle that you cannot solve a problem with the same state of consciousness that created the problem. You cannot free yourself from the consciousness of anti-christ by using the logic and the reasoning ability of the mind of anti-christ. This is the downfall of those who are trapped in this state of consciousness. In their arrogance they think the consciousness of anti-christ is superior to the consciousness of Christ, even to the mind of God. They think they have proven this by using their dualistic logic—which can "prove" anything. They are blind to the fact that the consciousness of anti-christ and its dualistic reasoning can never fathom the ultimate truth of the Christ mind. They think that by using the logic of the intellect and the rational mind, they can create a belief system that is absolutely true. In reality, any belief system created from the consciousness of duality is absolutely false. The dualistic mind can always come up with an argument that seemingly proves what it wants to believe. People trapped in the consciousness of anti-christ can always define an argument that convinces themselves that they are right. If *they* are right, why would they need a representative of the Christ mind, why would they need a spiritual teacher—especially if that teacher challenges their "absolute" beliefs? Why would they need a teacher who has ascended to a higher realm when they have the absolute truth right here in the material realm? Why would they need to recognize any authority above themselves when they know everything better than anyone else?

If you are to free yourself from the consciousness of duality, the consciousness of anti-christ, you can do so in only one way. You must be willing to take responsibility for the decisions you have made in the past. You must then be willing to realize that you made those decisions because you did not have the clear vision and the understanding of the mind of Christ. Any imperfect decision you have ever made was based on the dualistic reasoning of the mind of anti-christ. The *only* way to be free of that decision is to reach for the oneness, the single-eyed vision, of the Christ mind. As long as the Conscious You is still entangled with the consciousness of duality, you cannot see that higher truth on your own. That is why you need a teacher who can give you a morsel of truth from the higher perspective of the mind of Christ.

Imagine that you grew up inside a maze. Your world consists of walls of green leaves, forming passageways that seemingly lead nowhere. If you had been born in such a maze, you would think the world was a maze and that there was nothing outside of it. This is similar to the fact that most people think there is nothing beyond the material universe or nothing beyond the dualistic beliefs they have been brought up to see as infallible. When you go through the awakening that makes you realize there is a spiritual side to life, that there is a systematic path to a higher state of consciousness, you realize there is something outside the maze. This gives rise to the idea that there is a way out of the maze, yet because you are still inside the maze, you are no closer to finding that way. You still cannot see the forest for the trees, you cannot see the way out of the maze. Suddenly, you hear a voice calling you and as you look up, you see a person standing in the basket of a balloon that is hovering above the maze. The person looks at the maze from above and can clearly see your current position relative to the only exit. Would you take this person's advice or insist that you can find the way on your own?

Certainly, you can ignore the guide and fumble your way through the maze in the hope that you will some day discover the exit on your own. What if the maze is a trick maze that has no normal exit? If you keep following the open passageways, you will only end up back where you started. The only way out is to find your way to one of the outside walls and then forcefully break through the bushes that make up the wall. Would you ever think to do this? No person trapped in the duality consciousness could ever use the logic of that state of mind to reason that he or she needs to go beyond the duality consciousness in order to break out of the maze. Only the higher vision of the Christ mind can give you this concept. My beloved, please listen for the voice of the true teacher who is always there to guide you. Please realize that the true teacher is always trying to get you to break out of your current mental box. The true teacher will tell you what you *need* to hear, and not what your mortal self *wants* you to hear. Consequently, your mortal self will always object to what the true teacher tells you and will always seek to make you ignore or deny the instructions of a true teacher.

                              ***

   The only way to start the process of climbing back up the spiral staircase is to recognize the fact that you do not have the understanding you need, and therefore you must humble your-self and reach out to a spiritual teacher and ask for help. It is a universal law that if you ask, you will receive. There are spiritual teachers in the higher realm who are waiting for your call. You have your own personal inner teacher, what I have called your Christ self, who is ready to help you every step of the way that leads you back to the abundant life. Your Christ self was cre-ated as a counterbalance to your mortal self. Your mortal self was built by an accumulation of dualistic decisions that gradually took you down the spiral staircase. Your Christ self followed you each step of the way down, and therefore your inner teacher knows each of the dualistic decisions you made, each of the dual-istic beliefs you came to accept. Your Christ self has the antidote to each of these decisions. Your Christ self has the truth that will counteract each of the dualistic lies that make up your mortal self. Your Christ self has the truth that will make you free. Once you ask for help, you will begin to receive that help. You need to always keep in mind that when the teacher appears, you need to heed the teacher and follow the instructions. You need to recognize that when the true teacher appears, he or she comes to give you a truth that is beyond the dualistic beliefs of your mortal self. Your mortal self will come up with a very sophisticated reasoning in order to get you to reject that truth.

Your mortal self does not want you to change, it does not want you to accept the higher truth offered to you by a true spiritual teacher. A true teacher wants you to change, wants you to be free of the past, wants you to come up higher. What keeps you trapped in your current state of consciousness is the dualistic beliefs to which you are attached. When the true teacher comes to you, he comes to give you a truth that shatters one of your dualistic beliefs—which can sometimes be a shock to you. It is the very nature of the true teacher that he disturbs your pride, your arrogance, your attitude that you know everything or that you cannot or do not have to change. The true teacher will challenge your belief that everything can be explained by your current religion or belief system. As demonstrated by Jesus, the true teacher does not come to confirm your existing beliefs; he comes to challenge any aspect of your existing beliefs that is based on the dualistic reasoning of the mind of anti-christ. You can never allow yourself to get into the mode of thinking that a true teacher should be in complete compliance with the statements made by an outer religion or a religious scripture.

This will be shocking to some Christians, but the fact is that if you expect a true teacher to only tell you things that are in complete conformity with the Bible, or rather your particular interpretation of the Bible, you will inevitably prevent the true teacher from helping you. Jesus said and did many things that challenged the orthodox Jews and their interpretation of the Torah. If you ask for the help of a true spiritual teacher, you

should expect that the teacher will challenge many of your existing beliefs. If you are not willing to recognize the truth offered
by the teacher, even if it contradicts your existing beliefs, you will
not be able to accept the help of the teacher. You will remain
stuck in the arrogance and pride that makes you think that the
absolute truth of God can be confined to any scripture or belief
system found on earth. In essence, this subtle arrogance makes
you – or rather your mortal self – believe that it knows better
than God what is true and how you can be saved.

Millions of people claim to be devout religious people, yet
they are stuck in this trap of subtle pride, of spiritual pride. They
think their particular interpretation of a scripture, given in the
distant past, is better than any words a spiritual teacher might
give them today. This form of pride takes many subtle forms.
For example, many people have low self-esteem and look at
themselves as miserable sinners or as being incapable of doing
anything right. This does not seem prideful, but behind the tendency to tear yourself down, the inferiority complex, is the pride
of thinking you know better than God. In reality, God created
you as a unique and uniquely wonderful individual who is capable of doing anything you desire as long as you follow God's
law. If you replace that reality with a self-image that is less than
what God created, you are truly saying that you know better
than God who you are. Thinking you know better than God can
only come from the pride of the mortal self.

***

I see millions of people who come to the conclusion that
they are stuck, that they need to change their lives. I see many
people who cry out for help, and often their cries are sincere.
They truly do want to change, yet they are stuck in either fear
or pride. They are unwilling to consider an understanding that

132 ❖ *Your Life's Plan for Abundance*

contradicts or goes too far beyond their existing belief system. I have experienced – millions of times – that a person has cried out to me for help, I have offered them a higher understanding and they have rejected that understanding. There are many people who will start studying this course but who will encounter a statement that contradicts their outer belief system, and they will use it as an excuse for rejecting the entire course. This is indeed one of the greatest problems we run into as spiritual teachers. We want to set people free, but we cannot because they are too attached to some dualistic belief. One of the main things that causes these attachments to existing beliefs is precisely the pride and arrogance of the mind of anti-christ that makes people believe they already know everything, that they already have the ultimate truth, the ultimate religion. Even when people cry out for help, they want the answers to fit into their mental boxes. How can the answer set you free from your current mental prison if it conforms to the beliefs that make up that mental box? This simply cannot happen; it is a catch-22.

Jesus said that the meek shall inherit the earth (Matthew 5:5), and the meek are those who are willing to humble themselves and recognize that they do not know everything, that they do not have the understanding they need in order to free themselves from their current limitations. The meek are those who are willing to ask for help from Above, help from a teacher who knows more than they do, help from a teacher who has already escaped the downward pull of the mind of anti-christ. You want a teacher who has already risen above duality and can therefore give you the one truth of the Christ mind. Those who follow a true teacher will eventually inherit the earth because the people who remain stuck in the mind of anti-christ will inevitably self-destruct. They will be so consumed by their own pride and negativity that they can no longer remain on earth but must descend to a lower realm.

When you sink into the duality consciousness, this state of mind will pull you towards one of two extremes. Whatever extreme you go into, the contracting force of the Mother will form an opposing force that will seek to pull you back to the middle way. It is a sad fact that there are many people on this earth who go through life being trapped in the subtle pride of thinking they have everything figured out. They are not willing to ask for a higher understanding, they are not willing to ask for the help of a true spiritual teacher. What can bring such people to the point of humility where they are willing to ask for help? In many cases, the only thing that can bring people to that point is a crisis that is so devastating that it finally shatters these people's pride and makes them willing to humble themselves and ask for help. If you take an honest look at the people you know, you will see this pattern at work. You will see many people who have lived an entire lifetime without paying any attention to the spiritual side of life. Suddenly, they experience a crisis, which might be a severe illness, the loss of a loved one or other calamities, and now they turn to God and ask for help. In many cases, these people have not truly humbled themselves. They simply look at God as the genie in the bottle who is supposed to jump out and solve their problems and remove their pain. They are still trapped in the pattern of running away from the true teacher, and therefore they are not willing to ask for directions for how they can change themselves. They are not willing to see that they have actually created the crisis by going into a dualistic extreme, thereby generating a counter force from the Mother Light. The more they push against that force, the deeper the crisis becomes. They see themselves as victims of circumstances beyond their control, and they are not willing to acknowledge that there is a message behind the situation, namely that they need to change themselves. I sincerely hope you will take a different approach. I sincerely hope you will not wait for a crisis before you turn around and ask for the help of a true teacher. I hope you will adopt the approach that you are willing to be God-taught, that you are willing to turn your back to the false teacher and again face the true teacher that you abandoned so long ago but who has never abandoned you.

I hope you will also follow one of the mottos held by the spiritual teachers of humankind. It is this: "If the teacher be an ant, heed him!" The true teacher will not conform to your existing beliefs but will challenge your expectations. In many cases, a true teacher will not appear in the form of a heavenly being that gives you the truth as letters of living fire. A true teacher might very well appear in a humble disguise, as someone you think is not a spiritual teacher or perhaps is of a lower status than yourself and has nothing to teach you. That person or that book might indeed have a message that you need, and if you remain trapped in the pride of thinking that the real teacher could not possibly appear in this or that form, you will miss the message. Why do you think Jesus was born in humble circumstances and did not belong to the religious establishment? Why do you think he so often shattered people's expectations? Why do you think the Bible says: "Be not forgetful to entertain strangers: for thereby some have entertained angels unawares" (Hebrews 13:2).

***

My beloved, I encourage you to adopt the attitude that no matter who you are and how much you know, you are always willing to reach for a higher understanding of any aspect of life. Many people have been brought up to think that a particular religion or belief system has the absolute truth. I encourage you to see through this lie, which is truly based on the pride that springs from the mind of anti-christ. God's absolute truth is beyond what can be expressed in words in the material universe. The material universe currently has so much darkness left in it that it simply is not possible to give forth God's absolute truth in the form of a particular religion or belief system. If you want to know truth, you must be willing to reach beyond anything found in the material world, including an outer scripture or belief system. You must be willing to reach beyond the duality consciousness and reach for the true teacher who can give you the truth of Christ, even though that truth cannot be expressed in words. If you want truth, you must stop looking for it outside yourself. You must be willing to use the Key of Knowledge to find truth in the kingdom of God within you. It is not that truth is found only within your higher self. It is simply that the Conscious You can find truth only by looking within yourself.

I am not saying that the religions found in this world are completely false or that they have no truth. Several religions on this planet have a high degree of truth and they present a valid path to the self-transcendence that is the key to salvation. It is not wrong to consider yourself a Christian or a Buddhist or a Hindu. But once you fall into the trap of thinking that your religion is the *only* true religion, and that it has a complete, absolute and infallible understanding of life, you have cut yourself off from the true teacher. You have refused the true teacher, and you have said that you would rather confine your search for truth to a particular outer framework than reach for the Living Truth.

The essence of God is self-transcendence. God's creation is the River of Life which is always moving, and therefore God's truth is always self-transcending. If you confine your search for truth to a fixed outer framework, you can never find the Living Truth, which cannot be captured into a man-made doctrine or belief system. Such a system will indeed become a graven image, a non-moving image, that obscures the true God, the

Living God. You will be worshiping a false God, and as long as you insist on dancing around that golden calf, the true teachers must leave you alone. In contrast to the false teachers, the true teachers do respect your free will. Their law is: "Ask and you shall receive." If you do not ask, or if you do not ask with an open mind and heart that is willing to look beyond your present beliefs, the true teachers cannot teach you anything.

My beloved, I am not here to tell you that you need to become a member of a particular religion. I am not here to tell you that you need to adopt a certain set of outer beliefs and doctrines. I am not so much concerned about what you believe at this very moment. My real concern is your willingness to transcend your current beliefs by reaching for a higher understanding. As long as you maintain the willingness to reach for a higher vision, you are on the path that leads to the abundant life. The moment you close your mind and heart to a higher understanding, you pull yourself out of the River of Life, and thereby you block the abundant life from descending through your four lower bodies.

The key to turning your life into an upward spiral is to reach up for something higher. The Conscious You must reach for a higher part of your Being, the part that is anchored in the universal Christ mind. Only when you make contact with this I AM Presence – and realize that it is the real you – will you be able to separate yourself from your entanglement with the mortal self. No lifestream can exist without a sense of identity. You cannot give up your mortal sense of identity until you have something with which to replace it. You cannot bear the thought of existing in a vacuum, of being nothing or nobody. In order to fully free yourself from your identification with the mortal self, the Conscious You must reestablish its connection to the spiritual realm, to your I AM Presence, so that you know there is more to your Being than the mortal self.

You must begin by reaching beyond that mortal self. The Conscious You has the ability to do so because the Conscious You can, at any moment, decide to change its sense of identity, to stop identifying with some mortal limitation and instead reach for a higher sense of identity built upon the rock of Christ. I hope I have given you a deeper understanding of what it takes to reach for and build a new sense of identity. I will now move on and give you some practical tools that will empower you to be reborn into your true identity as a co-creator with your God.

6 | I INVOKE FREEDOM FROM LIMITING HABITS

In the name I AM THAT I AM, Jesus Christ, I call to all representatives of the Divine Mother and the Divine Father, especially Kuan Yin, Maitreya and Mother Mary, to help me clear the identity, mental, emotional and physical levels of my mind from all limiting habits and preprogrammed ways of reacting to life. Help me accept my creative powers and see the factors that block the flow of my God-given creativity, including...

[Make personal calls.]

1. I will stop running away

1. Mother Mary, help me see the subconscious habit pattern that is determining how the light flows in my four lower bodies. Help me break this habit and take back conscious control over my reactions to my situation.

Maitreya, I am truly meek,
your counsel wise I humbly seek,
your vision I so want to see,
with you in Eden I will be.

**Maitreya, kindness is the cure,
in fires of kindness I am pure.
Maitreya, now release the fire,
that raises me forever higher.**

2. I invoke the light of my I AM Presence to transform the energy in my emotional, mental and identity bodies that reinforce this habit pattern.

Maitreya, help me to return,
to learn from you, I truly yearn,
as oneness is all I desire
I feel initiation's fire.

**Maitreya, kindness is the cure,
in fires of kindness I am pure.
Maitreya, now release the fire,
that raises me forever higher.**

3. Mother Mary, help me see the decisions in both my long-term and short-term minds that originally formed this habit. I am building a positive habit rather than a limiting one.

Maitreya, I hereby decide,
from you I will no longer hide,
expose to me the very lie
that caused edenic self to die.

**Maitreya, kindness is the cure,
in fires of kindness I am pure.
Maitreya, now release the fire,
that raises me forever higher.**

4. Mother Mary, help me consume the energy impulse, the karma, that is reflected back to me by the cosmic mirror according to my past actions.

Maitreya, blessed Guru mine,
my heart of hearts forever thine,
I vow that I will listen well,
so we can break the serpent's spell.

**Maitreya, kindness is the cure,
in fires of kindness I am pure.
Maitreya, now release the fire,
that raises me forever higher.**

5. I am determined to break this spiral and create an upward, self-perpetuating spiral instead. My life is taking on an entirely new dimension. I am experiencing the abundant life in the form of both material and spiritual abundance.

Maitreya, help me see the lie
whereby the serpent broke the tie,
the serpent now has naught in me,
in oneness I am truly free.

**Maitreya, kindness is the cure,
in fires of kindness I am pure.
Maitreya, now release the fire,
that raises me forever higher.**

6. I realize that in order to break the negative spiral, my Conscious You must separate itself from the mortal self. I am uncovering and transcending the pattern of denial, the pattern of running away from situations or decisions that seem unpleasant or overwhelming.

> Maitreya, truth does set me free
> from falsehoods of duality,
> the fruit of knowledge I let go,
> so your true spirit I do know.
>
> **Maitreya, kindness is the cure,**
> **in fires of kindness I am pure.**
> **Maitreya, now release the fire,**
> **that raises me forever higher.**

7. In the past, my Conscious You decided that it did not want to experience certain situations, that it did not want to experience the consequences of its past choices and that it did not want to experience the agony of making new choices in a situation that was already deeply affected by imperfect choices from the past—making it seem like there were no good options left.

> Maitreya, I submit to you,
> intentions pure, my heart is true,
> from ego I am truly free,
> as I am now all one with thee.
>
> **Maitreya, kindness is the cure,**
> **in fires of kindness I am pure.**
> **Maitreya, now release the fire,**
> **that raises me forever higher.**

8. My Conscious You withdrew from such situations and allowed the mortal self to make decisions, and this has established a very deep-seated and very subtle pattern of running away from decisions that are unpleasant or seem too difficult. This is a pattern of thinking that by ignoring or denying something, I can avoid experiencing that something.

Maitreya, kindness is the key,
all shades of kindness teach to me,
for I am now the open door,
the Art of Kindness to restore.

**Maitreya, kindness is the cure,
in fires of kindness I am pure.
Maitreya, now release the fire,
that raises me forever higher.**

9. Mother Mary, help me undo the dualistic choices that make up my mortal self and keep it alive and in control. Help me break this habit, this pattern, of turning my back upon anything that seems overwhelming. I am willing to make decisions. I am willing to turn around and face what I have not been willing to face up until now.

Maitreya, oh sweet mystery,
immersed in your reality,
the myst'ry school will now return,
for this, my heart does truly burn.

**Maitreya, kindness is the cure,
in fires of kindness I am pure.
Maitreya, now release the fire,
that raises me forever higher.**

2. I hear my inner teacher

1. As long as I maintain the habit of running away, of not wanting to take responsibility for the beliefs and decisions stored in my four lower bodies, I will keep myself in a catch-22.

> O Kuan Yin, what sacred name,
> fill me now with Mercy's Flame.
> In giving mercy I am free,
> forgiving all is magic key.

> **In Kuan Yin's sweet melody,**
> **I am set free my Self to be.**
> **In Kuan Yin's vitality,**
> **I claim my immortality.**

2. True salvation is oneness with my source. How can I ever get back to oneness with my source as long as I am running away from God? How can running away from home bring me back home?

> O Kuan Yin, I now let go,
> of all attachments here below.
> All pent-up feelings I release,
> free from emotional disease.

> **In Kuan Yin's sweet melody,**
> **I am set free my Self to be.**
> **In Kuan Yin's vitality,**
> **I claim my immortality.**

3. How could I ever wake up anywhere else but where I am? I hereby decide that I am willing to wake up right *here*, right *now*.

O Kuan Yin, why must I feel,
that life falls short of my ideal?
All expectations I give up,
my mind is now an empty cup.

In Kuan Yin's sweet melody,
I am set free my Self to be.
In Kuan Yin's vitality,
I claim my immortality.

4. If I had a clear vision that allowed me to see what is the best possible choice in every situation, it would not be so hard to make decisions. I am willing to hear the guidance of my Christ self and ascended teachers.

O Kuan Yin, transcend the past,
as all resentment gone at last.
From future nothing I expect,
eternal now I won't reject.

In Kuan Yin's sweet melody,
I am set free my Self to be.
In Kuan Yin's vitality,
I claim my immortality.

5. I know that for each step I need to take, my Christ self will present me with the guidance I need in order to make the best possible decision. I am willing to change myself, I am willing to see each dualistic belief that I need to overcome.

O Kuan Yin, uplifting me,
beyond Samsara's raging sea.
All safe inside your Prajna boat,
the farther shore no more remote.

In Kuan Yin's sweet melody,
I am set free my Self to be.
In Kuan Yin's vitality,
I claim my immortality.

6. I want help to help myself. I want the guidance that will help me make the right decisions. I want to become a self-sufficient co-creator who takes full responsibility for my life, solving my problems through my internal powers.

O Kuan Yin, your alchemy,
with miracles you set me free.
As I forgive, I am forgiven,
by guilt I am no longer driven.

In Kuan Yin's sweet melody,
I am set free my Self to be.
In Kuan Yin's vitality,
I claim my immortality.

7. I acknowledge that God has worked by creating me with a unique individuality, by giving me free will and by creating an entire universe in which I can exercise my free will. I accept my responsibility to build upon that foundation by making choices concerning what I will co-create.

O Kuan Yin, all worries gone,
with nothing done, no thing undone.
Through separate self I will not do,
and thus I rest, all one with you.

In Kuan Yin's sweet melody,
I am set free my Self to be.
In Kuan Yin's vitality,
I claim my immortality.

8. I give up the impossible dream of running away from making choices. I make the decision that I am willing to work on breaking this habit, and I know my inner guidance is becoming much clearer.

O Kuan Yin, your sanity,
now sets me free from vanity.
For truly, what is that to me;
I just let go and follow thee.

In Kuan Yin's sweet melody,
I am set free my Self to be.
In Kuan Yin's vitality,
I claim my immortality.

9. I know that as I follow my guidance, I am increasing my ability to hear my inner teacher. My life is turning into an upward spiral by me making decisions based on the true guidance of a true teacher.

O Kuan Yin, so sweet the sound,
that emanates from holy ground.
As I let go of ego's chore,
I find myself on farther shore.

In Kuan Yin's sweet melody,
I am set free my Self to be.
In Kuan Yin's vitality,
I claim my immortality.

3. I am learning from my mistakes

1. Every mistake I ever made was influenced by or entirely based
on the duality consciousness, the mind of anti-christ. This consciousness is not part of my true being, it is not an integral part
of my sphere of self. The real me, the immortal spiritual being
that I am, did not make those mistakes.

Maitreya, I am truly meek,
your counsel wise I humbly seek,
your vision I so want to see,
with you in Eden I will be.

Maitreya, kindness is the cure,
in fires of kindness I am pure.
Maitreya, now release the fire,
that raises me forever higher.

2. The mistakes were made because I had built a temporary
sense of identity based on the duality consciousness, and this
sense of identity is ultimately unreal.

Maitreya, help me to return,
to learn from you, I truly yearn,
as oneness is all I desire
I feel initiation's fire.

Maitreya, kindness is the cure,
in fires of kindness I am pure.
Maitreya, now release the fire,
that raises me forever higher.

3. The Conscious You did make the decisions but it did so because it was no longer identifying itself as a co-creator with God. I made those mistakes based on a specific view of the world, a view influenced by the duality consciousness.

Maitreya, I hereby decide,
from you I will no longer hide,
expose to me the very lie
that caused edenic self to die.

Maitreya, kindness is the cure,
in fires of kindness I am pure.
Maitreya, now release the fire,
that raises me forever higher.

4. I was looking through the filter of a lesser sense of identity. This filter, this sense of identity based on separation from God, is ultimately unreal and not a part of me. I am separating myself from that sense of identity by reaching up and reconnecting with my immortal identity.

Maitreya, blessed Guru mine,
my heart of hearts forever thine,
I vow that I will listen well,
so we can break the serpent's spell.

**Maitreya, kindness is the cure,
in fires of kindness I am pure.
Maitreya, now release the fire,
that raises me forever higher.**

5. Doing so must involve an act of conscious will. I am willing to stop running away from making decisions. I am willing to let the mortal sense of identity die.

Maitreya, help me see the lie
whereby the serpent broke the tie,
the serpent now has naught in me,
in oneness I am truly free.

**Maitreya, kindness is the cure,
in fires of kindness I am pure.
Maitreya, now release the fire,
that raises me forever higher.**

6. I cannot let the mortal sense of identity die if I have nothing to put in its stead. I am clearing my identity body and uncovering my highest sense of identity.

Maitreya, truth does set me free
from falsehoods of duality,
the fruit of knowledge I let go,
so your true spirit I do know.

Maitreya, kindness is the cure,
in fires of kindness I am pure.
Maitreya, now release the fire,
that raises me forever higher.

7. I know and fully accept that I am a co-creator with God. I am letting the mortal sense of identity die. I am building a true sense of self-esteem, a self-esteem built on the rock of Christ whereby I know who I am. I am a co-creator with my God and I know my Creator gave me the right to take dominion over the earth and bring his kingdom into manifestation.

Maitreya, I submit to you,
intentions pure, my heart is true,
from ego I am truly free,
as I am now all one with thee.

Maitreya, kindness is the cure,
in fires of kindness I am pure.
Maitreya, now release the fire,
that raises me forever higher.

8. I surrender all of my human, mortal expectations. I especially surrender the expectation that God requires me to be perfect. I surrender the belief that I have to live up to some otherworldly, superhuman standard in order to be acceptable in the eyes of God.

Maitreya, kindness is the key,
all shades of kindness teach to me,
for I am now the open door,
the Art of Kindness to restore.

Maitreya, kindness is the cure,
in fires of kindness I am pure.
Maitreya, now release the fire,
that raises me forever higher.

9. The beings who have ascended are not those who never made mistakes but those who were most willing to recognize their mistakes, to learn from them and then to let them go. I am learning from my mistakes and transcending them.

Maitreya, oh sweet mystery,
immersed in your reality,
the myst'ry school will now return,
for this, my heart does truly burn.

Maitreya, kindness is the cure,
in fires of kindness I am pure.
Maitreya, now release the fire,
that raises me forever higher.

4. I am following my true teacher

1. Mother Mary, help me see the pride that prevents me from rising again after I have fallen. Help me see through the ego illusion that I do not need to reach for the higher truth of the Christ mind because I already know what I need to know in order to be saved.

O Kuan Yin, what sacred name,
fill me now with Mercy's Flame.
In giving mercy I am free,
forgiving all is magic key.

In Kuan Yin's sweet melody,
I am set free my Self to be.
In Kuan Yin's vitality,
I claim my immortality.

2. I cannot free myself from the consciousness of anti-christ by using the logic and the reasoning ability of the mind of anti-christ. Mother Mary, expose to me any arrogance of thinking the consciousness of anti-christ is superior to the consciousness of Christ, even to the mind of God.

O Kuan Yin, I now let go,
of all attachments here below.
All pent-up feelings I release,
free from emotional disease.

In Kuan Yin's sweet melody,
I am set free my Self to be.
In Kuan Yin's vitality,
I claim my immortality.

3. I realize that freedom from past decisions can come only through the oneness, the single-eyed vision, of the Christ mind. As long as the Conscious You is still entangled with the consciousness of duality, I cannot see that higher truth on my own.

O Kuan Yin, why must I feel,
that life falls short of my ideal?
All expectations I give up,
my mind is now an empty cup.

In Kuan Yin's sweet melody,
I am set free my Self to be.
In Kuan Yin's vitality,
I claim my immortality.

4. I know I need a teacher who can give me a morsel of truth from the higher perspective of the mind of Christ. I know the true teacher is always trying to get me to break out of my current mental box. The true teacher will tell me what I need to hear, and not what my mortal self wants me to hear.

O Kuan Yin, transcend the past,
as all resentment gone at last.
From future nothing I expect,
eternal now I won't reject.

In Kuan Yin's sweet melody,
I am set free my Self to be.
In Kuan Yin's vitality,
I claim my immortality.

5. The only way to start the process of climbing back up the spiral staircase is to recognize the fact that I do not have the understanding I need. I hereby humble myself and reach out to a spiritual teacher and I am asking for help.

O Kuan Yin, uplifting me,
beyond Samsara's raging sea.
All safe inside your Prajna boat,
the farther shore no more remote.

In Kuan Yin's sweet melody,
I am set free my Self to be.
In Kuan Yin's vitality,
I claim my immortality.

6. My Christ self followed me each step of the way down the staircase, and therefore my inner teacher knows each of the dualistic decisions I made, each of the dualistic beliefs I came to accept. Beloved Christ self, give me the truth that will counteract each of the dualistic lies that make up my mortal self. Give me the truth that will make me free.

O Kuan Yin, your alchemy,
with miracles you set me free.
As I forgive, I am forgiven,
by guilt I am no longer driven.

In Kuan Yin's sweet melody,
I am set free my Self to be.
In Kuan Yin's vitality,
I claim my immortality.

7. I know I am receiving the help I need, and I will heed the teacher and follow the instructions. When the true teacher appears, he or she comes to give me a truth that is beyond the dualistic beliefs of my mortal self. My mortal self will come up with a very sophisticated reasoning, but I will still follow the guidance of the true teacher.

O Kuan Yin, all worries gone,
with nothing done, no thing undone.
Through separate self I will not do,
and thus I rest, all one with you.

In Kuan Yin's sweet melody,
I am set free my Self to be.
In Kuan Yin's vitality,
I claim my immortality.

8. I am willing to reach beyond the duality consciousness and reach for the true teacher who can give me the truth of Christ, even though that truth cannot be expressed in words. I want truth, and I am looking for it inside myself.

O Kuan Yin, your sanity,
now sets me free from vanity.
For truly, what is that to me;
I just let go and follow thee.

In Kuan Yin's sweet melody,
I am set free my Self to be.
In Kuan Yin's vitality,
I claim my immortality.

9. I am using the Key of Knowledge to find truth in the kingdom of God within me. I am turning my life into an upward spiral by reaching up for a higher part of my Being, the part that is anchored in the universal Christ mind. I have contact with my I AM Presence, and I realize this is the real me.

O Kuan Yin, so sweet the sound,
that emanates from holy ground.
As I let go of ego's chore,
I find myself on farther shore.

In Kuan Yin's sweet melody,
I am set free my Self to be.
In Kuan Yin's vitality,
I claim my immortality.

Sealing

In the name of the Divine Mother, I call to Kuan Yin, Maitreya and Mother Mary for the sealing of myself and all people in my circle of influence in the creative flow of the Divine Mother, the River of Life. I call for the multiplication of my calls by all representatives of the Divine Mother, so that we form the perfect figure-eight flow of "As Above, so below." Thus, I accept that this is fully manifest, because the mouth of the Lord, the Divine Mother that I AM, has spoken it. Amen.

7 | CHANGING WHO YOU THINK YOU ARE

My beloved heart, in this chapter I will give you some teachings that are specifically designed to help you clear the imperfect beliefs in your identity body. In a sense, everything I have said up to this point relates to clearing your identity body, but there are certain things that I have not explained in great detail, and we will go into them here. The most important aspect of clearing your identity body is that by doing so you will uncover your true identity, you will discover who you really are as the God-free being that your Creator originally designed as an extension of itself. The contents of your identity body relate specifically to what you came to do in the material universe. What you came here to do is an expression of who you really are, meaning the spiritual Being that sent down an individualization of itself.

One of the most common misunderstandings found on earth is the concept that God's will is outside of, is separate from and is even in opposition to your own individual will. This is a very dangerous and a very insidious illusion that has affected many spiritual seekers. Obviously, the will of God is always in opposition to the will of your mortal self and the will of the prince of this world. Your mortal self and the prince of this world are completely trapped in the duality consciousness, the consciousness that springs from a sense of separation from God. By their very nature, they see themselves as outside of and in opposition to the will of God. The will of your ego, the will of your mortal self, will always feel that it is being restricted by the will of God. Your mortal self will try to get you to believe in the illusion that in order to follow the will of God, you have to give up your own will. You have to surrender your own will to the will of God and submit yourself to this higher authority who wants to control you. This has even led to the belief that it was only in rebelling against the God in the Garden of Eden that human beings gained their own will. This is the ultimate attempt to justify the existence of the mortal self by using the dualistic logic of the mind of anti-christ. It actually implies that before Adam and Eve ate the forbidden fruit, they were mere robots. If they had truly been robots, how could they have disobeyed their "programming?"

You were created with free will from the very beginning, and in rebelling against God's will you did not gain the freedom to make your own choices. You lost that freedom by giving it to the mortal self and the prince of this world. Your greatest possession is your individuality, and you have a built-in longing to express that individuality. If the mortal self and the prince of this world can make you believe that expressing your individuality is incompatible with following the will of God, you will be a house divided against itself. You have a built-in longing for wholeness, which can only be attained by following the will of God, and you have a built-in longing to express your individuality. If you believe the two are incompatible, you will never be whole or fulfilled. The only way out is to realize that the seeming conflict between your individual will and the will of God is nothing but a dualistic illusion. This illusion has been heavily reinforced by many orthodox religions, namely the religions that present God as an angry being in the sky who is watching your every move and is ready to punish you for every mistake. It is a great burden to my heart that so many sincere spiritual people are trapped in this subtle belief that God's will is somehow in opposition to their own. This makes many spiritual people feel a subtle resentment against God for the very fact that they are alive. They somehow feel that God forced life upon them, and therefore God is responsible for their current misery and limitations. They feel they have no control over their own destiny. After all, God created them, God gave them free will, God sent them into this world and now God has abandoned them because they made a mistake in the past. All these beliefs spring from the mortal self, and not even your mortal self believes them. The mortal self is using them as tools to drive a wedge between you and your higher Being, between the Conscious You and your real identity as the greater spiritual Being that you are.

I truly understand why many people believe this lie. When you have imperfect, dualistic beliefs in your identity body, you simply cannot see beyond the level of your identity body. You cannot see beyond the material realm and discover the greater spiritual Being of which you are an individualization. How can you accept that God's will is actually *your* will? One of the greatest benefits of clearing your identity body is that you will come to the recognition and the full acceptance that God's will is indeed *your* will and your will is God's will. To help you resolve this seeming enigma, let me take you on a little journey beyond time and space.

***

There was once an immortal spiritual Being, residing in the spiritual realm, which is above and beyond the material universe.

After the Creator had created the sphere that is the material universe, this Being saw that for the process of creation to continue, someone had to descend into that material universe and bring the light of God. Someone had to take up the role of a co-creator so that the material universe could gradually become filled with light and thereby become another jewel in the crown of God's Being. This spiritual Being decided that it did indeed want to be part of the creative process, that it did indeed want to serve the Creator by sending a part of itself down into the material universe to radiate the light of God and raise the material universe to a higher vibration. This spiritual Being saw itself clearly as an extension of, as an individualization of, the Creator who started the entire process of creating this world of form. This greater spiritual Being decided to send a part of itself down into the material realm. An immortal spiritual Being cannot send the totality of itself into the material realm. It sent a part of itself, an individualization of itself, which then became an individual lifestream. This individual lifestream is not separated from or in opposition to its spiritual "parent." Even though it has individuality and free will, its original will is not separate from or in opposition to the greater will of its spiritual source and the even greater will of the Creator itself.

You were not created in a vacuum. You were not created by some external, remote God who then forcefully sent you into this material universe without any choice on your part. You are an extension of a greater spiritual Being, and you are an expression of the fact that this greater Being has a desire to extend itself into the material universe and bring the light and the kingdom of God to replace the darkness that covers the land. After you were created as an individual lifestream, you had a choice concerning whether you would actually descend to the material universe or whether you would seek growth in the spiritual realm. Because you clearly saw the purpose for which you were created, you lovingly chose to descend as an emissary of the greater Being that you are. You were not forced to come here. You came here as the result of a choice, and that choice was not made by some alien, remote being. It was made by you, the Conscious You, seeing itself as an extension of the greater Being that you are.

I am aware that this might sound abstract with your present level of self-awareness. I can assure you that as you grow in self-awareness, as you clear the dualistic images from your identity body, you will come to see and accept the truth of what I am telling you here. You are here because you chose to come here, and you made that choice out of love. You are here because you want to be here. I am aware that there are many aspects of your present situation that are not in alignment with your original desire and your original purpose for coming here. Those imperfections are the results of choices that the Conscious You made because it was influenced by the duality consciousness. Once you separate the Conscious You from those dualistic beliefs, you will indeed come back to a clear recognition of why you came here in the first place.

Oh my beloved, I can assure you that once you reconnect to your original purpose for coming here, your life will take on an entirely new dimension. You will attain such a deep and joyful sense of purpose that you will indeed connect to the original meaning, the original purpose, behind God's creation. You will know who you are and why you truly came to this earth. You will know that you are an extension of a greater spiritual Being that embodies a particular quality of God. You will know that you are here to bring a particular God quality to this earth and thereby serve as one facet of the diamond mind of God that brings God's kingdom into manifestation on this planet. You will then reconnect to the whole of the Body of God and see that you are part of a great wave of Beings who came to this earth for a higher purpose. This will give you a sense of purpose, a sense of meaning, a sense of divine direction, that will truly be the ultimate fulfillment for which all spiritual people have a deep, inner longing.

Oh my beloved, what a pain it is to my heart that so many people on earth are wondering if life has a purpose or a deeper meaning. The answer is so obvious and so clear—once you have risen above the duality consciousness. I know that while you are still trapped behind the veil of illusions created by that state of consciousness, the answer seems illusive and impossible to grasp. I have no stronger desire than to see you, and all spiritual people, rise above that veil of illusion – that energy veil, that *evil* – in order to be free to know who you truly are and why you came to this universe. That is when you can begin to express your unique individuality and to bring your unique gift to this planet. This truly is the very foundation for experiencing the abundant life.

You do not seriously believe that the abundant life is all about money, do you? I can assure you that the true abundant life comes from knowing who you are and why you are here on this planet, from feeling that the light of God is streaming through your four lower bodies. It comes from knowing that every aspect of your lower being is in alignment with your original purpose for coming here. Every aspect of your life is an expression of that purpose and serves to fulfill that purpose. This is the ultimate state of abundance, the ultimate sense of being in the flow of the River of Life, the river of God's eternal self-transcendence that raises you to higher and higher levels and in so doing raises the vibration of the entire planet.

***

I have said that your identity body is the seat of your sense of identity, but it is also the body which focuses the power of will, the power of determination, the power of direction, the power of purpose. The basic impulse behind your coming into the material world was a decision. Your entire lifestream springs from an act of will. This act of will is an extension of the original decision made by your Creator, the decision that: *"I will create!"*

If you are to be ultimately successful in manifesting the abundant life, you need to reconnect to the higher will of your being, to a will that is beyond anything that could possibly be contained within your four lower bodies. You must connect to a will that is higher than the will of your conscious mind. Many people on this planet have made sincere attempts to conquer a destructive habit or to improve their lives in other ways. Yet after a long or short period of time, they have either given up or they have been pulled back into the old patterns of behavior. Many people, especially the more spiritually minded people on this planet, can see that there are so many things on earth that simply are not right, so many things that need to be improved. Some have put forth a sincere effort to improve life on this planet, to improve some aspect of their society. Many of them have found that there is an incredible opposition to change, an opposition to improvement, and so often their efforts fall short of the mark. They feel like they are fighting and fighting, but they are getting nowhere. There is always this opposition to every step they attempt to take. This is an opposition that comes from the mind of anti-christ, focused through the mortal selves of each human being on this planet, focused through the collective consciousness and focused through the prince of this world and all forces – in embodiment and out of embodiment – that are trapped by this consciousness of anti-christ.

There *is* a force on this planet that is a force of anti-will, a force that actively opposes God's will and the manifestation of God's kingdom on earth. The forces that can exist only in the shadow of darkness do not want you or anyone else to bring the light of God to this planet. When the shadows of the duality consciousness disappear, they can no longer hide. When they can no longer hide, they can no longer fool anyone, they cannot continue to exist on this planet. As a sincere spiritual seeker you cannot ignore the existence of this force of anti-will because if you do so, you simply cannot rise above it.

Your creative powers are depending on the force of the light that can flow through your four lower bodies, the force of the light that is available to your conscious mind. There is a force of anti-will in the matter realm. That force can work only with the energies that are already brought into the matter realm. Let us say that this force can work with energy around 1,000 Hz. If your conscious mind is able to direct light that vibrates at 500 Hz, how can you possibly overcome the force of anti-will that has the strength of 1,000 Hz? There is absolutely no way that you can do so. You can have the best intentions in the world, you can have a good spiritual teaching, perhaps even a good spiritual technique, but if the force of your will power, the force of the determination you can muster with your conscious mind, is weaker than the force of the anti-will that exists in the matter realm, how can you possibly overcome that force and move forwards? How can you possibly be successful in changing your society and changing this planet unless you can bring in a force that is stronger than the anti-will in the collective consciousness?

There is also a force of anti-will in the emotional realm, in the mental realm and in the identity realm. On each level this force reaches a certain strength. If you are to overcome that force of anti-will, both on a personal and on a larger scale, you need to bring a force of positive will that is stronger than the force of the anti-will. This is simply a matter of mathematics, and it does not take a genius to add up the numbers. If you have plus two and minus four and you add them up, what is the result? The result is that you are still in the minus, and thus how can you have a positive change? My beloved, I am not seeking to discourage you in any way by pointing this out to you. I am seeking to help you see that if you are to truly make progress in your life, if you are to manifest the abundant life, you need to discover a source of will power that is stronger than anything found in this world. That source of will power is to reconnect to the true identity that you are, to the greater spiritual being out of which you are an extension. Once you reconnect to that greater spiritual Being, you can reconnect to the original purpose for your coming here, and therefore you have access to the entire force of will power that goes all the way back to your Creator. There is absolutely no force in this world, there is no force created by your mortal self, by the collective consciousness or by the prince of this world, that can withstand the will power of God.

God's will power is so far beyond what most human beings have ever experienced that it can be almost shocking the first time you connect to this force of will. The will of God is absolute, is uncompromising, and it does not in any way cater to the dualistic reasoning of the mind of anti-christ. That is why the Bible says that in him is no variableness, neither shadow of turning (James 1:17). God's will simply does not compromise truth and it will not accept any opposition to the manifestation of God's kingdom. When you personally tie in to the will of your greater being, you will not accept any conditions on this earth that stand in the way of the fulfillment of your original purpose for coming here. This is precisely the force you need in order to break through the anti-will of your mortal self, the anti-will of people around you, the anti-will of the collective consciousness and the anti-will of the prince of this world.

The basic nature of the mind of anti-christ is a compromise with truth, with the reality of Christ. Everything that is influenced by the duality consciousness is a compromise. The master strategy of the prince of this world is to somehow tempt, fool or force you into compromising the truth. How can you overcome that tendency to compromise and the subtle temptation of the dualistic reasoning? You can overcome it only by reconnecting to a force that is completely beyond compromise, and that force is the will of God. The will of God will not compromise truth, and thus when you reconnect to that will, *you* will not compromise the original purpose for your coming here.

Reconnecting to the will of God for your lifestream will require some adjustment. It cannot be done overnight, and it will indeed take time and effort. You need to shed the dualistic beliefs that have caused you to build a separate will, a will that is separate from the original will that brought you into this universe. It is my intention here to give you a glimpse of the power of the will of God to which you have access. When you reconnect to that will of God, which is truly the will of your Self, your higher self, you can literally sweep aside and overcome all opposition to your creative expression, all opposition from your mortal self and the prince of this world.

Your four lower bodies form a hierarchical structure and your conscious mind is at the bottom level of that structure. You cannot use the conscious mind, the mind that is centered around the physical body, to overcome the force of the anti-will. The Conscious You can separate itself from the conscious mind and reconnect to its true identity. It can bring the determination of the will of God down to the level of the conscious mind. When you have *that* determination, you will not allow anything, be it within your own psyche or outside yourself, to stand in the way of the fulfillment of your purpose for being here on earth. Only when you have *that* determination, will you be able to sweep aside the opposition to your divine plan, to your reason for being.

***

Another advantage of connecting to your own higher will is that you will know that you have a God-given right to be here on planet earth and that you have a right to manifest and express the Christ consciousness. Many sincere spiritual seekers have a great love for God, but they are reluctant to acknowledge anything dark or evil. This is simply one aspect of the tendency to run away from that which seems overwhelming. Once you reconnect to the power of the will of God, you will never again fear any force in this world. You will know that they are no match for the power of God and that this power can protect you from any force in this world.

Only when you have the inner knowing that you were sent here by God to bring light into this dark world, can you withstand the onslaught of the prince of this world who will challenge you as he challenged and tempted Jesus. The prince of this world has such ultimate arrogance and spiritual blindness that he thinks he owns the entire material world. He thinks all people on earth belong to him and that he has them under complete control. The last thing he wants is for any person in embodiment to attain the Christ consciousness. Not only will this bring you outside the control of the forces of this world, but you will also serve as an example for others. This is the original purpose for Jesus' mission, and the prince of this world did everything possible to stop Jesus from fulfilling his mission. When that did not work, he changed tactics and sought to destroy Jesus' example so that no one else would dare to follow Jesus' own promise and do the works that he did (John 14:12).

The prince of this world will attempt to make you believe that you have no right to attain Christhood in this world. He will especially try to prevent you from exercising this Christhood by bringing the light of truth to other people and to your society. The prince of this world wants everyone to remain trapped in the duality consciousness without ever realizing that there is anything beyond that state of mind. He will use all kinds of clever ideas to make you doubt your ability or your right to radiate your light. One such scheme is the idea that by being the Christ in action, you interfere with the free will of other people. After all, most people on this planet seem content being asleep and they don't want to be awakened to the spiritual reality. While this might seem true, the reality is that people are not happy because deep within them they have a longing for wholeness, a longing that can never be fulfilled as long as they are trapped in the duality consciousness. They are only asleep because they have never been shown that there is an alternative to the dualistic state of consciousness, they have never been shown a viable path to attaining a higher state of consciousness.

In reality, it is the prince of this world who is interfering with people's free will. The simple fact is that people cannot make a free choice unless they know all their options and the consequences of those options. If people do not know that there is an alternative to the spiritual death of the duality consciousness, how can they possibly choose the life of the Christ consciousness? Don't you think most people would choose life, if they truly understood what is at stake?

Jesus was sent by God for the specific purpose of awakening people from their spiritual sleep, their spiritual death. It is true that because of the force of habit and their dualistic beliefs, many people resist being awakened. That is why so many people rejected Jesus and even plotted against him. This also explains why Jesus was sometimes very direct and forceful in order to cut through the prison walls of people's mortal selves. This was not a violation of people's free will. It was indeed mandated by God because God does not want people to remain asleep forever. God has mandated that they should be given spiritual teachers who can serve as examples. In this particular age, God wants to see a large-scale spiritual awakening on planet earth. This can come about only when a large number of people walk the path to Christhood and demonstrate how this path leads to a more abundant life. Only when people see someone from the same background as themselves manifest the abundant life, will they be awakened to their own Christ potential. All beings in heaven would love to see everyone on earth awakened so they can make a truly free choice between spiritual death and spiritual life.

My beloved, be aware that some of the people who might resist your spiritual growth are the ones closest to you. That is why Jesus said: "And a man's foes shall be they of his own household" (Matthew 10:36). The meaning is that the people closest to you are often reluctant to have you grow spiritually. They might be afraid of losing you, they might be jealous of you or they might not want to be awakened. After all, if *you* can manifest the abundant life, *they* can too, but in order to do so they must be willing to change themselves as you have been willing to change yourself. If they are not willing to confront the tendency to run away, they will seek to stop you from making progress that they cannot ignore.

I am not saying you need to look at other people as enemies. I am simply saying that you need to be aware that there will be opposition to your growth from your mortal self and the mortal selves of other people. The only way to overcome that opposition, which might be very subtle and sympathetic, is to be so anchored in the higher will of your own Being that you will not let any condition on earth prevent you from being who you are and letting "your light so shine before men, that they may see your good works, and glorify your Father which is in heaven" (Matthew 5:16).

There are two ways in which you can attempt to manifest the abundant life. One is that you start from the bottom and seek to work your way up by breaking through the opposition with the power available to your conscious mind. In doing so, you will be constantly fighting the anti-will of your mortal self, other people and the prince of this world. You are condemning yourself to a life that is a continuous struggle. You might make some headway, you might manifest some form of abundance, but it will not be the truly abundant life that God desires to give you. The only way to have *that* abundant life is to go directly to the top and reconnect to your true identity so that the power of the will of God can bring each of your four lower bodies into alignment with your original purpose. Thereby, you will make life so much easier for yourself. Once the vision of your higher purpose is anchored in your identity body, you will have set a firm foundation, you will have built your house on the rock of Christ (Matthew 7:24). Your thoughts will almost automatically fall into alignment with your original purpose. When your thoughts are in alignment with your true purpose, your emotions will not be divided and pulled in all directions by the lower dualistic desires. You will no longer be a house divided against itself and you will have the light of God flowing undiluted through your four lower bodies. This will increase your creative powers to the point where it becomes easy, it becomes effortless, to attain your true goal in life.

My beloved, look at the life of Jesus. It was not a struggle for him to turn the water into wine. He simply focused his outer mind within and brought himself into perfect alignment with his purpose for coming here. In that centeredness, he issued a command and – instantly – the water was turned into wine. Likewise, he was able to multiply the loaves and fishes and feed 5,000 people without any effort, without the toil of having to buy or bake the bread that was necessary for so many people. This is your true potential, and I know it might seem far beyond your present reach. I am giving you this vision to show you the advantage of going straight to the top and realigning your sense of identity with the greater purpose for which you came here.

Thereby, the will of your higher Being can take command, can take dominion, over each of your four lower bodies.

I know you are used to having to struggle in order to get what you need. I ask you to consider the concept of effortless manifestation. From the beginning of this course I have been saying that it is the Father's good pleasure to give you his kingdom. It is God's will that you have the abundant life. In order to get it, you only have to bring yourself into alignment with the higher will that truly is the will of your own higher Being, which is the will of God within you. When your four lower bodies are in alignment with your reason for being, the power of God will flow through them and effortlessly manifest what is needed in order to fulfill your divine plan.

***

My beloved heart, what will it take to bring yourself into alignment with the higher will of your own Being? You must be willing to realize that there is a force of anti-will that has managed to gain entry into your four lower bodies. This is what I have called your mortal self, and the mortal self has a will of its own, a will that is completely centered around itself. What will it take to escape the prison of that lower will? It will take that you begin to think beyond yourself, meaning the self that is focused around the physical body and the mortal self. You are an extension of a greater spiritual Being and you came here for a greater purpose, an eternal purpose.

Many people on earth are completely focused on themselves and spend an entire lifetime pursuing completely egotistical desires that are often centered around the pleasures of the physical body and its immediate needs. Many people have absolutely no attention left over for thinking about the long-term consequences for their own lives, such as their spiritual freedom and growth. Many people have no attention left over to consider how their actions affect other people, even their own loved ones. They commit the most selfish acts without ever feeling any sense of remorse or regret. Humankind has very little attention left over to consider how the modern way of life affects planet earth and its ability to sustain life in the long term. Only within recent decades have people begun to consider the effects of pollution on the environment, and they have done so only because they realized that it could have negative effects on themselves. Very few people have expanded their awareness to have a genuine love of the planet that gives them a platform for life.

Contrast this self-centeredness, this complete selfishness, with the greater vision of the Christ mind that sees the oneness of all life because it knows that all life came from the same source and is an expression of God's Being. The spiritual Being that sent you down here as an extension of itself did not have this limited, human, egotistical perspective. This Being is in perfect alignment with the will and the vision of the Creator, and thus it had a greater purpose for sending you into the material realm. That purpose is in perfect alignment with God's vision for the whole of creation, for planet earth and for humankind. If you are to attain ultimate happiness, ultimate fulfillment and a sense of ultimate purpose and self-worth, you need to look beyond this narrow sense of self that is focused in your mortal self. You need to reconnect to the greater sense of Self that you truly are. When you do, you will realize that you will never attain ultimate fulfillment by pursuing egotistical desires relating to the physical body. You will only be truly fulfilled when you reach beyond your body and give of your own true Being.

If you want a visual image of what I am talking about here, consider the sun. The sun is designed to radiate light, the light that gives life to everything on earth, and to do so unconditionally. The sun is not looking down at people on earth and judging whether they are receiving its light with the proper frame of mind. As Jesus said: "That ye may be the children of your Father which is in heaven: for he maketh his sun to rise on the evil and on the good, and sendeth rain on the just and on the unjust" (Matthew 5:45). The sun gives unconditionally. It gives without expecting a return, and it gives without attaching conditions to how people should receive its gifts. The sun finds its true fulfillment, its true joy, in radiating light. It is what goes out that is the source of fulfillment, not what comes in.

If the sun was to adopt the same self-centered state of consciousness that most people have today, the sun would begin to set up conditions for giving its light. It would say that: "If people do not receive my rays in the proper way, then I will no longer give my light to those people." This would cause the sun to shut off certain areas and no longer radiate light through those areas. What effect would that have on the sun's sense of fulfillment? The sun gains its fulfillment from radiating light. When the sun stops radiating light, it will no longer feel fulfilled, it will no longer be happy. Your true being, your I AM Presence and the Conscious You, are designed to be a spiritual sun radiating the light of God on planet earth. Your I AM Presence steps down the light of God and then sends it through your four lower bodies to be directed by the Conscious You in alignment with your original purpose for coming to earth.

You are designed to be a conduit through which the light of God can stream and then radiate on earth. This is the way to bring God's light into the material realm and thereby raise the vibration of the entire universe and fill it with light so that it can become another sphere in the spiritual realm—as is God's vision and plan. You are meant to direct God's light into specific conditions on earth in order to magnify, to accelerate, these conditions and help them transcend their current imperfect state. You are here to help everything on earth become more, and in so doing, *you* become more. You are here to give of your light, and it is in giving your light that you receive ultimate fulfillment. What happens when you stop giving your light, when you set up conditions which say that if people do not treat you a certain way, or if people do not give you the return that you want, you will shut off your light? When you shut off the flow of light through you, you also take away your own sense of fulfillment. If you shut off the light completely, you end up having no sense of fulfillment or purpose and your life becomes a continuous struggle.

What is the abundant life? It is that the light of God is flowing undiluted and unhindered through your four lower bodies, magnifying everything it encounters. Thereby, you will be surrounded by abundance. You will not be waiting to receive abundance from here below, you will be actively producing abundance by letting the light from Above accelerate everything you encounter. You will be multiplying your talents, and when you feel that light flowing through you, you will have the ultimate sense of fulfillment, the ultimate sense of abundance and nurturance. When you shut off that light – by accepting dualistic beliefs that define conditions for your giving – you are depriving yourself of the abundant life, you are depriving yourself of the sense of fulfillment, the sense of wholeness. You are truly impoverishing yourself because you can no longer feel the flow of light that is the key to happiness and abundance.

When you shut off the flow of God's light through your four lower bodies, you will not be sending an energy impulse of abundance into the cosmic mirror. The cosmic mirror simply cannot reflect the abundant life back to you in the form of physical conditions. The only way to truly manifest a materially abundant life is to first reestablish the spiritually abundant life that you were designed to have. When you follow Jesus' advice to seek first the kingdom of God and his righteousness – meaning the right use of God's energy – all things will be added onto you (Matthew 6:33) because the material universe has no other option but to reflect back to you the abundance that you are sending out.

***

God has created a universe that is one, interconnected whole. In God's original design there is no conflict, there is no contradiction, between each individual lifestream and the whole. What has happened on earth is that most of the lifestreams that call this planet home have fallen into the duality consciousness. Through this consciousness of separation they have created an almost infinite number of conflicts between individuals, between groups of people, between nations and even a conflict between humankind and Mother Earth. These conflicts spring from one main characteristic of the mind of anti-christ, namely selfishness. Selfishness is a product of the fact that an individual lifestream has separated itself from its source, has turned its back upon God. If you are not consciously connected to your source, you cannot realize that your spiritual brothers and sisters came from the same source. Consider the statement made by Jesus: "Inasmuch as ye have done it unto one of the least of these my brethren, ye have done it unto me" (Matthew 25:40). This is the statement of a Being who knows that it is not an island, that it does not exist in a vacuum, that it is not the only being that matters. This is the statement of a being who is connected to its source and who realizes that it is an extension of God. Everything else, including all other human beings, are also extensions of God. When you have this sense of expanded awareness, you realize that you are truly part of the Body of God. Through your connection to your source, you are connected to all other parts of the Body of God. What you do onto others, you are truly doing to yourself. I have so far stressed the image that the universe is a mirror that reflects back to you what you send out. I have said that the universe will do to you what you do to others. While this is indeed correct, there is a higher understanding. The higher understanding is that other people are not separate from you because *they* are part of the Body of God on earth and *you* are part of that body as well. We might go beyond the statement that the universe will do onto you what you do onto others and say that you are doing to yourself what you do onto others because others are part of your greater Self, namely the Body of God. What you do onto the Earth Mother, you are also doing onto yourself because even the physical planet is part of God's creation. As long as a part of you is focused on this planet, what happens to the whole will affect the individual part that is right now the center of your sense of identity.

The Conscious You has the ability to identify itself with and as anything of which it can conceive. The Conscious You can be ego-centered – by identifying itself as the mortal self – or it can be God-centered – by identifying itself as a spiritual being who is one with the Allness of God. The highest effect of clearing your identity body is that you will be able to see beyond the selfishness of your mortal self. You will be able to see beyond the sense of separation that originated with the prince of this world. You will be able to see beyond even your own identity as an individual being. You will be able to see that there is more to you than your individual lifestream because your individual lifestream is part of a greater whole, namely the All of God's consciousness. The Conscious You is an expression of that All and it has the capacity to reunite with the All, even while it is still focused through a physical body on a very small planet in a very large universe.

Ah my beloved, so many Christians ignore Jesus' statement: "Ye are gods" (John 10:34). Truly, ye are Gods in the sense that the Conscious You has the ability to identify itself with the All that is God. In so doing, you will experience the ultimate sense of wholeness, the ultimate sense of joy, the ultimate sense of bliss.

You will not simply *know* who you are—you will *be* who you are. You have then attained what the old Greeks called "gnosis," and the meaning of this word is that there is no longer any distance, any difference, any separation, between the knower and the known. For eons human beings have speculated about God and the nature of God. Many spiritual and religious people have made it their goal in life to know God, but the concept of knowing implies distance. The concept that you can know something that you are not experiencing implies that you are here and God is somewhere else. You are trying to connect to that remote God, and in your mind you build an image of what that remote God is like but you are still separated from that God. You might recall that the very essence of the mind of anti-christ is separation from God. The prince of this world can use even a sincere desire to know God as a tool for reinforcing the image of a remote God. There will come a time when a sincere spiritual seeker will have to transcend even the desire to *know* God, will have to transcend the concept of knowing something that you are not.

As long as you are separated from God, you cannot truly know God, you cannot know what God is like, what it is like to be God. Here is the thought that I will leave you to ponder: "The only way to *know* God is to *be* God!"

8 | I INVOKE MY HIGHER WILL

In the name I AM THAT I AM, Jesus Christ, I call to all representatives of the Divine Mother and the Divine Father, especially Gautama Buddha and Mother Mary, to help me overcome all lack of will and unwillingness to let God's power flow through me in a balanced manner, always staying on the Middle Way. Help me accept my creative powers and see the factors that block the flow of my God-given creativity, including...

[Make personal calls.]

1. I know how free will works

1. I surrender the illusion that God's will is outside of, is separate from and is even in opposition to my own individual will.

Gautama, show my mental state
that does give rise to love and hate,
your exposé I do endure,
so my perception will be pure.

Gautama, Flame of Cosmic Peace,
unruly thoughts do hereby cease,
we radiate from you and me
the peace to still Samsara's Sea.

2. The will of my ego, the will of my mortal self, will always feel
that it is being restricted by the will of God. I reject the illusion
that in order to follow the will of God, I have to give up my
own will.

Gautama, in your Flame of Peace,
the struggling self I now release,
the Buddha Nature I now see,
it is the core of you and me.

Gautama, Flame of Cosmic Peace,
unruly thoughts do hereby cease,
we radiate from you and me
the peace to still Samsara's Sea.

3. I surrender the illusion that God wants to control me and that
it was only in rebelling against the God in the Garden of Eden
that I gained my own will.

Gautama, I am one with thee,
Mara's demons do now flee,
your Presence like a soothing balm,
my mind and senses ever calm.

Gautama, Flame of Cosmic Peace,
unruly thoughts do hereby cease,
we radiate from you and me
the peace to still Samsara's Sea.

4. I was created with free will from the very beginning, and in rebelling against God's will I did not gain the freedom to make my own choices. I lost that freedom by giving it to the mortal self and the prince of this world.

Gautama, I now take the vow,
to live in the eternal now,
with you I do transcend all time,
to live in present so sublime.

Gautama, Flame of Cosmic Peace,
unruly thoughts do hereby cease,
we radiate from you and me
the peace to still Samsara's Sea.

5. I have a built-in longing to express my individuality. I know that expressing my individuality can be done within the framework of the will of God, which is the will of my own higher being.

Gautama, I have no desire,
to nothing earthly I aspire,
in non-attachment I now rest,
passing Mara's subtle test.

**Gautama, Flame of Cosmic Peace,
unruly thoughts do hereby cease,
we radiate from you and me
the peace to still Samsara's Sea.**

6. I know wholeness can be attained only by following the will of God. The seeming conflict between my individual will and the will of God is a dualistic illusion.

Gautama, I melt into you,
my mind is one, no longer two,
immersed in your resplendent glow,
Nirvana is all that I know.

**Gautama, Flame of Cosmic Peace,
unruly thoughts do hereby cease,
we radiate from you and me
the peace to still Samsara's Sea.**

7. I surrender any subtle resentment against God for the very fact that I am alive. I surrender any sense that God forced life upon me and therefore God is responsible for my current misery and limitations.

Gautama, in your timeless space,
I am immersed in Cosmic Grace,
I know the God beyond all form,
to world I will no more conform.

**Gautama, Flame of Cosmic Peace,
unruly thoughts do hereby cease,
we radiate from you and me
the peace to still Samsara's Sea.**

8. I am clearing my identity body and I have the recognition and the full acceptance that God's will is indeed my will and my will is God's will.

> Gautama, I am now awake,
> I clearly see what is at stake,
> and thus I claim my sacred right
> to be on earth the Buddhic Light.

> **Gautama, Flame of Cosmic Peace,**
> **unruly thoughts do hereby cease,**
> **we radiate from you and me**
> **the peace to still Samsara's Sea.**

9. I was not created in a vacuum. I am an extension of a greater spiritual Being, and I am an expression of the fact that this greater Being has a desire to extend itself into the material universe and bring the light and the kingdom of God to replace the darkness that covers the land.

> Gautama, with your thunderbolt,
> we give the earth a mighty jolt,
> I know that some will understand,
> and join the Buddha's timeless band.

> **Gautama, Flame of Cosmic Peace,**
> **unruly thoughts do hereby cease,**
> **we radiate from you and me**
> **the peace to still Samsara's Sea.**

2. I came here out of love

1. After I was created as an individual lifestream, I had a choice concerning whether I would descend to the material universe or whether I would seek growth in the spiritual realm. I clearly saw the purpose for which I was created, and I lovingly chose to descend as an emissary of the greater Being that I AM.

> O Blessed Mary's Song of Life,
> consuming every form of strife.
> As I attune to sound so fair,
> each cell is healthy, I declare.

> **O Mother Mary, generate,**
> **the song that does accelerate,**
> **my mind into a peaceful state,**
> **God's perfect love I radiate.**

2. I was not forced to come here. I came here as the result of a choice, and that choice was not made by some alien, remote being. It was made by me, the Conscious You, seeing myself as an extension of the greater Being that I am.

> As life's own song I ever hear,
> it does consume all sense of fear.
> In tune with Mother's symphony,
> from all diseases I AM free.

> **O Mother Mary, generate,**
> **the song that does accelerate,**
> **my mind into a peaceful state,**
> **God's perfect love I radiate.**

3. I am here because I chose to come here, and I made that choice out of love. I am here because I want to be here.

> In Mother's love I do transcend,
> and all my struggles hereby end.
> For when with Mother's eye I see,
> no imperfection touches me.

> **O Mother Mary, generate,**
> **the song that does accelerate,**
> **my mind into a peaceful state,**
> **God's perfect love I radiate.**

4. I reconnect to my original purpose for coming here, and my life takes on an entirely new dimension. I have a deep and joyful sense of purpose and I am connected to the original meaning, the original purpose, behind God's creation.

> I see that healing must begin
> by finding Living Christ within.
> For as I see with single eye,
> each cell the light does amplify.

> **O Mother Mary, generate,**
> **the song that does accelerate,**
> **my mind into a peaceful state,**
> **God's perfect love I radiate.**

5. I know who I am and why I came to this earth. I am an extension of a greater spiritual Being that embodies a particular quality of God. I am here to bring a particular God quality to this earth and thereby serve as one facet of the diamond mind of God that brings God's kingdom into manifestation on this planet.

In Mother's music I am free,
from memories of a lesser me.
My vision in a perfect state,
that all my cells regenerate.

**O Mother Mary, generate,
the song that does accelerate,
my mind into a peaceful state,
God's perfect love I radiate.**

6. I reconnect to the whole of the Body of God and I see that I am a part of a great wave of Beings who came to this earth for a higher purpose. I have a sense of purpose, a sense of meaning, a sense of divine direction that is the ultimate fulfillment of my deepest longing.

O Mother's Love, sweet melody,
from imperfections I AM free.
O Mother Mary, sound of sounds,
within my heart your love abounds.

**O Mother Mary, generate,
the song that does accelerate,
my mind into a peaceful state,
God's perfect love I radiate.**

7. The true abundant life comes from feeling that the light of God is streaming through my four lower bodies. It comes from knowing that every aspect of my lower being is in alignment with my original purpose for coming here. Every aspect of my life is an expression of that purpose and serves to fulfill that purpose.

Through Mother's beauty so sublime,
transcending bounds of space and time.
All cells beyond the mortal tomb,
as they are whole in Mother's womb.

O Mother Mary, generate,
the song that does accelerate,
my mind into a peaceful state,
God's perfect love I radiate.

8. My identity body focuses the power of will, the power of determination, the power of direction, the power of purpose. The basic impulse behind my coming into the material world was a decision. My entire lifestream springs from an act of will. This act of will is an extension of the original decision made by my Creator, the decision that: *"I will create!"*

In resonance with life's own song,
in life's harmonics I belong.
The blueprint of my perfect state
does every cell reconsecrate.

O Mother Mary, generate,
the song that does accelerate,
my mind into a peaceful state,
God's perfect love I radiate.

9. I am reconnecting to the higher will of my being, to a will that is beyond anything that could possibly be contained within my four lower bodies. I am connecting to a will that is higher than the will of my conscious mind.

The tuning fork in every cell
is now attuned to Mother's bell.
From curse of death I AM now free,
I claim my immortality.

O Mother Mary, generate,
the song that does accelerate,
my mind into a peaceful state,
God's perfect love I radiate.

3. I transcend the force of anti-will

1. This planet has a force of anti-will, a force that actively opposes God's will and the manifestation of God's kingdom. I will no longer ignore the existence of this force of anti-will because I want to rise above it.

Gautama, show my mental state
that does give rise to love and hate,
your exposé I do endure,
so my perception will be pure.

Gautama, Flame of Cosmic Peace,
unruly thoughts do hereby cease,
we radiate from you and me
the peace to still Samsara's Sea.

2. I am discovering a source of will power that is stronger than anything found in this world. That source of will power is to reconnect to the true identity that I am, to the greater spiritual being out of which I am an extension.

Gautama, in your Flame of Peace,
the struggling self I now release,
the Buddha Nature I now see,
it is the core of you and me.

Gautama, Flame of Cosmic Peace,
unruly thoughts do hereby cease,
we radiate from you and me
the peace to still Samsara's Sea.

3. I am reconnecting to my greater spiritual Being, and I have access to the entire force of will power that goes all the way back to my Creator. There is no force in this world that can withstand the will power of God.

Gautama, I am one with thee,
Mara's demons do now flee,
your Presence like a soothing balm,
my mind and senses ever calm.

Gautama, Flame of Cosmic Peace,
unruly thoughts do hereby cease,
we radiate from you and me
the peace to still Samsara's Sea.

4. The will of God is absolute, is uncompromising, and it does not in any way cater to the dualistic reasoning of the mind of anti-christ. God's will does not compromise truth and it will not accept any opposition to the manifestation of God's kingdom.

Gautama, I now take the vow,
to live in the eternal now,
with you I do transcend all time,
to live in present so sublime.

**Gautama, Flame of Cosmic Peace,
unruly thoughts do hereby cease,
we radiate from you and me
the peace to still Samsara's Sea.**

5. I am reconnecting to the will of my greater being, and I will not accept any conditions on this earth that stand in the way of the fulfillment of my original purpose for coming here. I am breaking through the anti-will of my mortal self, the anti-will of people around me, the anti-will of the collective consciousness and the anti-will of the prince of this world.

Gautama, I have no desire,
to nothing earthly I aspire,
in non-attachment I now rest,
passing Mara's subtle test.

**Gautama, Flame of Cosmic Peace,
unruly thoughts do hereby cease,
we radiate from you and me
the peace to still Samsara's Sea.**

6. I am reconnecting to a force that is completely beyond compromise, and that force is the will of God. The will of God will not compromise truth, and I will not compromise the original purpose for my coming here.

Gautama, I melt into you,
my mind is one, no longer two,
immersed in your resplendent glow,
Nirvana is all that I know.

Gautama, Flame of Cosmic Peace,
unruly thoughts do hereby cease,
we radiate from you and me
the peace to still Samsara's Sea.

7. My Conscious You is separating itself from the conscious mind and reconnecting to my true identity. I am bringing the determination of the will of God down to the level of my conscious mind.

Gautama, in your timeless space,
I am immersed in Cosmic Grace,
I know the God beyond all form,
to world I will no more conform.

Gautama, Flame of Cosmic Peace,
unruly thoughts do hereby cease,
we radiate from you and me
the peace to still Samsara's Sea.

8. I will not allow anything, be it within my own psyche or outside myself, to stand in the way of the fulfillment of my purpose for being here on earth. I AM sweeping aside the opposition to my divine plan, to my reason for being.

Gautama, I am now awake,
I clearly see what is at stake,
and thus I claim my sacred right
to be on earth the Buddhic Light.

**Gautama, Flame of Cosmic Peace,
unruly thoughts do hereby cease,
we radiate from you and me
the peace to still Samsara's Sea.**

9. I am reconnecting to the power of the will of God, and I do not fear any force in this world. I have the inner knowing that I was sent here by God to bring light into this dark world, and I am withstanding any challenge from the prince of this world.

Gautama, with your thunderbolt,
we give the earth a mighty jolt,
I know that some will understand,
and join the Buddha's timeless band.

**Gautama, Flame of Cosmic Peace,
unruly thoughts do hereby cease,
we radiate from you and me
the peace to still Samsara's Sea.**

4. I claim my right to be the Christ on earth

1. I know I have the right to attain Christhood in this world. I am exercising this Christhood by bringing the light of truth to other people and to my society.

O Blessed Mary's Song of Life,
consuming every form of strife.
As I attune to sound so fair,
each cell is healthy, I declare.

O Mother Mary, generate,
the song that does accelerate,
my mind into a peaceful state,
God's perfect love I radiate.

2. I claim my right to demonstrate that there is an alternative to the dualistic state of consciousness, there is a viable path to attaining a higher state of consciousness. I am one among many people walking the path to Christhood and a more abundant life.

As life's own song I ever hear,
it does consume all sense of fear.
In tune with Mother's symphony,
from all diseases I AM free.

O Mother Mary, generate,
the song that does accelerate,
my mind into a peaceful state,
God's perfect love I radiate.

3. My true being, my I AM Presence and the Conscious You, are designed to be a spiritual sun radiating the light of God on planet earth. My I AM Presence steps down the light of God and then sends it through my four lower bodies to be directed by the Conscious You in alignment with my original purpose for coming to earth.

In Mother's love I do transcend,
and all my struggles hereby end.
For when with Mother's eye I see,
no imperfection touches me.

O Mother Mary, generate,
the song that does accelerate,
my mind into a peaceful state,
God's perfect love I radiate.

4. I am a conduit through which the light of God is streaming and radiating on earth. I am bringing God's light into the
material realm and thereby raising the vibration of the entire
universe, filling it with light so that it can become another sphere
in the spiritual realm.

I see that healing must begin
by finding Living Christ within.
For as I see with single eye,
each cell the light does amplify.

O Mother Mary, generate,
the song that does accelerate,
my mind into a peaceful state,
God's perfect love I radiate.

5. I am directing God's light into specific conditions on earth in
order to magnify, to accelerate, these conditions and help them
transcend their current imperfect state. I am helping everything
on earth become more, and in so doing, I become more. In giving my light, I receive ultimate fulfillment.

In Mother's music I am free,
from memories of a lesser me.
My vision in a perfect state,
that all my cells regenerate.

O Mother Mary, generate,
the song that does accelerate,
my mind into a peaceful state,
God's perfect love I radiate.

6. The abundant life is that the light of God is flowing undiluted and unhindered through my four lower bodies, magnifying everything it encounters. I am surrounded by abundance. I am actively producing abundance by letting the light from Above accelerate everything I encounter.

O Mother's Love, sweet melody,
from imperfections I AM free.
O Mother Mary, sound of sounds,
within my heart your love abounds.

O Mother Mary, generate,
the song that does accelerate,
my mind into a peaceful state,
God's perfect love I radiate.

7. I am multiplying my talents. In feeling the light flowing through me, I have the ultimate sense of fulfillment, the ultimate sense of abundance and nurturance.

Through Mother's beauty so sublime,
transcending bounds of space and time.
All cells beyond the mortal tomb,
as they are whole in Mother's womb.

O Mother Mary, generate,
the song that does accelerate,
my mind into a peaceful state,
God's perfect love I radiate.

8. I know who I am and I am *being* who I AM. I am experiencing gnosis and there is no longer any distance, any difference, any separation, between the knower and the known.

In resonance with life's own song,
in life's harmonics I belong.
The blueprint of my perfect state
does every cell reconsecrate.

O Mother Mary, generate,
the song that does accelerate,
my mind into a peaceful state,
God's perfect love I radiate.

9. I am no longer separated from God, and I know what God is like, I know what it is like to be God. The only way to *know* God is to *be* God!

The tuning fork in every cell
is now attuned to Mother's bell.
From curse of death I AM now free,
I claim my immortality.

O Mother Mary, generate,
the song that does accelerate,
my mind into a peaceful state,
God's perfect love I radiate.

Sealing

In the name of the Divine Mother, I call to Gautama and Mother Mary for the sealing of myself and all people in my circle of influence in the creative flow of the Divine Mother, the River of Life. I call for the multiplication of my calls by all representatives of the Divine Mother, so that we form the perfect figure-eight flow of "As Above, so below." Thus, I accept that this is fully manifest, because the mouth of the Lord, the Divine Mother that I AM, has spoken it. Amen.

9 | DISCOVERING YOUR
DIVINE PLAN

My beloved heart, it is now time to go from the over-all vision of your greater purpose to the more specific plan anchored in your mental body. I have briefly mentioned the concept of a divine plan, but it is now time to talk about this plan in more detail. This plan truly is the blueprint for your current lifetime but also a part of the blueprint for your entire sojourn in the material universe.

You are already well aware that you are more than the physical body, and I hope you are beginning to attain the awareness that you are more than the part of you that is designed to descend into the material universe. I hope you are beginning to glimpse that you are more than the contents of the four lower bodies you carry with you from lifetime to lifetime. What I would like to give you now is a sense for what exactly happens when your lifestream descends into a particular physical body. As the Conscious You begins this descent, it first integrates with your long-term mind. This is the mind that you carry with you from lifetime to lifetime, and as the Conscious You begins to integrate with it we might say that the Conscious You puts on a pair of glasses through which it sees everything.

When the Conscious You finally descends into the physical body, it puts on another pair of glasses, which represents your short-term mind, the mind that is centered around your current physical body.

When you are in a physical body, you – meaning your conscious mind – are looking at the world through two pair of glasses. The one pair of glasses is your long-term mind, your identity, mental and emotional body and even the part of the long-term mind that relates specifically to being in a physical body. The other pair of glasses represents your short-term mind, which also has four levels. The contents of this short-term mind are the ones that were put in that mind in this particular embodiment. What happens in this process is that the Conscious You can easily forget its true identity as an immortal spiritual being. It now begins to look at everything through the glasses of your long-term and short-term minds; it begins to identity itself *with* – identify itself *as* – the contents of your long-term and short-term minds. The Conscious You builds certain expectations and certain desires for how life should be and what it wants life to be like.

For example, most people have been programmed to accept certain expectations, desires and aspirations for their current lifetime, for what their lives should be like, what they should accomplish, what they want to do, what they want to have and what they want to experience. This programming is put upon all people by their families and societies, and it forms a set of expectations. These expectations might very well be in opposition to the expectations that are stored in your long-term mind, or they might be out of touch with what is either your true potential or your realistic karmic circumstances. This, of course, creates a division in your own being. An important consideration is how you can resolve such divisions in your being and avoid sabotaging your efforts to change your life and manifest more abundance. In order to explain this, I need you to step back and look beyond both your short-term and your long-term minds. Beyond those levels of the mind is an even higher level and this is where you find your divine plan. The Conscious You is more than the short-term and the long-term minds. It is simply looking through the filter of those minds while you are in a physical body and while you identify yourself with that body. After your physical body dies, the Conscious You separates itself from the body. If you are a spiritually aware person, the Conscious You can separate itself from the long-term mind and temporarily rise to the spiritual realm. Many of the more spiritual people on earth will, between their embodiments, attend educational and healing centers that are located in the lower spiritual realm. The Conscious You is not simply lying dormant somewhere between your physical embodiments. The Conscious You is always engaged in the process of learning, the process of self-transcendence. There are many people on earth who are so identified with the physical body that their conscious selves are not able to rise to the lower spiritual realms between embodiments. These people get stuck in lower realms, and some of them do indeed go into a kind of sleep that is almost like a spiritual coma. The more spiritual people have the ability to free themselves from identification with the material realm and thereby rise to the spiritual schoolrooms. In these learning centers your conscious self will meet with your Christ self and a set of spiritual teachers who serve as your personal guides. Before you come down into your next embodiment, you will have several councils with your spiritual teachers in which you will define a very specific divine plan for what you want to accomplish in your next lifetime.

Before you came down into your current embodiment, you met with your spiritual teachers and created a very detailed plan for what you want to learn, what you want to experience and what portions of your past karma you need to overcome in this lifetime. It is possible, in fact it is likely, that your outer expectations, the expectations you have built based on the programming from your family and society, are to a smaller or larger degree out of alignment with your divine plan. It is even possible that you have some expectations in your long-term mind that are out of alignment with your divine plan. Obviously, such expectations will make you a house divided against itself. The greatest advantage of clearing your mental body is that it will allow you to see beyond any expectations you have built in this current lifetime and any imperfect, dualistic expectations that have lingered in your long-term mind. When you clear out this debris, you will be able to get a much clearer vision of your divine plan, both the long-term plan and the specific plan for this lifetime.

The greatest joy you can experience is to know that you are fulfilling your divine plan, that every aspect of your life is in alignment with that plan. This truly is the abundant life. As the Conscious You descends into the dense energies of the physical body, it is almost inevitable that you forget your divine plan. Even the most spiritually aware people forget most of their divine plans, although many people have a strong intuitive sense, even as young children, of what they want to do in life. Due to the very dense energies that currently dominate the planetary energy field, it is normal to forget your divine plan. As a spiritual seeker you should expect that you need to make an effort to reconnect to your divine plan. This is, so to speak, simply the cost of doing business on a planet with such dense energies. Don't blame yourself, God or anyone else for the fact that you have forgotten your divine plan. Simply decide that you will put forth a determined effort to rediscover who you are and why you are here.

Why is it important to reconnect to your divine plan? Besides the goal of attaining greater peace of mind and a deep sense of meaning, it will also give you very specific directions for your current lifetime. This might be directions such as the right occupation, the right person to marry, the right place to live or what you need to study – such as a spiritual teaching – in order to learn the lessons you are meant to learn. Because you are a spiritually aware person, you probably already have some intuitive sense of the basic elements of your divine plan. Many spiritual people can look back at their lives and see that they have done certain things for which they had no outer, rational explanation. They simply knew that it was something they had to do. You might even look back at your life and see that you have had certain unpleasant experiences or have done certain things that might seem like mistakes. When you reconnect to your divine plan, you are likely to discover that this was something you had to do. The reason might be that you needed to learn a lesson, that you were trying to help other people learn a lesson or that you had some karma from past lives that brought about the experience. Regardless of the actual cause, this was a necessary part of your divine plan, and when you see this, you can be at peace about the experience. Instead of looking back at your life with sorrow and regret, you can look for the hidden lesson and use even your unpleasant experiences as a springboard for spiritual growth.

***

Your divine plan has two aspects. In the previous chapter I talked about the overall purpose for your coming into the material universe, namely that you wanted to bring the light of God and to bring about God's kingdom. At the more specific level, you have an overall, timeless divine plan for what you want to accomplish in the material universe. That plan relates to who you are, namely the spiritual Being out of which you are an individualization.

When Moses climbed the mountain to receive the ten commandments from God, he saw God as a living fire. That is why the Bible says that our God is a consuming fire (Hebrews 12:29). In the spiritual realm are a number of God Flames, and each God Flame represents a particular quality of God. For example, there is a flame of God's Will, there is a flame of God's Wisdom, there is a flame of God's love, there is a flame of Peace and so forth and so on. For each positive quality known to human beings, there is a certain God Flame that focuses that quality. Your lifestream was born out of such a God Flame, and your overall purpose for coming into the material universe is to bring the light and the qualities of your God Flame in order to displace the darkness on earth. The Creator will not send that God Flame from outside the material universe. It must come from within by a person on earth embodying that God Flame.

Your God Flame has two aspects, namely the expanding element of the Father and the contracting element of the Mother, the Alpha aspect and the Omega aspect. This is described in the Bible in the statement: "I am Alpha and Omega, the beginning and the ending, saith the Lord, which is, and which was, and which is to come, the Almighty" (Revelation 1:8). The Alpha aspect of your God Flame, the masculine aspect, is the flame out of which you sprang, and the feminine aspect is the gift you are here to bring to the world. You might be out of the God Flame of love, but you chose to come to earth to bring truth. In order to bring truth to earth, you have to bring truth in a loving manner. Likewise, you might be out of the God Flame of peace, but you are here to bring direction. You must bring a direction that helps people attain peace and that expresses the quality of peace.

As you clear your mental body and your identity body, you will begin to get an intuitive feeling for your particular God Flame, and it is a topic that you might meditate upon as you give the invocations in this course. Many spiritual people will already have some sense of their God Flame, even though you may never have heard about the concept. You might see that there are certain qualities that have always seemed important to you or been dear to your heart. You might even see that there are certain negative characteristics you have often encountered, and the reason is that they are in opposition to your God Flame. You are here to let your God Flame consume them, which means that you attract them to you so that they can be consumed by the fire of your greater Being. It is therefore important that you do not become emotionally involved with such situations or feelings but simply allow them to pass into the fire of your inner Being. This requires you to be non-attached so that you do not magnify these negative qualities with your emotional body.

I know this concept will seem abstract to many people, but I am bringing it up because as you begin to clear your higher bodies, you will get a better intuitive awareness of your God Flame. It is important for you to have the concept in the back of your mind so that as you grow in self-awareness you can begin to consciously tune in to your God Flame and your reason for being.

Beyond the more abstract, overall level that relates to expressing your God Flame, is the more concrete level of your divine plan. Again, there is a part of your divine plan that relates to what you came to bring to earth, and this plan will carry over from lifetime to lifetime. For example, you might feel an affinity for certain activities or a certain type of occupation. You might have a particular concern for certain problems on earth and a desire to see them alleviated. There may also be certain elements of this plan that relate to what you need to learn in order to become who you truly are, and these are also long-term goals. These long-term goals are crystallized into particular goals for your current lifetime, and these goals are the easiest for you to uncover. Here we do, once again, run into a problem I have discussed earlier, namely that your outer mind, your conscious mind and your mortal self, might have built certain expectations that are in opposition to your divine plan. If you are very attached to these outer expectations, your conscious mind might actually refuse to see your divine plan. The reason being that following your divine plan would require some major adjustments in your outer lifestyle, and a part of you does not want to make those adjustments.

Your mortal self will do everything it can think of to prevent you from acknowledging your divine plan. It will try to make you so attached to the expectations you have built in this lifetime, expectations that your mortal self has programmed into your mind, that you simply will not look beyond them. Your mortal self will want you to become so attached to temporary desires and pleasures that you will ignore the true desires of your lifestream, as expressed in your divine plan. In order to fully see your divine plan, you will often have to give up, to surrender, certain dualistic, temporary expectations and all emotional attachments to seeing these desires and expectations fulfilled. This is what Jesus described in the statement that you cannot serve two masters, that you cannot serve God – meaning your long-term spiritual goals – and mammon – meaning your short-term, mortal desires and expectations (Matthew 6:24). When you allow yourself to be pulled in two opposing directions, you might refuse to acknowledge your divine plan. You will see it as something that is external to your mortal will – which it *is* – and even something that is being imposed upon you by some higher authority that is out to control you—which it *is not*. As I explained in the last chapter, this is an illusion projected upon the Conscious You by the mortal self, and only an act of will by the Conscious You can overcome it. You cannot fulfill your divine plan as long as the Conscious You sees it as being outside of its own will. You need to make peace with your divine plan, and you can do that only by reaching beyond the mortal desires and expectations for what your life should be like. You need to be willing to "lose your life," to lose your attachments to your dualistic expectations.

You should not expect to have your entire divine plan revealed to you at once. The path is a gradual process, and in the beginning you will only see parts of your divine plan. As you are faithful over your intuitive revelations, you will prove yourself worthy to grasp more and more details until you will eventually have a very clear recognition of your plan. Some details may not ever be known to your conscious mind because how can you learn a particular lesson if you know the purpose for the test you encounter? There will always be some things your outer mind will not know, and you grow by making decisions without having full awareness. You also need to keep in mind that many details of your divine plan are not set in stone. They need to be decided by you as events unfold and could not be planned in advance.

***

In order to discover your divine plan, you have to make an effort to see beyond your short-term desires and expectations. You will have to go through a process in which you gradually shed the programming from the world that tells you who you are and how you should live your life. Only by doing so can you let go of the images that prevent you from seeing your divine plan, which is hidden behind the veil of expectations.

Almost every aspect of life on this planet has been influenced by the consciousness of duality, the consciousness of anti-christ. As you grow up in modern society, your mind will be programmed with images, desires, beliefs and expectations that are specifically designed to keep you tied to the treadmill of being a good consumer, a good member of society, who will not rock the boat, who will not go beyond the norm. You are being programmed to fit into a mold of how the powers that be define a "normal" and "productive" member of society. If you look at the lives of some of the people who have brought humanity forwards, you will see that they did not follow the expectations of society. Some of these people were called geniuses, but they did not have any more inherent genius than you have. They were simply more in tune with their divine plans and the greater purpose for why they came to earth. They reached beyond the programming of society to draw down the contents of their divine plans and express them in their lives. This is how they made a unique contribution to society, a contribution that you might think is beyond you, but this is simply another aspect of the programming that does not want you to rise and be who you truly are.

The prince of this world does not want you to fulfill your divine plan, does not want you to express your true being, your true genius, in this world. The prince of this world is engaged in an impossible quest of attempting to control every aspect of life on planet earth. The prince of this world knows that if you were to reconnect to who you truly are and begin to express who you are, begin to manifest your divine plan, you could not be controlled any more than Jesus could be controlled. Your mortal self and the prince of this world do not want you to reconnect to your divine plan. They want you to live your life as a normal, average human being who does not rock the boat and go beyond the norm.

Many people say there is a fine line between genius and madness. You can indeed see some people who might have had the potential for genius, but they crossed the line into various forms of mental illness or delusions. The reason for this was that these people had not purified their four lower bodies, and thus they did not have balance. They were in a somewhat dangerous position of having reached a certain purity of the mental body that allowed them to know that they had a greater potential and purpose than the norm. They had glimpses of their divine plan, but because they had not purified their other bodies, they were not able to balance the seeming contradictions between their inner vision and their daily lives.

In many cases, the problem was that while they had glimpses of their divine plan, they also had certain worldly expectations to which they had become attached. They were pulled in two different directions by their higher vision and by their lower expectations. Because they did not have a spiritual approach to life, they could not rise above the dualistic expectations. They ended up being torn apart to a point where they could not maintain a balanced existence. They became trapped by the dualistic mind that takes everything to one of two extremes. This has caused many gifted people to either deny their gifts or to express them in an unbalanced manner, and either way causes people to depart from their divine plans. It is also common – especially among more spiritually inclined people – that people have a clear vision of *what* they need to accomplish, but because of attachments to certain expectations, they have an unrealistic vision of *how* to accomplish it. They are striving towards a correct goal, but they are using inappropriate or inefficient means to get there. As always, the key is to reach for the balanced perspective, the middle way, of the Christ mind, which comes from purifying all of your four lower bodies.

The invocations I have designed will purify all of your four lower bodies so that you will not be pulled in different directions by conflicting desires and expectations. In order for this program to be ultimately successful, you need to be willing to let go of the dualistic expectations and desires that have entered both your long-term and your short-term minds.

***

There has always been a certain built-in conflict in many people's approach to religion. There are many people who feel drawn to religion and to the spiritual side of life. They also have to balance the fact that they want to live a normal life, be married, raise children and be part of society. You see millions, if not billions, of people in today's world who are struggling to balance this contradiction. How can you be a religious person, a spiritual person, and at the same time live a normal life with the obligations of family and making a living?

For some Christians this is exemplified in Jesus' statement that you cannot serve God and mammon (Matthew 6:24), and they interpret it to mean that you should avoid the temptations of everyday life. Some even see the entire material universe as the enemy of their spiritual growth, which has caused much unnecessary tension. As always, there is a higher meaning behind this statement. Mammon first of all means the duality consciousness and not worldly activities. Jesus was not saying that you cannot participate in normal life. He was saying that you need to overcome your emotional attachments and your expectations so that you will not let them stand in the way of your spiritual growth. It simply is not correct to say that all spiritual people should withdraw from normal life, for this is a highly individual matter. For some people it might be right to withdraw – perhaps only for a time – while for others this would not be their divine plan. You need to remain open to direction from your inner teacher, and you can maintain this openness only when you are not serving mammon, when you are not living your life according to a set of dualistic expectations.

The only way to find balance between spiritual and worldly desires and obligations is to reconnect to your divine plan so that you know your specific goals for this lifetime. All spiritual people have spiritual growth as a foundational part of their divine plans. Many spiritual people do not realize that a part of their divine plan also specifies that they have a family, that they have a certain occupation and that they take active part in society in various ways. There is a tendency among spiritual people that you need to understand so that you can avoid becoming unbalanced in your spiritual search.

On the one hand it is true that in order to grow spiritually you must be willing to reach beyond the normal way of life in which so many people are trapped. You must reach for something higher, yet this does not necessarily mean that you have to go into the opposite extreme and live in a monastery or a cave in the Himalayas. In this age, there are many spiritual people who are meant to live active lives, and the reason is that we are entering an age where humankind needs to integrate spirituality with everyday life. People need to spiritualize everyday life.

Many religious people have compartmentalized their lives. They go to church on Sunday and live a worldly life the rest of the week, often ignoring their spiritual beliefs. In this age, humankind needs to rise to a higher level where their spiritual beliefs are not simply taken out of the closet on Sundays. Instead, every aspect of people's lives needs to be infused with their spiritual beliefs whereby their lives become an expression of who they are as spiritual beings. Many spiritually minded people volunteered to take embodiment at this critical time in part to demonstrate how to integrate spirituality with everyday life. Please make an effort to reach beyond any sense of conflict you might have had about this and realize that it is indeed a part of your divine plan that you bring your spirituality into every aspect of your life—even if it goes beyond the expectations of your family and the norms of your society. The norms of a secular, non-spiritual society need to change, and they will only do so when some people refuse to fit into the mold, thereby demonstrating that you can be a spiritual person while living in the world. You can serve God even though you are taking active part in worldly activities because you are not tempted by the consciousness of mammon, the duality consciousness. You are *in* the world but not *of* the world.

What gives you the longing for something higher is the inner knowing that you are more than the physical body, you are more than the outer personality that you have built in this lifetime. When you reconnect to that "more" by clearing your identity body, you will know who you are. You will also begin to know why you came into this particular lifetime and why you chose your particular circumstances, including your family background and other outer conditions. Your divine plan does have overall aspects that relate to your long-term goals for coming to earth. Your plan is also very realistic in the sense that it takes into account the fact that your lifestream has fallen into the duality consciousness.

Before you came into this lifetime, you met with your spiritual teachers, and you outlined a very specific plan for how you could deal with the fact that you are somewhat identified with the duality consciousness and that you created karma in past lives that is coming due in this lifetime. The goal for this part of your divine plan is to help you overcome the karma before it becomes physical and learn the lessons you need to learn so that you can overcome your dualistic beliefs. The goal is to set you free from human limitations, but in order to be free of certain limitations, you will have to experience them and then rise above the outer conditions.

Your divine plan is very specific in terms of where you chose to be born, meaning your country, your family and even the characteristics of your physical body. You might indeed have karma from past lives with your parents and siblings, and it is part of your divine plan that you interact with these people and hopefully develop a more loving relationship that allows you to rise above that karma. The same holds true for your spouse and children who are also part of your divine plan. The purpose is always that all of the people in a certain karmic group rise above their limitations, rise above the state of consciousness and the attitude towards each other that they have built in past lifetimes. The goal is that you rise above any approach to each other that is based on negative feelings and replace it with an approach that is based on love.

It is possible that certain parts of your divine plan specify that you need to be in a situation where you do not have material abundance. If you do not currently have abundance, this might actually be part of your divine plan. It is unlikely that your divine plan specifies that you should remain poor for an entire lifetime. If you find yourself without material abundance, it is usually because your greater Being wanted you to learn a lesson from this situation. Instead of focusing your attention on making money, you should focus your attention on learning the lesson you are meant to learn from not having money. Once you have learned that lesson, you will transcend the need to be in a situation where you do not have abundant supply. You can open up for the descent of God's abundance into your life.

***

The overall message I want to convey in this chapter is that you need to switch your perception of life, your attitude towards life, your approach to life. It is extremely common that people grow up with a sense of being victims of circumstances beyond their control. You feel that life is throwing circumstances at you, and they are difficult and overwhelming circumstances so you are always in the process of trying to cope. You always feel that it is a little too much and that life is giving you more than you can handle. When you start clearing you four lower bodies, this feeling will gradually dissipate. You will get over the sense of feeling overwhelmed because this feeling comes from the fact that you are carrying too heavy of a burden of misqualified energy. It is these energies that make you feel overwhelmed so once you have used my invocations to transform those energies, the feeling of being overwhelmed will dissipate.

You can then begin to breathe more freely, and what you need to do at this point is to shift your attitude to life away from the sense of being a victim of circumstances beyond your control. You need to accept the reality that everything that happens in your life is an opportunity for growth. You chose those circumstances because they give you a unique opportunity to rise above your dualistic beliefs and your karma. No matter what circumstances you encounter, you should assume that they are part of your divine plan. The entire purpose for this plan is to put you into circumstances where you have the best possible opportunity for coming up higher, for taking another step up the spiral staircase, by overcoming some dualistic belief in one of your four lower bodies. Instead of seeing yourself as a victim of circumstances beyond your control, you need to see yourself as a person who is constantly in the process of learning your lessons in life. Every situation you encounter is an opportunity to learn a lesson and take another step up the spiral staircase. This is the entire purpose of life, and you will make life much easier for yourself if you adopt the attitude that every situation you encounter can be used as a stepping stone for growth. Thereby, you can overcome the very common expectation that life should be easy or live up to some man-made standard of perfection. You can build the realistic expectation that life is an opportunity for growth and that life should put you into situations where you have to overcome certain limitations. When you reconnect to your divine plan, you will see that all of the experiences you have had in this lifetime represented unique opportunities to learn a specific lesson, to overcome some dualistic expectations, and move a step closer to the abundant life. When you look at life as an opportunity to grow, it becomes so much easier for you to detach yourself from the emotional involvement with a particular situation. Instead of falling into the trap of running away, of not being willing to look at a situation, you can go into the positive approach of asking your Christ self to help you learn the lesson behind the outer situation. If you will ask with an open mind and heart, you *will* receive an answer and you will see what you need to learn. I can assure you that once you actually learn the lesson, your situation will change. In some cases you will no longer attract specific outer circumstances. In some cases the outer conditions might not change, but your experience of them will have changed fundamentally.

Many people run into the same problem, the same crisis, over and over again. For example, some people have one failed relationship after another. Every time they move out of one relationship and move into another, they attract the same kind of person and have the same kind of problem. Many of these people fail to understand why they keep attracting the same circumstances over and over again. They do so because their divine plan specifies that they need to learn a particular lesson in this lifetime. If they do not learn that lesson from one situation, the cosmic mirror will give them another situation that outpictures their dualistic beliefs—and they have another opportunity to see those beliefs and let them go. Once you learn the lesson, there is no longer any need for you to experience those kinds of situations. All of a sudden, you will see that problems which might have followed you for decades can be resolved overnight and you will not encounter them anymore.

Instead of always feeling like you are behind, feeling like you are a victim of life, you can get yourself into a totally positive

approach where you realize that you are not a victim of circumstances beyond your control. Instead, you see every circumstance
you encounter as part of you divine plan and as an opportunity
to learn your lessons so you can be permanently free of this type
of situation.

Right now you might look at your life through the filter of a
number of dualistic, human expectations and you think your life
does not measure up to those expectations. This might give you
a subtle or obvious sense that your life has been a failure because
it did not meet these expectations. When the Conscious You is
not looking through the filter of your long-term and short-term
minds, it is completely free of such unrealistic expectations. The
Conscious You did not design your divine plan according to
human expectations, and it is not the purpose of your current
lifetime to live according to such expectations. It is entirely possible that what might seem like a failure according to worldly
expectations is in accordance with your divine plan. Or perhaps
certain decisions you have made were not quite in harmony with
your divine plan, but by learning from those decisions you can
still come up higher and thus catch up to your divine plan.

The prince of this world and the mortal self want to make
you believe that you can never rise above the imperfections from
your past. No matter how imperfect your life might have been,
you can *always* use any mistake as an opportunity to see through
a dualistic illusion and therefore take another step up the spiral
staircase. If you grow spiritually, your life has not been wasted,
no matter what worldly expectations – your own or those of
other people – might say.

***

My beloved, we now need to take another step. We need to
consider how you can best overcome the limitations, the dualistic

beliefs, that are stored in your four lower bodies. There are two things you need to realize in order to fulfill the goals defined in your divine plan. The first one is that in order to overcome a specific limitation you will have to do something that you currently think you cannot do. That is why you are trapped by this particular limitation. Behind the limitation is a dualistic belief that makes you think there are certain things you cannot do. To use my earlier example, you might have a dualistic belief in your four lower bodies which says that you can't draw. In order to overcome that limitation, you will have to break through the belief that you cannot draw. You will have to prove to yourself that this belief is not true so you can fully accept that with God all things are possible.

In order to overcome a certain limitation, in order learn a certain lesson, you have to do something that seems impossible. You have to overcome the perception that certain things are not possible. You have to break through the programming of your mortal self, which is constantly projecting at your conscious mind that this particular limitation is impossible to overcome.

The other thing you need to realize is that you are never in a situation where you are facing a limitation that you cannot overcome. Your divine plan was designed by your spiritual teachers and the Conscious You. The entire purpose of your divine plan is to set you free from limitations. You may have many limitations you need to overcome before you are completely free of all dualistic beliefs. There might be some limitations that you can't overcome with your current level of awareness, but you don't have to face those limitations with your current level of awareness. Your divine plan is very carefully designed based on a realistic assessment of your current level of spiritual awareness, of self-awareness. You will not be presented with challenges that you are incapable of overcoming. You will not be presented with a lesson that you cannot learn.

In every situation you face, you do indeed have the potential to learn the lesson and thereby overcome the limitation that is holding you back and precipitating unpleasant or challenging circumstances. In order to learn your lesson, in order to overcome the limitation, you must be willing to do what seems impossible with your current level of awareness. You must realize that the sense that something is impossible is the actual problem.

For example, if you are facing the challenge of a difficult relationship, your conscious mind will often focus on the outer circumstances of the relationship. It is so easy to focus on the other person, thinking it is the other person's fault. If only the other person would change, the problem would be solved. In reality, the key to an improvement of your personal situation is that *you* must change. You must go within and discover the lesson that you are meant to learn from that particular situation. When you learn that lesson, the outer situation will magically change. Even if the other person does not change, the very fact that your attitude towards that person has changed will manifest an improvement in your experience of the relationship.

If you truly want to learn the lesson and be free of a particular type of challenge, you need to look beyond the outer circumstances. You need to look for the hidden lesson and you need to realize that the lesson you need to learn relates to a belief. Part of this belief is that you think it is impossible for you to overcome a certain limitation. For example, you might think it is impossible to find a partner with whom you can have a positive relationship. The reason this seems impossible is that there is a lesson you have not learned, and therefore you keep attracting to you persons who force you to confront the lesson. Because the underlying belief makes people think it is impossible to change and learn the lesson – and also because of the habit of running away from difficult situations – most people refuse to look for the lesson, they refuse to look in the mirror. They keep themselves in a catch-22 in which they keep attracting situations that force them to confront what they resist confronting.

This truly is the School of Hard Knocks, and I would love to see everyone who follows this course rise above that way of learning. I would like to see people rise to the school of reaching for inner guidance that helps them see what they need to learn in this lifetime. How can you do this? The master key is to ponder Jesus' statements: "I can of mine own self do nothing" (John 5:30) and "With men this is impossible; but with God all things are possible" (Matthew 19:26). There are many things in this world that you cannot do with the power that is available to your conscious mind. If you had the power of God, then all things would be possible. What keeps the power of God from flowing undiluted through your four lower bodies? It is the dualistic beliefs that cause you to shut off the flow of God's light. The real key to breaking free of human limitations is to overcome the dualistic beliefs that prevent God's light from manifesting the abundance that God wants you to have. Again, consider the saying: "We have nothing to fear but fear itself." It is only your fear-based beliefs – the beliefs that cause you to accept certain things as impossible – that prevent you from having the abundant life. The problem with fear is that it makes you unwilling to look at your beliefs, which makes it impossible for you to see that they are illusions. You feel trapped in a small prison cell, but all along the door has never been locked. You have simply been allowing an illusion to make you afraid to pull on the handle.

Once you start reconnecting to your divine plan, you will begin to see that there is method behind the seeming madness in your life. If your life has been chaotic, you will begin to realize that it is simply because you have particular lessons to learn. You keep attracting situations that force you to deal with the problem in your own psyche instead of running away from it. I understand that many people are not truly dealing with the problem, even though they run into it again and again. When you know why the history of your life is repeating itself, you can get yourself out of the tendency to run away. You can realize that while you were planning your life, you were outside your current beliefs and thus you actually planned to force yourself to learn a certain lesson. You did, in your greater awareness, plan to force yourself to face a particular limitation over and over again until you get it right.

The moment you accept that you have a lesson to learn and begin to look beyond the outer circumstances, you will see that the situation will change fundamentally. When you discover the hidden lesson and learn that lesson, you will suddenly find that you will no longer attract a certain type of situations or a certain type of people. You will then know that you have taken a major step up the spiral staircase. Be careful not to rest on your laurels. You need to always keep in mind that you have now learned an important lesson and it is time to look for the next lesson so you can take the next step.

Your divine plan is based on a realistic assessment of your potential for growth in this lifetime. It has a certain range for what could be accomplished. There is the lowest potential and there is the highest potential. If you truly adopt the right attitude, you can fulfill the highest potential for your divine plan instead of settling for the lowest potential. There are indeed many people on this earth who are stuck at a certain level of the spiral staircase because there is one particular lesson they refuse to learn. Sometimes it takes a number of lifetimes before a person has suffered so much that he or she finally says: "There must be a better way, there must be something I have not understood!" If you are willing to truly look for the lessons you are meant to learn in this lifetime, you can shorten the process. In one lifetime you will be able to learn the lessons that could otherwise have taken ten or twenty lifetimes to learn. This is truly what

I desire to see happen for you so that you can be free of your limitations and manifest the abundant life.

***

There is one more aspect of your divine plan that I would like you to understand. There are many of the more spiritual people on this earth who in past lifetimes have risen above the egotistical, self-centered state of consciousness. They have reconnected to the fact that they are here for a greater purpose, namely the purpose of raising the collective consciousness of humankind so that God's abundant life can become a planetary reality. This has caused many spiritual people to volunteer to take on certain burdens that are aimed at not only raising their own level of consciousness but raising the collective consciousness. This can be done only by transforming misqualified energy and by resolving blocks in the collective psyche. This is something you saw in the life of Jesus, and indeed Jesus has to some degree carried the sins of the world, meaning the karma of the world, in order to give humankind a reprieve in which they could rise to a higher level of consciousness without being so burdened by the negative energy from their past.

The universe is set up for you to learn so if Jesus took on your karma permanently, and you never had to deal with it again, how could you possibly learn your lessons? The orthodox concept that Jesus has taken upon himself not only the sins that were committed in the past but also all sins that could be committed in the future simply isn't correct. If Jesus had done this, how could people learn their lessons in life? The universe acts like a mirror that reflects back what you send out. It is in experiencing what comes back that you have an opportunity to learn. That is to say, you must learn through experience only when you are not willing to follow the spiritual path and learn before your past actions come back to haunt you. Because the earth is currently burdened by so much misqualified energy, it is indeed common that the more spiritual people will volunteer to take on a certain amount of the energy or karma in the collective consciousness. This is done in order to lighten the burden of other people so they are not so overwhelmed and have a greater opportunity to make spiritual progress in the current lifetime. There are many spiritual people who have taken on a karma that can manifest as limiting circumstances in their current lifetime. For example, some people carry diseases in their bodies as an outpicturing of the burden of misqualified energy they carry for humankind. Other people might experience lack of material abundance as a result of carrying the energies of humankind. You do not carry this energy or karma as some kind of sacrifice that pays back people's karma. You carry it in order to demonstrate to other people that you can overcome such burdens by taking a more spiritual approach to life. It is not your task to carry this burden forever. You are not meant to be overcome by this burden, it is indeed your task to demonstrate how to overcome all burdens.

Unfortunately, many people do not remember that they have voluntarily taken on these burdens, and this might cause people to feel some resentment or a sense of injustice over the fact that they carry these burdens. Some spiritual people are divided within themselves because they have an intuitive sense that the burdens they carry are not their own. They do not have the clear vision to realize that they chose to take on these conditions in order to help other people. They feel a sense of injustice because they think God must have unjustly put this upon them—a belief that is reinforced by these people's mortal selves and the prince of this world. By reconnecting to your divine plan, you can overcome this negative attitude and be totally at peace, even though you are experiencing certain outer limitations and burdens. You can see that you have taken on these burdens for a greater purpose, and even though they give you discomfort in this lifetime, you can realize that your current lifetime is only a very short interval in the eternity of the River of Life. By carrying this burden for others, you will indeed lay up for yourselves treasures in heaven. You will reap your just reward in your next lifetime or as you rise to the spiritual realm.

I am not saying that you should resign yourself to carrying your present burdens and never seek to overcome them. I am encouraging you to use the tools I give you, including my invocations, to consume the misqualified energy so that you no longer have to carry the physical burden. God has no desire to punish anyone. It is simply a law that all misqualified energy must be returned to its source and that it must be re-qualified. There are many ways to balance misqualified energy. One is to take it on as actual physical circumstances. If you can consume the energy before it descends into the matter realm, you don't need to carry the physical burdens. You can use my invocations to transform the energy so that you do not have to carry or continue to carry this physical burden.

***

The true purpose behind Jesus' mission was to serve as an example for humankind, an example of the fact that even a person born in seemingly humble circumstances can rise above those outer limitations and manifest the Christ consciousness, thereby winning his or her eternal freedom. Many of the spiritual people on earth have volunteered to take on certain burdens and limiting conditions in order to set forth the example for other people that it is possible to rise above any physical condition and manifest a more spiritual form of life. You might have volunteered to take on your present circumstances in order to show the people around you that they too can rise above these limitations. The prince of this world has managed to destroy the example of Jesus, and most people cannot identify with him or they think they cannot follow in his footsteps. The current plan of the ascended masters is to send many mature lifestreams to this earth in order to demonstrate how putting on the mind of Christ empowers you to rise above all human limitations. When thousands upon thousands of people demonstrate this, the prince of this world will not be able to destroy the examples of all of them. It is easy to put one person on a pedestal by saying he was unique, but it is far more difficult to turn 10,000 people into exceptions.

If you look at your current life, you might indeed see certain limiting conditions. Those conditions are not necessarily meant to be permanent, they are not meant to last for the rest of your lifetime. You might be meant to demonstrate the path of overcoming such conditions, and this is part of your divine plan. You might be meant to demonstrate that you can remove the physical limitations, or that by adopting a spiritual approach to life you can live with the conditions without having them stop you from being who you are and doing what you came here to do. In either case, you transcend the limitations to the point where they no longer matter, they no longer prevent you from being who you are and letting your light shine before the world.

When you attune to your divine plan, you can also begin to attune to the specific ways whereby you can overcome the limitations you are facing. God never requires you to face a limitation that you cannot overcome—if you are willing to transcend yourself, to overcome the dualistic belief that makes it seem impossible to transcend the limitation. It is part of your divine plan that you uncover this dualistic belief, resolve it and rise above it.

When you overcome a particular dualistic belief, you will open a pathway through the jungle of the collective consciousness.

You carve a trail and it will become possible for other people to follow that trail. As more and more people follow the trail you have blazed, it will become wider, making it even easier for others to follow. You might have volunteered to take on a certain limitation because you wanted to be the trailblazer who demonstrated to other people how to overcome that particular limitation. For example, many people have volunteered to take on the disease of cancer in order to demonstrate that this disease is not incurable, as many people have come to believe. In order to fully demonstrate this, you need to uncover the dualistic beliefs that give rise to the disease of cancer or any other limitation. This is indeed part of the greater divine plan for planet earth. You are living in a time when the spiritual teachers of humankind, the ascended masters, are longing to bring forth many new discoveries and revelations for how people can overcome their limitations. You might have volunteered to take on a certain limitation because you wanted to be part of that overall plan. By clearing your own mental body and reconnecting to your divine plan, you will also reconnect to the greater plan for the planet. You will then know how you can play your individual part, and this will empower you to discover the insights you need in order to overcome the dualistic beliefs that are the hidden cause behind your current limitations.

***

Life is not a random game of chance or the punishment of an angry God. Life is not a chaotic process that seems to have no meaning or direction. If you will look beyond the surface appearances on this planet, you will see that behind them is the River of Life, which is moving humankind forwards with an unstoppable force. People can slow down this movement, but they cannot stop it forever. Take a look at the history of the last

2,000 years and see that, even though humankind often falls prey to the force that wants to prevent them from changing, there is a certain force of progress that nothing can stop. Neither the collective consciousness of humankind nor the prince of this world can stop the force of progress, the River of Life, that brings humankind towards a higher level of awareness. Surely, there are many problems in today's world that did not exist 2,000 years ago, and in a sense the world is a more dangerous place than it was back then. Beyond these outer appearances, humankind has indeed progressed to a much higher level of awareness, to a greater understanding of life.

This understanding of the reality behind surface appearances is the highest potential of your mental body. Your mental body is the body that focuses the wisdom of God, and you might recall the statement in the Bible: "Wisdom is the principal thing; therefore get wisdom: and with all thy getting get understanding" (Proverbs 4:7). This is the highest goal for clearing your mental body, namely to get an understanding of the true purpose of life and the specific purpose for your present lifetime. It is also through your mental body that you can come to understand the laws that God used to design this universe. You can then align yourself with those laws, thereby fulfilling your role of using those laws to bring God's kingdom into manifestation.

Ah my beloved, can you sense the joy that comes from knowing that you are not disconnected from the whole, that you are not condemned to live in a chaotic world that has no purpose? Can you sense that when you uncover your divine plan, you will discover a deeper sense of purpose and meaning? It is not a sense of meaning that is so abstract that it is disconnected from your daily life. On the contrary, this sense of meaning carries into the most minute details of your daily life. It helps you realize that even seemingly mundane conditions carry an opportunity to learn a lesson and to overcome a limitation. You can demonstrate to others that it is possible for humankind to rise to a higher level and come ever closer to bringing God's kingdom into manifestation on earth.

This is the overall lesson that humankind needs to learn in this age, namely that it is possible to rise above the entire consciousness of limitation, the consciousness of duality, the consciousness of mammon, and bring God's kingdom – namely the sense of joy that comes from being in the flow of the River of Life – into people's everyday lives. The outer limitations that you see are simply the temporary projections of the duality consciousness. They are products of the fact that most human beings have an imperfect filmstrip in their minds, and through that filmstrip they are projecting imperfect images into the cosmic mirror. When people raise their consciousness and throw out the dualistic beliefs, they will uncover the true filmstrip, the filmstrip of their higher Beings and their divine plans. They will then begin to project perfect images into the cosmic mirror, and inevitably the cosmic mirror will reflect back those images in the form of perfect physical conditions on this planet. Planet earth can return to its original purity and beauty, which is so far beyond its current state of imperfection that most human beings cannot grasp that high of a vision. As you begin to clear your mental body, you will begin to grasp the true potential for your own life and the true potential for planet earth. This will indeed give you the peace of mind that is the natural state of your mental body.

Your mental body is the focus for God's peace, the peace that passes understanding, meaning the understanding of the human intellect and the dualistic state of mind. Your mental body can anchor God's peace by grasping the higher understanding that cannot be grasped by the consciousness of duality. When you see that higher vision, that immaculate concept, you will have the discernment to know what is real and what is unreal, what is in alignment with God's law and what is not, what is part of your divine plan and what is not. As you attain that discernment, you can make right choices, and thereby you can realign your thoughts with the reality of your divine plan and your true identity. You can ensure that, as the light of God flows into your emotional body, it does not have any internal divisions, any internal conflicts. It will not give rise to the conflicting emotions that plague so many people and stop them from manifesting God's abundance.

The higher wisdom will penetrate all of the dualistic illusions that prevent you from knowing who you are and prevent you from seeing your divine plan. When you grasp that wisdom, you will see that every aspect of your life serves a greater purpose. You will then know that nothing is wasted, nothing is for naught. You will know that no matter what you have gone through, you can turn your life around and use your past experiences as a springboard for winning your eternal victory.

Follow me as I lead you towards that victory and follow me as I give you the teachings of how to carry that sense of victory into your emotional body. The emotional body is the focal point for the illusions created by your mortal self and the prince of this world. Your emotions can so easily be stirred, and it is only when you have the clarity of God's wisdom that you can see through the temptations presented by the prince of this world—the temptations that are aimed at making you accept imperfect conditions as real or unavoidable. You can look the prince of this world straight in the eye and say with all the power of your higher Being: "Evil is not real, and its appearances have no power—in my consciousness and on this planet!"

10 | I INVOKE THE VISION OF MY DIVINE PLAN

In the name I AM THAT I AM, Jesus Christ, I call to all representatives of the Divine Mother and the Divine Father, especially the Great Divine Director, the Goddess of Liberty and Mother Mary, to help me overcome all lack of ability or willingness to see and make peace with my divine plan. Help me accept my creative powers and see the factors that block the flow of my God-given creativity, including...

[Make personal calls.]

1. I have a vision of my divine plan

1. Before I came down into my current embodiment, I met with my spiritual teachers and created a very detailed plan for what I want to learn, what I want to experience and what portions of my past karma I need to overcome in this lifetime.

Divine Director, I now see,
the world is unreality,
in my heart I now truly feel,
the Spirit is all that is real.

**Divine Director, send the light,
from blindness clear my inner sight,
my vision free, my vision clear,
your guidance is forever here.**

2. I am clearing my mental body in order to see beyond any expectations I have built in this current lifetime and any imperfect, dualistic expectations that have lingered in my long-term mind. I have a clear vision of my divine plan, both the long-term plan and the specific plan for this lifetime.

Divine Director, vision give,
in clarity I want to live,
I now behold my plan Divine,
the plan that is uniquely mine.

**Divine Director, send the light,
from blindness clear my inner sight,
my vision free, my vision clear,
your guidance is forever here.**

3. I have a clear vision of my God Flame and how to bring the light and the qualities of my God Flame in order to displace the darkness on earth.

Divine Director, show in me,
the ego games, and set me free,
help me escape the ego's cage,
to help bring in the golden age.

Divine Director, send the light,
from blindness clear my inner sight,
my vision free, my vision clear,
your guidance is forever here.

4. I have a clear vision of the more concrete level of my divine plan, the particular goals for my current lifetime.

Divine Director, I'm with you,
my vision one, no longer two,
as karma's veil you do disperse,
I see a whole new universe.

Divine Director, send the light,
from blindness clear my inner sight,
my vision free, my vision clear,
your guidance is forever here.

5. Mother Mary, help me see any expectations in my outer mind that are in opposition to my divine plan. I surrender my attachments to these outer expectations, and my conscious mind is indeed willing to see my divine plan.

Divine Director, I go up,
electric light now fills my cup,
consume in me all shadows old,
bestow on me a vision bold.

> **Divine Director, send the light,**
> **from blindness clear my inner sight,**
> **my vision free, my vision clear,**
> **your guidance is forever here.**

6. I am willing to make any adjustments to my outer lifestyle in order to fulfill my divine plan. I am willing to give up, to surrender, my dualistic, temporary expectations and all emotional attachments to seeing these desires and expectations fulfilled.

> Divine Director, heart of gold,
> my sacred labor I unfold,
> o blessed Guru, I now see,
> where my own plan is taking me.

> **Divine Director, send the light,**
> **from blindness clear my inner sight,**
> **my vision free, my vision clear,**
> **your guidance is forever here.**

7. I am making peace with my divine plan. I am reaching beyond the mortal desires and expectations for what my life should be like. I am willing to "lose my life," to lose my attachments to my dualistic expectations.

> Divine Director, by your grace,
> in grander scheme I find my place,
> my individual flame I see,
> uniqueness God has given me.

**Divine Director, send the light,
from blindness clear my inner sight,
my vision free, my vision clear,
your guidance is forever here.**

8. I am seeing beyond my short-term desires and expectations. I am shedding the programming from the world that tells me who I am and how I should live my life. I am letting go of the images that prevent me from seeing my divine plan.

Divine Director, vision one,
I see that I AM God's own Sun,
with your direction so Divine,
I am now letting my light shine.

**Divine Director, send the light,
from blindness clear my inner sight,
my vision free, my vision clear,
your guidance is forever here.**

9. I have a clear vision of what I need to accomplish, and I have a clear and balanced vision of how to accomplish it. I have the balanced perspective of the middle way, and I am letting go of the dualistic expectations and desires that have entered both my long-term and short-term minds.

Divine Director, what a gift,
to be a part of Spirit's lift,
to raise mankind out of the night,
to bask in Spirit's loving sight.

**Divine Director, send the light,
from blindness clear my inner sight,
my vision free, my vision clear,
your guidance is forever here.**

2. Everything is an opportunity for growth

1. I see how to live a balanced life and integrate spirituality with everyday life. Every aspect of my life is infused with my spiritual beliefs. My life is an expression of who I am as a spiritual being.

O Liberty now set me free
from devil's curse of poverty.
I blame not Mother for my lack,
O Blessed Mother, take me back.

**O Cosmic Mother Liberty,
conduct Abundance Symphony.
My highest service I now see,
abundance is now real for me.**

2. I see how my divine plan is designed to help me overcome my identification with the duality consciousness and my past karma. I see how to overcome the karma before it becomes physical and learn the lessons I need to learn so that I can overcome my dualistic beliefs.

O Liberty, from distant shore,
I come with longing to be More.
I see abundance is a flow,
abundance consciousness I grow.

O Cosmic Mother Liberty,
conduct Abundance Symphony.
My highest service I now see,
abundance is now real for me.

3. I see how to overcome any karma from past lives with my parents, siblings, spouses, children and other people I meet. I am developing a more loving relationship that allows me to rise above that karma.

O Liberty, expose the lie,
that limitations can me tie.
The Ma-ter light is not my foe,
true opulence it does bestow.

O Cosmic Mother Liberty,
conduct Abundance Symphony.
My highest service I now see,
abundance is now real for me.

4. I see if certain parts of my divine plan specify that I need to be in a situation where I do not have material abundance. I am focusing my attention on learning the lesson I am meant to learn. I am transcending the need to be in a situation where I do not have abundant supply.

O Liberty, expose the plot,
projected by the fallen lot.
O Cosmic Mother, I now see,
that Mother's not my enemy.

O Cosmic Mother Liberty,
conduct Abundance Symphony.
My highest service I now see,
abundance is now real for me.

5. I am shifting my perception of life, my attitude towards life, my approach to life. I accept the reality that everything that happens in my life is an opportunity for growth.

O Liberty, with opened eyes,
I now reject the devil's lies.
I now embrace the Mother realm,
for I see Father at the helm.

O Cosmic Mother Liberty,
conduct Abundance Symphony.
My highest service I now see,
abundance is now real for me.

6. I chose my present circumstances because they give me a unique opportunity to rise above my dualistic beliefs and my karma. No matter what circumstances I encounter, I know they are part of my divine plan.

O Liberty, a chalice pure,
my lower bodies are for sure.
Release through me your symphony,
your gift of Cosmic Liberty.

O Cosmic Mother Liberty,
conduct Abundance Symphony.
My highest service I now see,
abundance is now real for me.

7. The purpose of my divine plan is to put me into circumstances where I have the best possible opportunity for coming up higher by overcoming some dualistic belief in one of my four lower bodies.

O Liberty, the open door,
I am for Symphony of More.
In chakras mine light you release,
the flow of love shall never cease.

O Cosmic Mother Liberty,
conduct Abundance Symphony.
My highest service I now see,
abundance is now real for me.

8. I am a person who is constantly in the process of learning my lessons in life. Every situation I encounter is a stepping stone for growth. I surrender the expectation that life should be easy or live up to some man-made standard of perfection. Life is an opportunity for growth and life should put me into situations where I have to overcome certain limitations.

O Liberty, release the flow,
of opulence that you bestow.
For I am willing to receive,
the Golden Fleece that you now weave.

O Cosmic Mother Liberty,
conduct Abundance Symphony.
My highest service I now see,
abundance is now real for me.

9. All of the experiences I have had in this lifetime represented unique opportunities to learn a specific lesson, to overcome some dualistic expectations, and move a step closer to the abundant life. I am free from the emotional involvement with particular situations. I am asking my Christ self to help me learn the lesson behind any outer situation.

> O Liberty, release the cure,
> to free the tired and the poor.
> The huddled masses are set free,
> by loving Song of Liberty.
>
> **O Cosmic Mother Liberty,**
> **conduct Abundance Symphony.**
> **My highest service I now see,**
> **abundance is now real for me.**

3. I break free from limiting beliefs

1. I know that when I keep attracting the same circumstances over and over again, it is because I have not yet learned a particular lesson. I am asking my Christ self for guidance, and I know I will receive an answer. When I learn the lesson, the outer situation *will* change.

> Divine Director, I now see,
> the world is unreality,
> in my heart I now truly feel,
> the Spirit is all that is real.

Divine Director, send the light,
from blindness clear my inner sight,
my vision free, my vision clear,
your guidance is forever here.

2. I surrender any sense that my life is a failure. I surrender any dualistic, human expectations. I did not design my divine plan according to human expectations. What might seem like a failure according to worldly expectations can be a victory according to my divine plan.

Divine Director, vision give,
in clarity I want to live,
I now behold my plan Divine,
the plan that is uniquely mine.

Divine Director, send the light,
from blindness clear my inner sight,
my vision free, my vision clear,
your guidance is forever here.

3. No matter how imperfect my life might have been, I am using any mistake as an opportunity to see through a dualistic illusion and therefore take another step up the spiral staircase. When I grow spiritually, my life has not been wasted, no matter what worldly expectations might say.

Divine Director, show in me,
the ego games, and set me free,
help me escape the ego's cage,
to help bring in the golden age.

Divine Director, send the light,
from blindness clear my inner sight,
my vision free, my vision clear,
your guidance is forever here.

4. Part of my divine plan is to overcome my human limitations. In order to overcome a specific limitation, I will have to do something that I currently think I cannot do. The belief that something is impossible keeps me trapped by a particular limitation.

Divine Director, I'm with you,
my vision one, no longer two,
as karma's veil you do disperse,
I see a whole new universe.

Divine Director, send the light,
from blindness clear my inner sight,
my vision free, my vision clear,
your guidance is forever here.

5. Behind any limitation is a dualistic belief that makes me think there are certain things I cannot do. I am transcending the perception that certain things are not possible. I am breaking through the programming of my mortal self, and I know that with God all things are possible.

Divine Director, I go up,
electric light now fills my cup,
consume in me all shadows old,
bestow on me a vision bold.

Divine Director, send the light,
from blindness clear my inner sight,
my vision free, my vision clear,
your guidance is forever here.

6. Any limitation I face can be overcome when I am willing
to transcend my current level of awareness. My divine plan is
designed based on a realistic assessment of my current level of
spiritual awareness. I can overcome any challenge and learn any
lesson by rising to a higher level of awareness.

Divine Director, heart of gold,
my sacred labor I unfold,
o blessed Guru, I now see,
where my own plan is taking me.

Divine Director, send the light,
from blindness clear my inner sight,
my vision free, my vision clear,
your guidance is forever here.

7. The sense that something is impossible is the actual problem
I need to overcome. The key to improving my personal situation
is that *I* must change. I am going within and discovering the lesson. When I learn that lesson, the outer situation will magically
change.

Divine Director, by your grace,
in grander scheme I find my place,
my individual flame I see,
uniqueness God has given me.

Divine Director, send the light,
from blindness clear my inner sight,
my vision free, my vision clear,
your guidance is forever here.

8. I am looking beyond the outer circumstances, seeing the hidden lesson. The reason I think it is impossible to overcome a certain limitation is that there is a lesson I have not learned.

Divine Director, vision one,
I see that I AM God's own Sun,
with your direction so Divine,
I am now letting my light shine.

Divine Director, send the light,
from blindness clear my inner sight,
my vision free, my vision clear,
your guidance is forever here.

9. There are many things in this world that I cannot do with the power that is available to my conscious mind. When I have the power of God, all things are possible. I am breaking free of human limitations by overcoming the dualistic beliefs that prevent God's light from manifesting the abundance that God wants me to have.

Divine Director, what a gift,
to be a part of Spirit's lift,
to raise mankind out of the night,
to bask in Spirit's loving sight.

Divine Director, send the light,
from blindness clear my inner sight,
my vision free, my vision clear,
your guidance is forever here.

4. I reconnect to the divine plan for this planet

1. I see whether I have volunteered to take on a certain amount of the energy or karma in the collective consciousness. I see whether this is manifesting limiting circumstances in my life, such as an illness or lack of abundance.

O Liberty now set me free
from devil's curse of poverty.
I blame not Mother for my lack,
O Blessed Mother, take me back.

O Cosmic Mother Liberty,
conduct Abundance Symphony.
My highest service I now see,
abundance is now real for me.

2. I carry this energy or karma in order to demonstrate to other people that I can overcome such burdens by taking a more spiritual approach to life. I am reconnecting to my divine plan and I am totally at peace, even though I am experiencing certain outer limitations and burdens.

O Liberty, from distant shore,
I come with longing to be More.
I see abundance is a flow,
abundance consciousness I grow.

O Cosmic Mother Liberty,
conduct Abundance Symphony.
My highest service I now see,
abundance is now real for me.

3. I see that I have taken on these burdens for a greater purpose, and even though they give me discomfort in this lifetime, my current lifetime is only a short interval in the eternity of the River of Life. By carrying this burden for others, I am laying up for myself treasures in heaven. I will reap my just reward in my next lifetime or as I ascend to the spiritual realm.

O Liberty, expose the lie,
that limitations can me tie.
The Ma-ter light is not my foe,
true opulence it does bestow.

O Cosmic Mother Liberty,
conduct Abundance Symphony.
My highest service I now see,
abundance is now real for me.

4. Instead of resigning myself to carrying my present burdens, I am using the tools to invoke spiritual energy and consume the misqualified energy so that I no longer have to carry the physical burden.

O Liberty, expose the plot,
projected by the fallen lot.
O Cosmic Mother, I now see,
that Mother's not my enemy.

O Cosmic Mother Liberty,
conduct Abundance Symphony.
My highest service I now see,
abundance is now real for me.

5. I see whether I have volunteered to take on certain limiting conditions in order to set forth the example for other people that it is possible to rise above any physical condition and manifest a more spiritual form of life. I see whether I am meant to remove the physical limitations or live with them without having them stop me from being who I am and doing what I came here to do.

O Liberty, with opened eyes,
I now reject the devil's lies.
I now embrace the Mother realm,
for I see Father at the helm.

O Cosmic Mother Liberty,
conduct Abundance Symphony.
My highest service I now see,
abundance is now real for me.

6. I am attuning to the specific ways whereby I can overcome the limitations I am facing. God never requires me to face a limitation that I cannot overcome—if I am willing to transcend myself. I am transcending the dualistic belief that makes it seem impossible to transcend the limitation.

O Liberty, a chalice pure,
my lower bodies are for sure.
Release through me your symphony,
your gift of Cosmic Liberty.

O Cosmic Mother Liberty,
conduct Abundance Symphony.
My highest service I now see,
abundance is now real for me.

7. By overcoming a particular dualistic belief, I am opening a pathway through the jungle of the collective consciousness. I carve a trail and it will become possible for other people to follow that trail. I am a trailblazer who is demonstrating how to overcome a particular limitation.

O Liberty, the open door,
I am for Symphony of More.
In chakras mine light you release,
the flow of love shall never cease.

O Cosmic Mother Liberty,
conduct Abundance Symphony.
My highest service I now see,
abundance is now real for me.

8. I am clearing my mental body and reconnecting to my divine plan and the greater plan for the planet. I know how I can play my individual part, and this empowers me to discover the insights I need in order to overcome the dualistic beliefs that are the hidden cause behind my current limitations.

O Liberty, release the flow,
of opulence that you bestow.
For I am willing to receive,
the Golden Fleece that you now weave.

O Cosmic Mother Liberty,
conduct Abundance Symphony.
My highest service I now see,
abundance is now real for me.

9. I am attaining an understanding of the true purpose of life and the specific purpose for my present lifetime. I am feeling the sense of joy that comes from knowing that I am rising above the entire consciousness of limitation, the consciousness of duality, the consciousness of mammon, and bringing God's kingdom into my everyday life.

O Liberty, release the cure,
to free the tired and the poor.
The huddled masses are set free,
by loving Song of Liberty.

O Cosmic Mother Liberty,
conduct Abundance Symphony.
My highest service I now see,
abundance is now real for me.

Sealing

In the name of the Divine Mother, I call to the Great Divine Director, Goddess of Liberty and Mother Mary for the sealing of myself and all people in my circle of influence in the creative flow of the Divine Mother, the River of Life. I call for the multiplication of my calls by all representatives of the Divine Mother, so that we form the perfect figure-eight flow of "As Above, so below." Thus, I accept that this is fully manifest, because the mouth of the Lord, the Divine Mother that I AM, has spoken it. Amen.

11 | FIND YOUR EMOTIONAL FREEDOM

My beloved heart, we are now ready to talk about the emotional body, and I can tell you that the emotional body is the greatest weapon used by the prince of this world in his efforts to prevent you from manifesting the Christ consciousness and through that consciousness manifest the abundant life. The emotions are a powerful force because without feelings you cannot give momentum and direction to your thoughts, and therefore your thoughts cannot be translated into physical actions and physical manifestations. Because the emotions are easily moved, just as the ocean is easily stirred by a powerful wind, it is not that difficult for the prince of this world and your mortal self to change the direction of your emotions so that they take a slightly wrong path. Many people see a higher vision for their lives and truly desire to change their lives, but they simply cannot bring it into physical manifestation; they cannot make it happen. These people have a certain purity in their identity and mental bodies so they can see a higher vision for their lives. They can see that their lives should be better than they are. Because they have not purified their emotional bodies, have not taken dominion over their feelings, their emotions will often distort or sabotage their best efforts.

Imagine a thought being like an arrow. You put the arrow on the bow, you draw back the string and then you release the arrow. This is what happens in the mental body. You grasp an idea, you make it more specific and then you let it fly into the emotional body. Now imagine that when the arrow is in flight, a strong wind blows. The arrow might have been aimed perfectly at the target, but oh how easy it is for the wind to blow it off course so that it misses the mark. This is what happens to so many spiritual people who grasp a higher vision in their mental bodies and who make an effort to change their lives with the best of intentions. Because they have not taken dominion over their emotional bodies, their mortal selves and the prince of this world can so easily give the arrows of their thoughts a slight misdirection so that they always miss the mark. Or perhaps there is a strong headwind – in the form of emotional turmoil – that causes the arrow to fall short of the mark. People's emotional bodies are pulled in different directions by conflicting desires. Their best efforts lose steam before they ever reach the matter plane. Taking dominion over your emotional body is truly a crucial element of your efforts to manifest the abundant life.

When I say "take dominion," I mean that the Conscious You must decide to take dominion over the emotional body, as a good parent must take dominion over a child while it is not yet able to make right decisions for itself. Your emotional body can be compared to a child. As is the case with a child, your emotions are easily excitable, and they do not consider long-term consequences. The child does what it wants to do and what seems attractive at the moment. Your emotions are not able to consider what is best for you in the long-term or what is right according to a higher standard, such as the laws of God and your divine plan. The motto of your emotional body is: "If it feels good, do it." Unless the Conscious You steps into the role of the loving but firm adult who can guide the child of your emotions, the child is likely to hurt itself and create unpleasant long-term consequences.

How do you take dominion over your emotions? I have already given you the master key, which is to reach up for the higher will that brought you into the material universe in the first place. When you have that will, you allow it to filter through to your thoughts. When all your thoughts are in alignment with that will, you need to let the will power carry into the emotional body and make sure that all of your feelings are in alignment with the higher will and the higher vision embedded in your divine plan. You need to see yourself as a person with a higher purpose rather than a happy-go-lucky person who is driven hither and yon by the waves of his or her emotional body. You need to have the firm resolve that simply will not allow feelings that are out of alignment with your divine plan and work against your goal for coming to earth. You need to come to the resolve that you are the one who decides what feelings should arise in your emotional body. You cannot allow any other force, be it your mortal self, other people, the institutions of society, the media or the prince of this world to control which emotions arise in the ocean of your feelings.

***

Because the emotions are volatile, your mortal self and the prince of this world have long ago realized that using the emotions is one of the best ways to control your actions. If you can control people's feelings, you can control their actions because their actions spring from feelings. If you can create enough chaos in people's emotional bodies, you can prevent their higher thoughts from ever reaching the matter realm and their conscious minds. Emotional control starts in your identity body with the belief that you are a mortal human being who is ultimately out of control of your own destiny and is incapable of doing anything beyond certain boundaries. If you believe this, you see yourself as a victim of life. You think you have been thrust into a situation in which you are constantly being forced to respond to circumstances that you did not design and thus could not influence. You constantly feel that you are being attacked and pushed in unwanted directions by the "slings and arrows of outrageous fortune," as Shakespeare put it.

This puts you into a reactionary frame of mind. You are in the mode of reacting to life instead of taking dominion over life. This, of course, is precisely where your mortal self and the prince of this world want you. They can now control you by throwing at you ideas and circumstances to which you feel you must react.

Beyond the control in the identity body is, of course, certain thought patterns that are programmed into your mind by your mortal self. Or rather, they are part of your mortal self and have therefore entered your sphere of self where they can influence your thought process. The problem is that your mental body might contain a certain image of what life should be like. Based on this image, you have built a set of expectations of what your life should be like; what should and should not happen to you. What has happened in your emotional body is that your mortal self has built upon the mental images and the expectations in your mental body. It has created a very subtle belief that if your expectations are not met, then it is not only necessary and unavoidable, but it is indeed perfectly justified that you respond with certain negative emotions. Your mortal self has set up a subconscious computer, and when a certain button on the screen of your conscious mind is pressed, it will automatically release a particular emotion, a particular reaction.

For example, many people have an expectation that life should be easy and effortless. Many people expect that life should give them certain material things and certain bodily pleasures. If they do not get them, they feel deprived. This gives rise to a variety of emotions which usually include anger against God, against their parents, against society or against specific other people whom they feel are preventing them from having what they think they are entitled to have. This anger can easily be used by the mortal self to justify certain actions that people know are wrong and not in their long-term interest. Once they are caught in a vortex of anger, they can easily justify overruling their deeper moral beliefs or their concern for future consequences. Many people will in a fit of anger commit acts they normally would have avoided and that they deeply regret later. Even though people might regret such actions, they can often be manipulated into the same type of actions through another fit of intense anger, triggered by a situation that does not meet their expectations.

Many people are in a state of greed or envy of others, feeling they should have what others have or have more than others. They might go through life being jealous of other people, and this might push them to take certain actions that they know are wrong. This is indeed what causes some people to steal what they feel they should have but are not willing to work to obtain. Another common emotion is pride that causes people to go through life in a constant attempt to prove that they are better than others, that they are always right, that they know better than anybody else. Such people are literally trapped in emotional patterns over which they have no control, and these patterns deprive them of all sense of happiness, fulfillment and peace of mind. They deprive them of the abundant life.

***

The majority of human beings on this planet are virtually robots when it comes to emotional reactions. They have certain buttons in their subconscious minds, and when someone pushes one of their buttons, it automatically releases a particular emotion that causes these people to lose control over their thoughts, their feelings and their actions. Since you have followed this course up until this point, you are obviously not completely trapped in such a dysfunctional emotional pattern. If you will do some honest self-examination, you might see that you still have certain buttons in your emotional body. When someone pushes those buttons, you easily snap into a particular pattern of thoughts and feelings. I am not saying this to make you feel bad about yourself, for truly it is virtually impossible to grow up anywhere on earth without having such emotional programs projected into your mind. I am simply saying this because if you are to take dominion over your emotional body, you need to become aware of these programmed responses so that you can rise above them. How do you rise above them? You do so by becoming aware of them and then by making the conscious decision not to engage in such robotic responses to life's challenges.

The people who act like robots will say to you that they are not making the decision to fly into a fit of anger or guilt or whatever the emotion might be. In a sense they are correct because they have long ago given their mortal selves control over their minds. These people are not consciously making a decision to engage in a particular emotion. It is quite possible for anyone to reclaim their ability to make conscious decisions concerning how to respond to life. How can you ever take control over your life unless you take control over your reactions to outer circumstances?

Take a realistic look at this planet. You have a very volatile situation because the entire planet is burdened by misqualified energies. Even nature is out of balance, as evidenced by the rising number of natural disasters. At the same time you have many people who are programmed to respond with negative feelings so it is foreseeable that there will be many conflicts between people. There are many abundance gurus who will tell you that unless you approach every situation with a positive mental attitude, you will not be able to manifest the abundant life. These gurus are correct, but it must be added that a positive mental attitude will not influence your actions unless you use your higher will and the power of thought to take dominion over your emotional body. If your positive mental attitude stays at the mental level and does not descend to your feelings, how can it help you find the best response to situations that do not meet your expectations? The most successful people are not the ones who have their outer circumstances under control but the ones who can control their inner circumstances and can thus respond to any situation in the most constructive manner possible. Those who do not have such self-control will often respond to unexpected situations in a way that makes the situation worse and thus creates or reinforces a downward spiral. You may have heard the old saying that it is better to conquer yourself than to conquer a city, and this refers to taking control over your emotional reactions to life.

If you are in control of yourself, if you have taken dominion over your four lower bodies, you will be able to choose your reaction to any situation. You will be able to choose the reaction that is best for you in the long run, meaning that it is in harmony with the laws of God and your divine plan. You will be able to choose to turn the other cheek instead of responding with negative emotions. If you are not able to consciously choose your reaction to any situation, you know that someone else is in control. That "someone" is your mortal self and the prince of this world who are seeking to prevent you from manifesting the abundant life and fulfilling your divine plan.

The way to take control over your reactions is by expanding your awareness of the processes in your mind. In order to explain this, let me start at the lowest level, namely the level of physical actions. Many people will commit actions they later regret, and when they look back at the situation they will say: "But I had no other choice." If you had no other choice, you really had no choice at all, did you? If you have only one option, only one way to respond to a given situation, then you truly do not have a choice. The idea that you have no choice or have no other choice is always an illusion. It is based on the fact that you have allowed your mortal self to manipulate you into a situation where it seems like you have only one possible response. You are being completely controlled by your mortal self and most likely by the prince of this world through your mortal self. It *seems* like you have only one possible way to respond to a given situation. You seemingly cannot chose a different reaction than what is programmed into your emotional body.

I have talked about the need to take responsibility for your situation and the need to stop running away from making decisions. When people have allowed themselves to be manipulated into a situation where they think they have no choice, they have refused to take responsibility for their lives and they are trapped in a pattern of running away from making their own decisions. The brutal fact is that you always have more than one option, you always have more than one way to respond to a situation. The lie perpetrated by those who want to control you is that in some situations you have to respond with violence or force. This is a very insidious lie.

Virtually every religion on this planet (in its pure form) attempts to help you avoid being trapped by this lie. Jesus did so by giving people the Golden Rule as a model for behavior. That is why he told people to turn the other cheek instead of resisting evil, instead of responding to force with force (Matthew 5:39).

Take a look at the world and see how many conflicts there are between people. Some of these conflicts have been going on for thousands of years, and no one can remember how they started. The real question is why no one has stopped the spirals of violence, and the reason is that they have not broken the pattern of thinking that if someone is violent towards you, it is justified that you respond with violence. Such spirals of violence will never stop until someone decides to turn the other cheek and no longer respond with violence no matter what has been done to them. In order to break this pattern of violence, you have to go into the emotional body and break the programming which says that if other people do something to you, you can only respond with anger. You must take dominion over yourself so that instead of responding with negative emotions, you can respond to a situation with love. Only then will you have risen above the spiral of violence, and only then will you be free to pursue the spiritually abundant life instead of wasting your life in a senseless conflict that never ends.

***

How do you adopt a nonviolent approach to life, how do you get out of a pattern of responding to life with negative emotions? How do you make it possible for yourself to respond to life with love? The first step is to realize the simple fact that before you take any action, there is an interval, a pause, between your thoughts and feelings and the action. It is in this interval that the Conscious You has the opportunity to stop a self-destructive action. This interval is beyond time and there is always a split second where you have the opportunity to stop that action or allow it to move forwards. You have the opportunity to choose a better response – a nonviolent, love-based response – to the situation. By training your conscious mind to become more aware of what is going on in your four lower bodies, you can reclaim your ability to stop an action before it crosses the line into the matter realm and releases unavoidable consequences.

Before you take an action, someone has to make the decision to translate your thoughts and feelings into a physical action. You can allow your mortal self to make that decision, and it will always follow its programming, which means that your action will create unpleasant long-term consequences. The only other option is that the Conscious You fills its proper role and reclaims its power to make decisions. Only by doing so can you stop actions that are out of alignment with who you are and that work against your divine plan.

You might have heard the old advice that before you take action in a heated situation, you should count to ten. While this is good advice, it is not even necessary to count to ten. What you need to do is center in your heart and ask yourself whether this action is truly an expression of your inner being, of your real identity as an immortal spiritual being. Consider the action and ask yourself: "Is this who I am? Would the spiritual being that I truly am respond in this way?" If you have clarity in your identity, mental and emotional bodies, you will instantly be able to stop any action that is not in alignment with who you are and does not support your divine plan.

All people find themselves in unexpected and chaotic situations in which they have to make quick decisions. The prince of this world loves nothing better than forcing you into a situation where it seems like you have very few options and you have to make a decision right now. It is only by forcing you to make decisions without considering long-term perspectives that you can be fully controlled. The way to avoid such control is to establish a stable center, an immovable point of reference, for all your decisions. In the ultimate sense, this is the rock of the Christ consciousness. A more immediate goal is to consider whether your reaction is truly nonviolent. Only nonviolent responses will prevent you from blocking the descent of God's abundance into your life. After all, how can you accept what God gives you freely as long as you think you have to respond to life with violence? The spiritual Being that you truly are will respond to every situation with love. If you find yourself responding to a situation with less than love, you know that you are not acting upon your highest potential. Only your mortal self will respond with anything less than love, and this is a good way to expose when your mortal self is in control.

What prompts most people to take violent actions are violent feelings. Once a feeling has been unleashed and has been allowed to stir your emotional body into a frenzy, it is more difficult to prevent it from releasing an action. It can be done but would it not be better to prevent the negative feeling from arising in the first place? In order to do this, you need to go one step further and expand your awareness of the fact that all of your feelings arise from certain thoughts. The only real way to avoid the emergence of negative feelings is to resolve the thoughts that trigger them. The thoughts are at a higher level and are more fluid. They are easier to change but harder to see with the conscious mind. The thoughts that give rise to negative feelings are the imperfect expectations and the false desires you have in your mental and higher emotional bodies.

What is an unrealistic expectation? It is an expectation that is out of alignment with the reality of life. I earlier mentioned the statement by Albert Einstein that if you keep doing the same thing and expect different results, you are insane. Most people have expectations programmed into their mental bodies that make them believe they can keep doing the same thing, and one day the universe will magically reflect back different outer circumstances. I am fully aware that your mortal self cannot see the folly of this line of reasoning, cannot see that such expectations

are completely out of touch with reality. The Conscious You
has the ability to see this and therefore overrule the mortal self.
You can separate yourself from the unreality of the mortal self
and fully integrate the reality that the universe is a mirror which
will reflect back to you whatever you send out. When you understand this, you see that you cannot change your outer situation
without changing yourself.

***

There is an even deeper level to consider here. Many of your
expectations do not seem to be out of touch with the reality of
life. They seem to become self-fulfilling prophecies. For example, if you have an expectation that life is a struggle and that you
need to fight for everything you get, the universe will reflect
circumstances back to you that force you to fight for everything.
Such circumstances are not ultimately real because they are out
of alignment with God's highest vision for you. Your expectations take on a temporary reality, but they will seem real only as
long as you are trapped in the duality consciousness.

You have two types of unrealistic expectations. There are
expectations that can never be fulfilled and there are expectations that become self-fulfilling prophecies. For example, many
people have an expectation that they can keep doing the same
thing and get different results, that they can change their outer
circumstances without changing themselves. This is a completely unrealistic expectation because the universe will reflect
back what you send out. Some people expect that others are out
to take from them what they have, and such an expectation will
become a self-fulfilled prophecy. Such people attract to them
the type of people who want to take from others instead of getting it from the infinite supply of abundance that is available
within themselves.

The dualistic expectations you have in your mental body will give rise to false desires in your emotional body. What is a false desire? A false desire has two main characteristics:

•   The first one is that it is based on lack; it is based on a sense that you are deprived of something that you really should have. You think you are entitled to have certain things in life, you desire to have them, and when you don't have them, you feel a sense of lack, you feel deprived. This is what gives rise to negative feelings, such as anger, envy or greed.

•   The other aspect of a false desire is that it can never be fulfilled, it can never be satisfied. A false desire is truly like a bottomless pit, like a black hole in your emotional body that can never be filled. If you have heard about black holes in space, you know that they are areas of intense gravitational force that pulls everything into them, and nothing ever comes out. That is a good visualization of a false desire because you can keep putting energy into it without ever filling up the black hole.

Many people are trapped in an endless quest for more money, more power, more sex, more food, more pleasure. No matter how much they get, it is never enough. They are never satisfied and they always want more. This becomes a downward spiral that swallows up their lives without giving them anything in return because they never reach a state of fulfillment, happiness or peace of mind. There are many people on earth whose entire lives are consumed by this endless quest of seeking to fulfill false desires that can never be satisfied. The more spiritually inclined people are not completely trapped in this pattern. Yet you need to take a look at your life and see if you can identify certain desires that have the characteristics I have described. If you do identify them, you need to be honest with yourself and examine them more closely. Unless you take dominion over these desires and remove them from your being, they will always pull on your emotions and sabotage your best efforts to manifest a truly spiritual life.

What is the key to overcoming your false desires? Let us start by considering who wants to keep you stuck in a pattern of endlessly seeking to fulfill false desires. The brutal fact is that such desires are created by your mortal self and the prince of this world, and they have two goals for doing this. One goal is to keep you stuck in pursuing worldly desires so you cannot manifest Christhood and fulfill your divine plan. The other goal is to keep you in a spiral of always wanting something you can't have, thereby continually misqualifying energy, which your mortal self and the prince of this world need for their sustenance. They look at you as a cow that can be milked for energy and then discarded when you are no longer producing.

Does that mean you should forcefully try to suppress all false desires in order to escape this control? This is not the right approach; it is simply going from one extreme to the other yet still being trapped in the duality consciousness. The real key is to realize that a false desire really is a perversion of a true desire. One of the main characteristics of a true desire is that it is not based on lack but on a sense of abundance. You do not feel deprived, you feel you have so much that you desire to share it with others. The other main characteristic of a true desire is that you are not seeking to get anything; you are seeking to give. It is in giving that you attain a sense of fulfillment because the act of giving carries its own emotional reward.

All desires spring from an attempt to produce a certain feeling. Ultimately, that feeling is what I have talked about earlier, namely the feeling of wholeness, the feeling of being complete, of being filled. A false desire springs from your mortal self. Your mortal self was born out of separation from God. It can never give you a sense of wholeness. Your mortal self cannot overcome its separation from God, and only when you feel one with God and feel the light of God flowing through your being will you feel whole. Your mortal self has some rudimentary recognition of the fact that the Conscious You desires wholeness. It is trying to give you this feeling of wholeness, but it can do so only by using the dualistic state of mind and the things of this world. Your mortal self sees wholeness as a static state where you have enough of something from this world and where you have set yourself up so you can never lose what you have. That is why your mortal self defines false desires and seeks to make you believe that if only you had enough money, material possessions, power or pleasure, you would feel whole, you would be filled. Your mortal self truly believes that if only you had enough of the things of this world, you would feel whole. This is obviously an illusion because nothing from this world can give you a true sense of wholeness. You can be whole only by knowing who you are and feeling the light of God streaming through your Being.

When the Conscious You realizes the impossible quest of the mortal self, you can separate yourself from it. You cannot separate yourself from the mortal self until you have something to put in its stead. You cannot fully overcome a false desire until you reconnect to the true desires of your higher being.

***

There is a large group of spiritual Beings who are serving as the spiritual teachers of humankind. Among those beings is the Buddha who, like Jesus, descended to earth to bring forth a new spiritual teaching, which today is known as the religion of

Buddhism. One of the central tenets of Buddhism is that life is suffering and that suffering is caused by wrong desire.

It is beyond this course to go into an in-depth teaching about Buddhism. Many people have misunderstood the central concept and think the Buddha was saying that they should over-come all desires and have no desires left. In reality, the Buddha was saying that you need to overcome all *attachments* to anything in this world. A false desire is a desire that makes you attached to something in this world, making you think you cannot be whole without having the object of the desire. It is this attachment that gives rise to suffering.

If you had no desires, how could you possibly grow and become more than you are today? The basic force of creation is God's desire to become more and fill up the void with light. If you cut off all desires, you are cutting off the flow of the River of Life through your Being. This is no more constructive for your spiritual growth than to allow yourself to be completely absorbed in trying to fulfill the false desires of your mortal self. People who have taken the teachings of the Buddha to the extreme of suppressing all desires have forgotten the most cen-tral aspect of the Buddha's teachings, namely the Middle Way. The Middle Way does not mean that you suppress all desires but that you rise above the false desires that spring from your mortal self, you rise above the duality consciousness that pulls you away from the Middle Way. In doing so, you will reconnect to the true desires of your higher Being, the desires that brought you to earth in the first place. Those desires relate to giving of yourself, of your God Flame. They relate to expressing your divine indi-viduality and bringing God's kingdom to this realm.

Some desires spring from your lifestream's wish to expe-rience certain conditions on earth. These are the desires that are most easily perverted by your mortal self. These are the desires that can become worldly or carnal desires, related to the pleasures of the physical body. When such desires become physical and self-centered, they become a bottomless pit that can never be filled. For each such lower desire there is a higher desire. The difference is that the higher desire can be fulfilled in an ultimate sense whereby the Conscious You no longer desires to experience this particular condition in the material universe. You now desire more, and therefore you desire to rise above the material universe rather than remain in it indefinitely. You are simply no longer satisfied by lower desires and they are replaced by a higher desire. You are not forcefully and willfully suppressing a desire. You come to recognize it as a limited desire, you see beyond it to discover the true desire, and the true desire naturally and effortlessly replaces the false desire.

One desire that confuses many spiritual people is the desire for sexual union. Most people on earth engage in sex based on a false desire that springs from their mortal selves. This is a desire that can never be filled. No matter how much sex they have, they will never be satisfied. Behind this desire for physical pleasure is a higher desire of experiencing a state of wholeness that comes when two lifestreams, with opposite polarities, come together in a true, spiritual union.

Everything is born out of the interaction of the expanding force of the Father and the contracting force of the Mother. When the two come together, new life is created through their union and wholeness. It is possible that a lifestream can desire to experience such wholeness in the material realm. This springs from the true desire for a greater union, and this desire can be fulfilled. It is possible to come to a point where you feel that you have experienced enough of this form of union, and now you desire something beyond what can be attained through a physical body and the faculties of that body. You desire a spiritual union that can be found only by finding a true polarity in your own Being, namely by establishing union between the Conscious

You and your I AM Presence as the true Father-Mother polarity of your Being.

***

You literally have a choice to make. You can choose whether you will serve God or mammon, and with that I mean that you can choose whether you will let the rest of your life be consumed by the impossible quest to fill false desires, the desires that Jesus called mammon. Or you can decide to serve the true desires of your higher Being and seek to fulfill your divine plan by expressing your God-given individuality and creativity.

All false desires spring from the sense of lack, and the only way out of false desires is to transcend the sense of lack. How do you transcend the sense of not having enough? You do so by allowing your four lower bodies to be filled with the light of God, which burns away all sense of lack and fills you with a sense of ultimate nurturance. You must follow the process I have described and start by reaching up to your identity body, reconnecting to your true identity. When you know who you are, namely that you are a spiritual Being who has access to the infinite abundance of God's light, you can truly overcome the sense of lack that springs from your mortal sense of separation from God's abundance. You can bring the light of God through your identity body, into your mental body and then into your emotional body. When you bring the light of God into your emotional body, you will produce a feeling of being nurtured. This gives rise to the sense of being whole, and as I said earlier the desire for wholeness is behind both false and true desires. When you have that sense of wholeness, you will have transcended the false desires because you will no longer feel lack. You will no longer feel deprived but will feel nurtured in an ultimate sense. You will realize that you do not need anything from outside yourself in order to fulfill your true desires.

The essence of a false desire is that you feel you are not whole and that you think you need something from outside yourself in order to obtain wholeness. This opens you up to being controlled by your mortal self, other people or the prince of this world. They can control you because you think you need something from outside yourself in order to obtain wholeness, in order to feel nurtured. When you reconnect to your true identity and open the flow of God's light through your being, you realize that you need nothing from outside yourself in order to be whole. It is the stream of God's light through your being that gives you the sense of true and ultimate wholeness. When this state of wholeness takes dominion over your emotional body, you no longer have a desire to *receive* something from other people. You have a true desire to *give* to other people, to share with other people.

This gives rise to a most beautiful situation in which all people realize the truth behind one of Jesus' most profound statements: "Freely ye have received; freely give" (Matthew 10:8). When you understand the reality of life, namely that God is the source of all good and perfect things and that it is the Father's good pleasure to give you the kingdom, you will have a feeling of inner wholeness. Through this feeling of being nurtured, you will overcome the fear of giving to others. When most people in a society freely give what they have received from God, people's combined efforts will bring forth more abundance than any of them could produce alone. This is described in the statement that the whole is more than the sum of its parts, and this truly is the abundant life on earth. The abundant life on earth will come about when people begin to freely give here below what they freely receive from Above.

Look at planet earth today and consider how almost every aspect of society and almost every aspect of human interactions is based on the sense of lack, the lack of nurturance. This causes people to hold back from giving, to hold on to what they have. This causes many people to focus all of their attention on receiving rather than giving. If no one is giving, how can anyone receive? People who are trapped in the false desires, the self-centered egotistical desires, cannot see this obvious truth. That is why an entire society, indeed an entire planet, can descend into a negative spiral where everyone feels deprived, everyone has desires based on lack and everyone is trying to get rather than to give.

One of the main problems that prevents the manifestation of God's kingdom on earth is that so many people are trapped in the desire for control. They feel deprived, they feel a sense of lack and they think other people are out to take from them what they have. They think they can only get abundance if they take it by force. In order to get what they want and avoid losing what they have, they think they have to control other people and their physical circumstances.

Many of the most powerful people on earth are completely swallowed up by this desire to control everyone and everything. Throughout history, you have seen some people who attained a very high degree of power, meaning the false power that is based on controlling others. The wheels of time inevitably ground to dust any control they had attained. None of these people could control their destiny, and eventually the towers of Babel they had built through control crumbled and were turned back into the dust of the earth from which they had come. That which springs from the mortal self comes from the dust of the earth, and it shall return to dust instead of being resurrected into the immortal life of the Christ consciousness.

***

One of the main weapons used by the mortal self and the prince of this world is that they take advantage of the volatility of your emotions to inject the element of doubt into your being. When the Serpent tempted Eve in the Garden of Eden, this was done by injecting the element of doubt. The effect is that you doubt God. You doubt that if you multiply your talents, God will reward you. You doubt that if you freely give, you will freely receive more. You doubt the very essence of the relationship between yourself and God, namely that if you are faithful over a few things, God will make you ruler over many things. You doubt that it is the Father's good pleasure to give you his kingdom.

This is the very essence of what prevents you from receiving God's abundance. It prevents you from acting as the co-creator you are meant to be. When you have this doubt in God's willingness to give you abundance or doubt that God's laws actually work to multiply what you give, you sabotage the process whereby God's abundance descends through the four levels of the material universe. You effectively shut yourself off from the flow of the River of Life. Instead of being in the River of Life that constantly brings more abundance into the matter realm, you are shutting yourself off from this flow. That is why you become a self-fulfilling prophecy. Your very doubt in God's law and in the process of manifestation will become outpictured in the matter realm. Your consciousness of doubt and lack will be reflected back to you by the cosmic mirror. As long as you remain in that illusion, as long as you allow yourself to be ruled by the doubts injected by the prince of this world, the cosmic mirror will seem to confirm your belief that God is an unjust master who is reaping where he has not sown (Matthew 25:24).

God is a God of unconditional love, which is why he has given you free will. You have the ability to set yourself outside of the River of Life, the flow of God's nurturance. God allows you to do this, yet at any moment God is ready to receive you back into his kingdom—if you are willing to let go of the doubt that caused you to leave that kingdom in the first place. How do you overcome doubt? There is only one way. You must first reconnect to your true identity so that you know with an absolute, inner knowing that you are more than a miserable sinner, more than a mortal human being who is separated from your God by some chasm that you cannot breach. How can you know this? You can know this only through direct experience. The first two commandments say that you should have no other gods before the true God and that you should not take onto yourself any graven image. The essence of the duality consciousness is that you see yourself as separated from God. This means that you no longer have a direct experience of God's Presence, and thus you do not experience the reality of God. This is how God becomes a topic that can be debated by the dualistic mind, by your mortal self. When you experience the reality of something through direct experience, where is the room for doubt? When the direct experience is missing, God now becomes a theoretical concept whose reality can be debated endlessly by the human intellect and the mind of duality. The mind of duality can never solve the question of God's existence, for how can a mind that springs from separation from God ever have the direct experience of God's Being?

Imagine yourself sitting in your home and someone tells you about the South Pole and what it looks like down there. Obviously, you are not on the South Pole so you cannot directly experience what it is like to be there. You can use the description given to you, and even photographs, to build a mental image of what it is like on the South Pole. Your mental image might be quite detailed and accurate, but it never *can* be and it never *will* be a substitute for direct experience. You will not truly know what it is like to be on the South Pole until you actually stand there and experience it with all elements of your being, by which I mean more than your physical senses. Only when you are actually there, will you know what it feels like to be you in that location. The very essence of the duality consciousness is that you have separated yourself from the direct experience of God's being. You no longer experience your I AM Presence as the Presence of God within your sphere of self. This is what gives rise to the sense that God is a remote Being, the external being in the sky.

We now have the sense that you are separated from God, and for the more spiritual people on earth we have the desire to know God, to know what God is like. Once again, we have a false desire and a true desire. A false desire is based on lack, and what is the cause of lack? The essence of lack is fear. You think: "I don't have this and because I don't have it, something bad can happen to me and if I don't get what I think I need, the worst will happen. I don't know what I need to know about God and salvation, and if I don't get that knowledge, my soul will burn forever in hell." This is what has given rise to every fear-based religion found on this planet. A fear-based religion is truly the way that seems right onto a human, but the ends thereof are the ways of death.

What is the false desire that drives fear-based religions? At the lower level, it is the idea that you can make a bargain with God, that you can *buy* your way into heaven. If you do the right things, you will please God and he will allow you to enter his kingdom. I have earlier explained why this is an impossible dream so I will not go into it again. At the higher levels of fear-based desires, you have the desire to know God. This is still a self-centered desire based on the fear of what will happen to you if you don't know what you need to know about God. Many sincere religious people spend an entire lifetime seeking to fulfill the desire to know God and to know all about God through an outer religion. Knowing something implies distance between you and what you are seeking to know. If the object was right here, you could simply experience it without "knowing" it.

When you seek to know something that you think you cannot experience directly, you are building a mental image of it. If that mental image is influenced by the consciousness of duality, it will be a false image, a graven image. If you seek to know a remote God, you are driven by a dualistic approach and this will prevent you from experiencing God directly. You might build the mental image that you know everything there is to know about God – as did the Pharisees – yet your outer knowledge of God prevents you from having the direct, inner experience of God's Presence. Your outer knowledge can actually prevent you from entering the kingdom of God within you, which is why God told you not to create any graven images.

The concept of knowing and the desire to know the remote God can become a trap that actually reinforces the sense of separation from God. I am *not* saying that it is wrong for people to strive to know God because at a certain level of your spiritual path it is necessary to seek to expand your understanding of God. The desire to know God can easily become a blind alley that stops your progress. Most people fail to realize this, and thus so many religious people get caught in the very subtle trap of spiritual pride. They feel they know so much about God, about their particular religion and that they have done all these outer deeds prescribed by their religion. They feel they are above other people and that God simply has to accept them into his kingdom. As Jesus said, the kingdom of God is within so you will not enter that kingdom by simply knowing something about God or a religious doctrine. No amount of outer knowledge can bring you into God's kingdom. You cannot enter God's kingdom through knowledge; you can enter only by being there. The sense of being there can only be obtained by going beyond knowledge of the remote god and actually experiencing the God who is All and in all—including in you.

The key is to know that there will come a point on your path where it is absolutely essential that you transform the fear-based desire to know the remote god into a love-based desire to be one with the internal God. If you do not do this, you will become stuck on the way that seems right onto a human, and this is exactly what had happened to the scribes and Pharisees who failed to recognize the Christ in Jesus. As Jesus said: "Except your righteousness shall exceed the righteousness of the scribes and Pharisees, ye shall in no case enter into the kingdom of heaven" (Matthew 5:20). Is it not obvious that in order to enter God's kingdom, you have to overcome the sense of being outside that kingdom? The only way to *know* God is to *be* God.

I do not mean this in a blasphemous sense, in the insane, inflated sense that makes you think you are better than everyone else and can do whatever you want. I mean this in the true sense that you realize you are an individualization of God and that the Conscious You is out of the greater Being, the Presence, of God. It has the ability to experience God's Being, God's Presence. The Conscious You can experience God's Being by identifying itself with God's Being. This is not a theoretical knowledge based on a mental image of what God is like. This is a direct experience of God's Being. This experience is beyond words or any images that could be defined in the world of form. That is why no outer religion can possibly describe this experience and that is why no religion can give an accurate description or image of God. The higher form of religion does not seek to help people *know* God. The true form of religion, the inner universal religion, seeks to help people *experience* God's Presence. When you experience that Presence, you know who you are. You know, through direct experience, that you are an extension of God because you have experienced the direct connection between your lifestream and God.

Go back to my image of the South Pole. You might be able to close your eyes and think very intensely about the South Pole. You might actually give yourself the impression that you are *on* the South Pole. But will this bring you to that location? It might give you an illusion of being on the South Pole, but until you actually travel there, it will still be a mental image. No matter how much knowledge you have about God, you are still trapped by a mental image that portrays God as a remote Being. Only when you transcend the mental image and experience God's Presence, thereby experiencing yourself as an extension of God's Being, will you have the true inner knowledge of who you are. When you have that knowledge, it will filter through your identity body, your mental body and your emotional body. This will eradicate doubt from your being because now you know – through direct experience – and you no longer have a mental image that the mortal self and the prince of this world can manipulate with all the subtlety and sophistication of the dualistic mind. This is the only way to fully overcome doubt. This is the only way to ultimately take control over your four lower bodies so that your sense of identity, your thoughts, your feelings and your actions become an expression of who you are and an expression of the true desires that brought your lifestream into the material universe and thereby created your four lower bodies.

My beloved, who are you really? You are designed to be an extension of God's Being. You are designed to be a transformer for God's light, stepping it down in vibration and bringing it into the material realm. You are designed to be a spiritual sun that radiates the light of your particular God Flame and thereby brings those qualities into manifestation through everything you encounter in the material universe. This is why God told you to multiply your creative talents, to multiply your individuality, to multiply your light and then take dominion over the earth. You are not here to be a passive spectator to the drama of life. You are not here to simply sit by and watch as the people who are controlled and possessed by the prince of this world carry on their senseless, endless games of seeking power and control. You are not here to watch this planet slide into a downward spiral that will eventually lead to the extermination of humankind and possibly even to the destruction of the entire planet. You are here to infuse everything you encounter with spiritual light. You are here to spiritualize every aspect of your life. You are here to bless everything you encounter and thereby raise it up to its highest potential. You are here to set the Ma-ter Light free from all imperfect images imposed upon it through the mortal selves of the people on earth and the prince of this world. You are here to set the Mother Light free to outpicture the perfection of God so that the abundant life can be manifest on earth.

How do you fulfill your highest potential? By being who you are, by overcoming the distance between who you think you are and who you truly are. Go back to the difference between having an image of God and experiencing God's Presence. God is not standing still, God is the River of Life that is constantly transcending itself and becoming more. If you hold on to a mental image of God, and if you refuse to go beyond that image, you have created a graven image, an unchanging image. You can know God only by being in the River of Life, by flowing with the ever-moving stream of God's abundance. In order to flow with that stream of life, you must overcome the false desires that make you want to stop the clock, to hold on to something you think you own. You must be willing to lose your limited sense of life in order to remain in the everlasting life that is the eternal flow of becoming more.

***

The master key to taking dominion over the emotional body is to adopt the attitude that every situation you encounter is an opportunity to express the light of your true Being, the light of your God Flame, thereby magnifying every condition you encounter. You are here to infuse every situation you encounter with light so that no matter how imperfect or dark the situation might seem, it will be raised to a higher level by your very presence. What is the key to letting that light flow? Ultimately, the key is to reclaim your true identity as I have explained above. I know this might seem like a distant goal in your present situation so I will give you an intermediate key that can work wonders in terms of opening the flow of God's light through your being. That key can be summed up in one word, and that one word is "gratitude."

When you feel gratitude towards God for creating you and for giving you the opportunity to descend into the material universe as an extension of itself, you will be able to lock yourself on the path that will lead you above all doubts. I am aware that I have defined a high goal for you when I talk about attaining the inner experience that you are an extension of God. You might not be quite ready for this experience, and if you will begin by contemplating and cultivating an "attitude of gratitude," you will take an all-important step towards having the inner knowing that eradicates all doubt.

Gratitude is a feeling that you can cultivate even if you still have some sense of lack or doubt. We have talked about people who felt like they had no other choice. They had no other choice because they were blinded by the programming of their mortal selves. You need to separate the Conscious You from that programming. When you do so, you realize that you always have more than one option for responding to a situation. No matter what situation you encounter, no matter how difficult that situation might seem, there is always something for which you can be grateful. If you are willing to consciously cultivate the habit of always looking for a reason to be grateful, you will have taken a most important step towards attracting more abundance.

What is gratitude? Gratitude is the lower aspect of the inner knowing that I have talked about in this chapter. Gratitude is the willingness to trust that when you freely give, you will receive more, even though you currently have no outer proof of this. Gratitude is knowing that you are not deserted by God, that God is here with you and that God has given you what you need to transcend your current situation and rise to the next step on the spiral staircase. You might not have everything you want, but you have what you need in order to take the next step, and for that you have reason to be grateful. Gratitude is the feeling that you have what it takes to rise higher, and when you do make the best use of what you have, God will surely give you more. This is what Jesus promised in his parable about the talents, and it is a true promise.

Given that the universe is a mirror, people who bury their talents in the ground are actually saying: "God, I am deprived of your abundance and therefore I have no reason to feel grateful. If you want me to stop feeling ungrateful, give me your abundance and then I will automatically feel grateful." This approach can never work and it is the result of a programming by the prince of this world. It is based on the illusion that feelings are the result of outer conditions. As I have attempted to explain to you in many different ways, your feelings should be controlled only by your thoughts that are controlled by your sense of identity. When you take responsibility for your life, you realize that you are responsible for your own feelings and that you cannot use outer conditions as an excuse for allowing impure feelings. Everything is brought into manifestation by flowing through the four levels of the material universe. The emotional realm is above the matter realm, which means that the feeling must come before the physical manifestation. If you are waiting for God to give you abundance before you feel gratitude, you will never be able to bring that abundance into the matter realm. You are like the person expecting his mirror image to smile before he smiles at the mirror. It is the feeling of gratitude – based on the inner knowing that it is the Father's good pleasure to give you his kingdom – that is the vehicle for bringing abundance into the matter realm. Only when you feel gratitude for what you already have, can God give you more.

Expecting God to give you abundance before you feel gratitude is expecting that God would violate his Law of Free Will. God has given everyone free will, and the reason certain people feel deprived and ungrateful is that they have used their free will to give away their free will, to give control over their lives to the mortal self and the prince of this world. It is truly because they have given away control of their lives that they have been manipulated into a sense of lack. What they are now saying to God is that they want God to fix their sense of lack, and in essence they are saying that they want God to take control of their free will rather than the mortal self and the prince of this world. This is imposing a false image upon God, an image based on the duality consciousness, an image that God wants to control them and that God is like the prince of this world. I consider such a dualistic image of God to be blasphemy in the true sense of the word.

There are many religious and spiritual people who are sincere in wanting to do what is right according to an outer religion. What these people are really saying is that they now want God to take control of their free will, that they want God to take back his gift. This is a complete misunderstanding of the reason God gave you free will in the first place. God did not want to create you as a robot, God did not want to control you. God wants you to grow by making your own choices, and therefore God will never control your free will. He will never take that free will away from you. If your situation is to improve, you must take back your power to make choices. You must stop running away from making choices, even to the point that you will not use an outer religion as a justification for not taking dominion over your four lower bodies. You must take responsibility and accept the fact that your outer situation can improve only when you use your higher will and the vision of your divine plan to produce the positive feeling that becomes the vehicle for letting God's abundance flow into the matter realm.

The way to start this process is to be grateful for being alive, for being self-aware, for having the opportunity to make choices. Instead of feeling like you have to make these choices all alone, you can realize that God has sent you a comforter. You have a Christ self, which is your inner teacher. You have spiritual beings in a higher realm who serve as your personal teachers. They are ready at any moment to guide you so that you can make better choices, but they will not make choices for you. You must be willing to help yourself. You must be willing to overcome the feeling of lack, the feeling of fear, the feeling of being deprived, the feeling of injustice, the feeling of ingratitude. You must be willing to put forth the effort of will power and find something for which you are grateful. Then you must build on that something by asking your spiritual teachers for inner direction so that you can make better choices that will give you more things for which you can be grateful.

As the prophets of old said: "Choose you this day whom ye will serve" (Joshua 24:15). Choose whether you will serve life or death: "Choose life!" (Deuteronomy 30:19). Choose to choose for yourself. We, who are your spiritual teachers, have an unconditional love for you, and we will do everything we can to help you make the best possible choices. But we *cannot* and we *will not* choose for you, neither can we produce a feeling in your emotional body. You are the one who must get in the driver's seat and take command over the unruly child of your emotions. If you will first clear your identity and mental bodies, you will have the will power and vision needed to tame the beast, to slay the dragon, of untamed emotions.

This brings us to the point where we can take the final step and discuss what needs to happen at the level of the physical mind, the conscious mind, at the level of action. For thousands of years, spiritual people have had a tendency to withdraw from the world, to set themselves apart from mundane activities. It is time to go beyond this approach. It is time to realize that spiritual people are not here to withdraw from the world but to take dominion over the world and spiritualize *everything*.

12 | I INVOKE EMOTIONAL FREEDOM

In the name I AM THAT I AM, Jesus Christ, I call to all representatives of the Divine Mother and the Divine Father, especially Saint Germain, Portia and Mother Mary, to help me take command over my emotional body and reconnect to my true desires. Help me accept my creative powers and see the factors that block the flow of my God-given creativity, including...

[Make personal calls.]

1. I take command over my emotional body

1. I am taking dominion over my emotions by allowing the higher will power of my I AM Presence to carry into my emotional body. I am bringing all of my feelings into alignment with the higher will and the higher vision embedded in my divine plan.

O Saint Germain, you do inspire,
my vision raised forever higher,
with you I form a figure-eight,
your Golden Age I co-create.

**O Saint Germain, what love you bring,
it truly makes all matter sing,
your violet flame does all restore,
with you we are becoming more.**

2. I am the one who decides what feelings arise in my emotional body. I will not allow any other force, be it my mortal self, other people, the institutions of society, the media or the prince of this world to control which emotions arise in the ocean of my feelings. I am having dominion over my life.

O Saint Germain, what Freedom Flame,
released when we recite your name,
acceleration is your gift,
our planet it will surely lift.

**O Saint Germain, what love you bring,
it truly makes all matter sing,
your violet flame does all restore,
with you we are becoming more.**

3. I see and surrender the belief that if my expectations are not met, then it is necessary, unavoidable or justified that I respond with negative emotions. I am in control of my subconscious computer, and I do not allow any external force to control my emotions.

O Saint Germain, in love we claim,
our right to bring your violet flame,
from you Above, to us below,
it is an all-transforming flow.

O Saint Germain, what love you bring,
it truly makes all matter sing,
your violet flame does all restore,
with you we are becoming more.

4. I am taking dominion over my emotional body. I am becoming aware of programmed responses, and I am rising above them by making the conscious decision not to engage in robotic responses to life's challenges.

O Saint Germain, I love you so,
my aura filled with violet glow,
my chakras filled with violet fire,
I am your cosmic amplifier.

O Saint Germain, what love you bring,
it truly makes all matter sing,
your violet flame does all restore,
with you we are becoming more.

5. I am reclaiming my ability to make conscious decisions concerning how I respond to life. I am taking control over my inner circumstances and I am responding to any situation in a way that is in harmony with the laws of God and my divine plan.

O Saint Germain, I am now free,
your violet flame is therapy,
transform all hang-ups in my mind,
as inner peace I surely find.

O Saint Germain, what love you bring,
it truly makes all matter sing,
your violet flame does all restore,
with you we are becoming more.

6. Before I take any action, there is an interval between my thoughts and feelings and the action. I am training my conscious mind to become more aware of what is going on in my four lower bodies. I am reclaiming my ability to stop an action before it crosses the line into the matter realm and releases unavoidable consequences.

O Saint Germain, my body pure,
your violet flame for all is cure,
consume the cause of all disease,
and therefore I am all at ease.

O Saint Germain, what love you bring,
it truly makes all matter sing,
your violet flame does all restore,
with you we are becoming more.

7. My Conscious You is filling its proper role and reclaiming my power to make decisions. Before I take action, I center in my heart and ask myself whether this action is truly an expression of my inner being, of my real identity as an immortal spiritual being.

O Saint Germain, I'm karma-free,
the past no longer burdens me,
a brand new opportunity,
I am in Christic unity.

O Saint Germain, what love you bring,
it truly makes all matter sing,
your violet flame does all restore,
with you we are becoming more.

8. All feelings arise from thoughts. I am avoiding the emergence
of negative feelings by resolving the thoughts that trigger them.

O Saint Germain, we are now one,
I am for you a violet sun,
as we transform this planet earth,
your Golden Age is given birth.

O Saint Germain, what love you bring,
it truly makes all matter sing,
your violet flame does all restore,
with you we are becoming more.

9. I am reclaiming my ability to overrule the mortal self. I am
separating myself from the unreality of the mortal self and inte-
grating the reality that I cannot change my outer situation without changing myself.

O Saint Germain, the earth is free,
from burden of duality,
in oneness we bring what is best,
your Golden Age is manifest.

**O Saint Germain, what love you bring,
it truly makes all matter sing,
your violet flame does all restore,
with you we are becoming more.**

2. I take command over my desires

1. Dualistic expectations in my mental body give rise to false desires in my emotional body. A false desire is based on lack, and it can never be satisfied. It is like a black hole in my emotional body that can never be filled.

O Portia, in your own retreat,
with Mother's Love you do me greet.
As all my tests I now complete,
old patterns I no more repeat.

**O Portia, opportunity,
I am beyond duality.
I focus now internally,
with you I grow eternally.**

2. Mother Mary, help me take a look at my life and identify false desires. I am examining my false desires, taking dominion over them and removing them from my being.

O Portia, Justice is your name,
upholding Cosmic Honor Flame,
No longer will I play the game,
of seeking to remain the same.

O Portia, opportunity,
I am beyond duality.
I focus now internally,
with you I grow eternally.

3. A false desire is a perversion of a true desire. A true desire is not based on lack but on a sense of abundance, the desire to share with others. It is in giving that I attain a sense of fulfillment. The act of giving carries its own emotional reward.

O Portia, in the cosmic flow,
one with you, I ever grow.
I am the chalice here below,
of cosmic justice you bestow.

O Portia, opportunity,
I am beyond duality.
I focus now internally,
with you I grow eternally.

4. All desires spring from an attempt to produce the feeling of wholeness. A false desire springs from my mortal self trying to give me the feeling of wholeness by controlling the things of this world. My mortal self believes that if I had enough of the things of this world, I would feel whole.

O Portia, cosmic balance bring,
eternal hope, my heart does sing.
Protected by your Mother's wing,
I feel at one with everything.

O Portia, opportunity,
I am beyond duality.
I focus now internally,
with you I grow eternally.

5. I am whole by knowing who I am and feeling the light of God streaming through my Being. I am separating myself from the impossible quest of the mortal self. I am reconnecting to the true desires of my I AM Presence.

O Portia, bring the Mother Light,
to set all free from darkest night.
Your Love Flame shines forever bright,
with Saint Germain now hold me tight.

O Portia, opportunity,
I am beyond duality.
I focus now internally,
with you I grow eternally.

6. I am walking the Middle Way where I do not attempt to suppress all desires. I am reconnecting to the true desires that brought me to earth, the desires for giving of my God Flame, expressing my divine individuality and bringing God's kingdom to this realm.

O Portia, in your mastery,
I feel transforming chemistry.
In your light of reality,
I find the golden alchemy.

O Portia, opportunity,
I am beyond duality.
I focus now internally,
with you I grow eternally.

7. Mother Mary, help me see the desires that spring from my lifestream's wish to experience certain conditions on earth. I am willing to see how these desires have been perverted by my mortal self and have become a bottomless pit that can never be filled.

O Portia, in the cosmic stream,
I am awake from human dream.
Removing now the ego's beam,
I earn my place on cosmic team.

O Portia, opportunity,
I am beyond duality.
I focus now internally,
with you I grow eternally.

8. I am reconnecting to the higher desires that can be fulfilled in an ultimate sense whereby the Conscious You no longer desires to experience this particular condition in the material universe. I desire more, and I desire to rise above the material universe rather than remain in it indefinitely.

O Portia, you come from afar,
you are a cosmic avatar.
So infinite your repertoire,
you are for earth a guiding star.

O Portia, opportunity,
I am beyond duality.
I focus now internally,
with you I grow eternally.

9. I am no longer satisfied by lower desires and they are replaced by a higher desire. I am not forcefully and willfully suppressing a desire. I recognize it as a limited desire, I see beyond it to discover the true desire, and the true desire naturally and effortlessly replaces the false desire.

O Portia, I am confident,
I am a cosmic instrument.
I came to earth from heaven sent,
to help bring forward her ascent.

O Portia, opportunity,
I am beyond duality.
I focus now internally,
with you I grow eternally.

3. I have an attitude of gratitude

1. I am choosing that I will no longer serve mammon. I will not let the rest of my life be consumed by the impossible quest to fill false desires. I decide to serve the true desires of my higher Being, and I seek to fulfill my divine plan by expressing my God-given individuality and creativity.

O Saint Germain, you do inspire,
my vision raised forever higher,
with you I form a figure-eight,
your Golden Age I co-create.

**O Saint Germain, what love you bring,
it truly makes all matter sing,
your violet flame does all restore,
with you we are becoming more.**

2. I am transcending the sense of lack by allowing my four lower
bodies to be filled with the light of God, which burns away all
sense of lack and fills me with a sense of ultimate nurturance. I
am bringing the light of God through my identity body, into my
mental body and then into my emotional body.

O Saint Germain, what Freedom Flame,
released when we recite your name,
acceleration is your gift,
our planet it will surely lift.

**O Saint Germain, what love you bring,
it truly makes all matter sing,
your violet flame does all restore,
with you we are becoming more.**

3. I am feeling nurtured and whole. I feel nurtured in an ultimate
sense. I do not need anything from outside myself in order to
fulfill my true desires. The stream of God's light through my
being is giving me the sense of true and ultimate wholeness.

O Saint Germain, in love we claim,
our right to bring your violet flame,
from you Above, to us below,
it is an all-transforming flow.

**O Saint Germain, what love you bring,
it truly makes all matter sing,
your violet flame does all restore,
with you we are becoming more.**

4. I am here to spiritualize every aspect of my life. I am here to
bless everything I encounter and thereby raise it up to its highest
potential. I am here to set the Ma-ter Light free from all imperfect images imposed upon it through the mortal selves of the
people on earth and the prince of this world.

O Saint Germain, I love you so,
my aura filled with violet glow,
my chakras filled with violet fire,
I am your cosmic amplifier.

**O Saint Germain, what love you bring,
it truly makes all matter sing,
your violet flame does all restore,
with you we are becoming more.**

5. I am fulfilling my highest potential by being who I am, by
overcoming the distance between who I think I am and who I
truly am. I am willing to lose my limited sense of life in order to
remain in the everlasting life that is the eternal flow of becoming
more.

O Saint Germain, I am now free,
your violet flame is therapy,
transform all hang-ups in my mind,
as inner peace I surely find.

O Saint Germain, what love you bring,
it truly makes all matter sing,
your violet flame does all restore,
with you we are becoming more.

6. Every situation I encounter is an opportunity to express the light of my true Being, the light of my God Flame, thereby magnifying every condition I encounter. I am infusing every situation I encounter with light. No matter how imperfect or dark the situation might seem, it is raised to a higher level by my very presence.

O Saint Germain, my body pure,
your violet flame for all is cure,
consume the cause of all disease,
and therefore I am all at ease.

O Saint Germain, what love you bring,
it truly makes all matter sing,
your violet flame does all restore,
with you we are becoming more.

7. I am opening the flow of light from my I AM Presence by cultivating an attitude of gratitude. I feel gratitude towards God for creating me and for giving me the opportunity to descend into the material universe as an extension of itself.

O Saint Germain, I'm karma-free,
the past no longer burdens me,
a brand new opportunity,
I am in Christic unity.

O Saint Germain, what love you bring,
it truly makes all matter sing,
your violet flame does all restore,
with you we are becoming more.

8. No matter what situation I encounter, no matter how difficult
that situation might seem, there is always something for which
I am grateful. I am consciously cultivating the habit of always
looking for a reason to be grateful, and thereby I am attracting
more abundance.

O Saint Germain, we are now one,
I am for you a violet sun,
as we transform this planet earth,
your Golden Age is given birth.

O Saint Germain, what love you bring,
it truly makes all matter sing,
your violet flame does all restore,
with you we are becoming more.

9. Gratitude is the lower aspect of the inner knowing that when
I freely give, I will receive more, even though I currently have
no outer proof of this. I know that I am not deserted by God.
God is here with me and God has given me what I need to
transcend my current situation and rise to the next step on the
spiral staircase.

O Saint Germain, the earth is free,
from burden of duality,
in oneness we bring what is best,
your Golden Age is manifest.

O Saint Germain, what love you bring,
it truly makes all matter sing,
your violet flame does all restore,
with you we are becoming more.

4. I take command over unruly emotions

1. I know I have what it takes to rise higher, and when I do make the best use of what I have, God will surely give me more. This is what Jesus promised in his parable about the talents, and it is a true promise.

O Portia, in your own retreat,
with Mother's Love you do me greet.
As all my tests I now complete,
old patterns I no more repeat.

O Portia, opportunity,
I am beyond duality.
I focus now internally,
with you I grow eternally.

2. I surrender the illusion that feelings are the result of outer conditions. My feelings are controlled only by my thoughts that are controlled by my sense of identity. I take responsibility for my feelings, and regardless of the outer conditions, I produce only love-based feelings.

O Portia, Justice is your name,
upholding Cosmic Honor Flame,
No longer will I play the game,
of seeking to remain the same.

O Portia, opportunity,
I am beyond duality.
I focus now internally,
with you I grow eternally.

3. Everything is brought into manifestation by flowing through
the four levels of the material universe. The emotional realm is
above the matter realm, which means that the feeling must come
before the physical manifestation. If I wait for God to give me
abundance before I feel gratitude, I will never be able to bring
that abundance into the matter realm.

O Portia, in the cosmic flow,
one with you, I ever grow.
I am the chalice here below,
of cosmic justice you bestow.

O Portia, opportunity,
I am beyond duality.
I focus now internally,
with you I grow eternally.

4. I have the inner knowing that it is the Father's good pleasure
to give me his kingdom, and this feeling is the vehicle for bringing abundance into the matter realm. I am feeling gratitude for
what I already have, and God is giving me more.

O Portia, cosmic balance bring,
eternal hope, my heart does sing.
Protected by your Mother's wing,
I feel at one with everything.

**O Portia, opportunity,
I am beyond duality.
I focus now internally,
with you I grow eternally.**

5. I am taking back my power to choose my feelings. I am improving my outer situation by using my higher will and the vision of my divine plan to produce the positive feeling that becomes the vehicle for letting God's abundance flow into the matter realm.

O Portia, bring the Mother Light,
to set all free from darkest night.
Your Love Flame shines forever bright,
with Saint Germain now hold me tight.

**O Portia, opportunity,
I am beyond duality.
I focus now internally,
with you I grow eternally.**

6. I am grateful for being alive, for being self-aware, for having the opportunity to make choices. I realize that God has sent me a comforter. I have a Christ self, which is my inner teacher, and I have ascended masters in a higher realm who serve as my personal teachers.

O Portia, in your mastery,
I feel transforming chemistry.
In your light of reality,
I find the golden alchemy.

O Portia, opportunity,
I am beyond duality.
I focus now internally,
with you I grow eternally.

7. My teachers are guiding me so that I can make better choices, but they will not make choices for me. I am willing to help myself. I am transcending the feeling of lack, the feeling of fear, the feeling of being deprived, the feeling of injustice, the feeling of ingratitude.

O Portia, in the cosmic stream,
I am awake from human dream.
Removing now the ego's beam,
I earn my place on cosmic team.

O Portia, opportunity,
I am beyond duality.
I focus now internally,
with you I grow eternally.

8. I am using my will power to find something for which I am grateful. I am building on it by asking my spiritual teachers for inner direction. I am making better choices that give me more things for which I am grateful.

O Portia, you come from afar,
you are a cosmic avatar.
So infinite your repertoire,
you are for earth a guiding star.

O Portia, opportunity,
I am beyond duality.
I focus now internally,
with you I grow eternally.

9. I am getting into the driver's seat and taking command over
the unruly child of my emotions. I have the will power and vision
needed to tame the beast, to slay the dragon, of untamed emotions. My emotional body is the perfect vehicle for the expression of the love-based emotions of my I AM Presence.

O Portia, I am confident,
I am a cosmic instrument.
I came to earth from heaven sent,
to help bring forward her ascent.

O Portia, opportunity,
I am beyond duality.
I focus now internally,
with you I grow eternally.

Sealing

In the name of the Divine Mother, I call to Saint Germain, Portia and Mother Mary for the sealing of myself and all people in my circle of influence in the creative flow of the Divine Mother, the River of Life. I call for the multiplication of my calls by all representatives of the Divine Mother, so that we form the perfect figure-eight flow of "As Above, so below." Thus, I accept that this is fully manifest, because the mouth of the Lord, the Divine Mother that I AM, has spoken it. Amen.

13 | GIVING IS THE KEY TO RECEIVING

My beloved heart, we have traveled a long way. This course has been quite a journey through many different topics, most of which, I am sure, go far beyond what you were told by your outer teachers, be they in a religious or a secular setting. I am grateful that you have been willing to endure with me on this long journey. We are now at a very fortunate point where we can talk about the master key to manifesting abundance in your life. What I have talked about throughout this course is the need to reclaim your true identity as a spiritual being who is here for a higher purpose, namely to bring God's kingdom into manifestation by using the perfect vision of the Christ mind and the light of God. You can direct the light of God to flow through the vision – the filmstrip – of the Christ mind in your four lower bodies, thereby imposing a perfect image upon the Ma-ter Light that makes up the entire material universe. In order to reclaim that position, in order to multiply your divine individuality and take dominion over the earth, you need to first reach up and reestablish the flow of God's light through your being, through your four lower bodies. You need to recapture the vision of Christ as the highest vision for your lifestream, for your potential, for your divine plan. Then you need to bring them down through your four lower bodies until you reach the level of the physical mind, the conscious mind. Yet, it is not enough to simply bring the vision and the light down to the matter realm. The real key to manifesting the abundant life is what you do with that light and that vision.

Many spiritual people are very sincere in their spiritual striving. Some of them have put in decades of effort with various forms of study, meditation or spiritual practices, and they have indeed made much progress. They have raised their own consciousness far beyond where they were when they started. If you will take an honest look at these people, you will discover two tendencies:

- Some people have a very strong vision of what needs to happen in order to improve planet earth and make it a better place for all. They are very good at grasping that vision, they are good at explaining it, but oftentimes the vision stays in their heads and is not easily transferred into action.

- Some people have established a certain flow of God's light. They can be very strong, very powerful or they can be very loving and able to fill a room with a positive energy. Such people are often good at taking action, but they sometimes lack the greater vision and are focused on the trees without seeing the forest. They do not always have the vision of what to do with their energy and enthusiasm, thus taking unbalanced actions that do not produce the desired results. Such people often think it is enough to love everyone and accept everything as being good.

There are many people on earth today who have a certain spiritual attainment. They have come to a point where they have the potential to do much good and have an impact on a planetary scale. They have not yet crossed the essential line that needs to be crossed before they can take their attainment out of the realm of potentiality and bring it into the realm of actuality.

Many spiritual people are close to breaking through to the point where they can have a major positive impact on this planet, an impact that will raise the collective consciousness and propel society forwards into a golden age. They have not made a decisive impact, neither in their own lives in terms of manifesting the abundant life, nor at the level of society in terms of raising the quality of life for all. I am in no way trying to diminish people's sincere efforts. I am only trying to point out that there is a vast potential that is on the brink of breaking through but has not yet been pulled into the matter realm. What is missing, what is the key that is lacking, that people have not discovered or have not internalized? In order to give you this key in its simplest possible form, let me ask you to contemplate the number 8, the figure eight. This is indeed a symbol for what needs to happen in order for you to establish the truly abundant life.

***

When you look at the figure eight, you can start at the very top, which represents the Creator itself. You can envision that the light is flowing from the Creator down through the levels of the spiritual realm, represented by the upper figure. The light then reaches the nexus of the figure eight, and that nexus is a symbol for your identity body, the very highest point of your identity body. This is the meeting point between spirit and matter, between your higher Being, through which the light of God streams, and your lower being, your four lower bodies, through which you act in this world. What I have taught you in these last several chapters is the way to bring that flow of God's light from the nexus all the way down to the bottom of the figure eight, which is your conscious mind, your outer mind, and your physical body. In order to truly manifest God's abundance in your life, you need to complete the circle, to complete the figure-eight flow. You cannot simply let the light sit down here and do nothing, neither can you use it for selfish purposes. Doing so is burying your talents in the ground.

The real question is what you do with the light after you bring it down. You have a choice between the way that seems right onto a human and the true way to the eternal life. The way that seems right onto a human is to reason that since you have put forth an effort to bring the light down, you are entitled to use it for your own gratification. You do indeed see many people who have spiritual attainment, but they are using it only for their own gain or pleasure. Some are on a never-ending quest to raise their own consciousness, perhaps seeking so-called supernatural abilities or peak experiences, yet they are doing this only for their own gratification. Look at the life of Jesus and the life of the Buddha. If they had chosen the path of self-gratification, they would have stayed in the forest or the wilderness, working on raising their own consciousness. Instead, they came to a turning point and returned to the world, spending the rest of their lives working to help others.

I told you about the two types of people who have not brought things into manifestation, and this is truly caused by the fact that these people have not done something with their light, something that reaches beyond themselves. I am not necessarily saying that these people are selfish or egotistical in the lowest sense of the word. I *am* saying that there are a number of spiritual people on this planet who have become focused on themselves, who have become almost completely absorbed in themselves and their quest for spiritual growth—however they define it. These people are not openly egotistical in the sense that they do whatever they want without considering how it affects other people. Many of them are truly living according to spiritual principles and are not harming other people or the environment. Many of them are found in both the New Age community and in traditional religions, including Christian churches. These people are, from an outer perspective, living a good life, and they are not violating any of God's laws, at least not any of the outer laws that are described in various religious or spiritual philosophies. They have not truly stepped up and considered what they can do with their spiritual attainment in order to bring God's kingdom to earth, in order to find their place in the greater, timeless work that is God's creation. Because they have not reached beyond themselves, they cannot complete the circle so that the light flows back to God.

This is what Jesus described in his parable about the multiplication of the talents. Only when you put your talents to good work, will you multiply them. Only when the talents, or rather the light, is multiplied, can you complete the figure-eight flow so that God can multiply from Above what you have multiplied here below. There will be even more light flowing down the figure eight to your conscious mind. The key to manifesting the abundant life on a permanent basis is to complete the circle by giving freely what you have freely received.

This is an absolutely crucial point. Many spiritual people have not fully understood this point. Many of them are close to understanding it, but they do not have the full, correct and complete understanding. If you do not fully grasp this point, my attempts to help you manifest the truly abundant life will come to naught. Some people have taken their spiritual progress and turned it into a downward spiral without even realizing that they have taken the wrong road, the way that seems right onto a human. They have used their light for self-centered purposes instead of rising to the greater vision that since all life came from the same source, they are one with all life. What they are doing onto others, they are truly doing to themselves. The brutal fact is that such people often think they are doing everything right, yet they are following the path that will inevitably lead to spiritual death, the black hole of becoming more and more self-centered rather than God-centered.

All life is one. As you begin your spiritual journey, you are trapped in the duality consciousness and cannot see this fact. You are too focused on your physical body and mortal self to consider the big picture, to have any sense of oneness with the all. You must begin where you are and seek to raise your own consciousness. Because the collective consciousness on this planet is in such a low state, it is indeed necessary for any spiritual seeker to separate himself or herself from the mass consciousness. You need to be focused on yourself and your own growth in order to escape the downward pull of the mass consciousness. It is indeed valid to be focused on yourself and your own growth, but the crucial point is that this is valid only for a time. You must focus on yourself in order to regain a direct, inner connection to your higher Being. Once you regain that connection, you need to take it to the next level and realize that you are an extension of your Creator and so is every other human being.

When you reach a certain level of oneness with God, you need to develop a sense of oneness with all life. You are no longer simply seeking to raise your own consciousness, you are seeking to raise the consciousness of other people and even the collective consciousness. Only when you give of your light to help others, will you have completed the figure-eight flow, which is what Jesus described when he said: "My Father worketh hitherto and I work" (John 5:17). You are now using your attainment, your light, to work for God's greater plan, which is to raise everyone to the Christ consciousness. If you do not make the transition from a self-centered to a God-centered view, you will use your light to reinforce the self-centeredness of the mortal self. As shocking as it might seem, many sincere spiritual people have indeed taken this self-centered path. They think they are doing everything right, but their righteousness is falling short of the mark. Instead of multiplying their light and spiritual attainment by helping others, they have turned the light into darkness that only reinforces their mortal selves.

This is what Jesus talked about in a remark that has often been misinterpreted or ignored: "The light of the body is the eye: if therefore thine eye be single, thy whole body shall be full of light. But if thine eye be evil, thy whole body shall be full of darkness. If therefore the light that is in thee be darkness, how great is that darkness!" (Matthew 6:22-23). If your eye is single, you see the oneness of all life. If your eye is evil, meaning divided, you see everything through the consciousness of separation, and thus you see your own interests as being in opposition to or superior to the whole. As you grow spiritually, you will reach a turning point. If you do not start using your spiritual attainment to raise up the whole, you will inevitably pervert your light and attainment, turning it into the darkness of the mind of anti-christ—which denies its oneness with its Creator and with all life.

***

Let me talk about the motives behind people's actions and even their approach to spirituality. There are many religious people on this planet who believe that in order to be saved and in order to be good religious people they have to worship God. Some of them even believe they have to worship Jesus. Many of them believe that in order to be saved, in order to be accepted into God's kingdom, they have to do something for God, they have to do something that pleases God. They have to obey the laws of this external being in the sky who has set forth a strict law that needs to be observed without compromise.

If God has created this entire universe, is it likely that this God will need something from a human being who lives on this small planet? What could you possible give to God that God would need, that God does not have already? Why would God need to be worshiped by anyone when God is the All and therefore is complete in himself? God is so complete that he is constantly giving out of himself, as the sun is constantly letting its light shine. The people who think they need to do something for the external God or give something to that God are like people who think they need to build a giant search light and shine it on the sun in order to give the sun light. First of all, you could never build a search light big enough to have any impact on the sun. Secondly, why would you need to give light to the sun when the sun's reason for being is to give light to earth? These people are not thinking logically and are, in fact, trapped in the consciousness of wanting to buy their salvation?

God – in the form of the Creator – needs nothing from you. God does not want you to worship him. Jesus does not want you to worship him, and that is indeed why he said: "Why callest thou me good? there is none good but one, that is, God" (Matthew 19:17). God does not need you to go into a church or a temple and worship him or burn incense or make sacrifices. God does not need you to build elaborate cathedrals and call them God's house. God needs none of this. What is it that God wants you to do with the light that he gives you?

Let us look at the many spiritual and religious people who have already come up higher. They have realized that religion is not really about worshiping a remote God who does not need their worship. Religion is about taking your spiritual beliefs and putting them into practice by helping others. For example, there are many sincere and devout Christians who have great attainment in this area and who have dedicated their lives to helping others in the name of Jesus. There are also many people in other religions and in the spiritual and New Age community who are likewise seeking to help raise the entire planet by invoking positive energy through many different rituals. Some of these people truly have the pure sincerity of heart. Others have not yet transcended the tendency to be focused on doing things for the remote God in the sky. Many people are still working to help others because they think it pleases God. They are doing it because they feel like they have to; they are doing it out of a sense of obligation or duty or because they feel it will obligate God to save them. Some even do it out of a subtle pride of wanting to show God that they have done so much more than other people. These people are giving only to get something in return, they are not giving for the love of giving, for the pure love of seeing life flow.

I have talked about fear as a poor motivator. I have talked about the necessity to have will power in order to break through the opposition to the manifestation of God's kingdom on earth. If your will power is based on fear, it will not be powerful enough to break through the opposition created by the mass consciousness and the prince of this world. There are many people who have overcome fear and who are not truly acting out of fear. They still have a sense of obligation and duty, and this sense is not truly selfless. It is not based on the one thing that can overcome all opposition. That one thing is the force of love.

If you are to break through the opposition to the manifestation of the abundant life, you need a will power that is based entirely on love. Love is the most powerful force in the universe. In order to rise above fear and self-centeredness, you need to understand what love is, and this is a problem for many people, even many spiritual people. Many people have made great spiritual progress, but many of them have reached a plateau. For a time they were growing and making great progress, but then they came to a point where they started feeling that they had understood enough, that they knew enough, that they were doing enough. Many of them felt they had found the ultimate truth, the ultimate organization, teaching or guru. All they needed to do was to stay in that teaching, stay in that organization, keep following that guru and then they would one day be saved. This is a very subtle version of the dream of an automatic salvation, and it is still focused on themselves. The driving force of all life is self-transcendence, the drive to become more than you are right now. If you think you know enough and are doing enough, you will inevitably set yourself outside the River of Life, and thus you cannot close the figure-eight flow.

There will come a turning point on the spiritual path. When you reach that point, you cannot – and you *will* not – make further progress until you reach beyond yourself. You will not make further progress until you start giving of what you have and what you have learned. Instead of focusing on your own spiritual growth, you must look beyond your own growth and look at the planet as a whole. You must start considering how you can use what you have learned, what you have discovered, what you have internalized, in order to raise the consciousness of other people. If you do not give out what you have learned, you will not grow beyond a certain point. You will inevitably stagnate, yet there is no stagnation. You are either growing through self-transcendence or collapsing through self-absorption, the gravitational force described in the second law of thermodynamics. Many people on earth feel that they are very spiritual, feel that they are doing the right thing, yet they are not growing. They have reached a level where they feel they are righteous because they belong to this or that organization.

They look back at their lives, and they see how much they have done, either for a particular organization or for raising the consciousness of the planet. Even though they have done much, they have allowed their growth to come to a halt. They are not truly considering how they can transcend the outer organization or the outer teaching. First of all, they are not considering how they can transcend themselves, their attitude and their approach to life. They are satisfied with the understanding they have and they are not looking for the higher understanding that can take them to the next level. They have not understood that as long as you are in embodiment here on earth, there is always a next level. You will only rise permanently from earth by being willing to always reach for the next level.

These people are trapped in the righteousness that Jesus denounced when he said that unless your righteousness exceeds the righteousness of the scribes and Pharisees you cannot enter heaven (Matthew 5:20). This poses a very difficult dilemma for us, who are your spiritual teachers, because it often causes us to lose the very people who have the highest spiritual attainment. This dilemma is simple. Many of the people who will be open to the teachings of this course are people who are already open to the spiritual path and have made significant progress on the path. The problem is that many of these people are content with their progress. They might read this course out of curiosity and they will pick up some ideas that they feel are very good because they confirm what they already believe. Many will find it difficult to use this course to look in the mirror and see where they have not transcended a certain level of understanding and attainment. Many will be reluctant to acknowledge the fact that even though they have made much spiritual progress, they still have not taken the ultimate step to establishing the abundant life. That ultimate step is to freely give what you have received, using it to help others by inspiring them to come up higher.

***

Why are so many people standing at this turning point where they have all the knowledge and the understanding they need, but they somehow cannot put it into practice, they cannot put it into action and truly manifest the spiritually abundant life for themselves and others? The reason is that so many people have not understood the true nature of love. This is caused by the fact that they have grown up in a society that is based on a completely distorted view of love, namely a dualistic view of love, a view that is based on the consciousness of anti-christ. Human love has nothing to do with divine love. It is not that human love is *opposed to* divine love. It is simply that human love is *disconnected from* divine love. Divine love is the very force that drives God's creation, and it is the force of self-transcendence, the force of becoming more. In contrast, human love seeks to possess, seeks to own, seeks to control, seeks to make things stand still by stopping the flow of life. When you own something, you want to keep it. This automatically gives rise to a fear of loss, and to avoid loss you think you have to control your circumstances by preventing them from changing.

You are essentially caught in a form of insanity that seeks to prevent something from becoming more by holding it in a limited state. You think what you have is all you could possibly have so you would rather hold on to a limited state than allow it to become more. You are essentially saying to God, who is offering you unlimited abundance: "Leave me alone, God, I want to keep what I have; I don't want it to become more." Many human relationships might from a surface perspective seem to be loving, but in reality they are based on a desire to own other people or to control what you get from other people. Underneath the seemingly loving relationship is the desire to control something so that it can remain the same, so you can keep owning it.

Should it not be obvious by looking at the transitory nature of everything on earth that you cannot ultimately own anything? What is there that you could possibly keep? Think about the popular saying that you cannot take it with you, meaning that none of your material possessions can be taken with you when you die. There *is* something you can take with you, namely the spiritual attainment that you have internalized. That spiritual attainment requires that you understand the nature of love, which is that love is a constant flow, namely the River of Life which never stands still. The River of Life never seeks to own or possess anything; it is constantly giving, it is constantly flowing—changing, transcending itself and becoming more. It does not seek to own any one thing because it sees itself as one with every good and perfect thing. It knows that only in becoming more – in being one with The River of Life – can you truly own anything. Only when you do not seek to possess and control one thing, can you allow the All to become more. Only by giving of yourself, can you multiply your talents and become more. It is only in self-transcendence that you have true ownership because only when you transcend yourself will you stay in the River of Life. Only when you stay in that river, can you have abundance, the true abundance that is constantly growing and becoming more. That is why you need to raise your understanding of love so you realize that true love, divine love, never stands still and never seeks to own, possess or control anything. True love is always giving of itself and it is precisely in the giving of itself that it is becoming more.

This is the central key to manifesting abundance, and it is a truth that most spiritual seekers have not fully understood, have not fully internalized or have not fully put into action. In order to maintain the figure-eight flow, you must give out here below what you have received from Above. The Creator wants you to freely give what you have freely received, but he does not want you to give it to him because he does not need it. If the Creator needed anything from you, why would he be constantly giving his light to you? God does not need you to give back to him by worshiping a remote being in the sky, by doing for others in order to please that remote being or by focusing on raising your own consciousness to impress that remote God.

What God needs you to do is to look around you and consider the conditions currently found on earth. God needs you to go through a realistic assessment and say: "With all I know about God, as a completely self-contained Being who is constantly giving of himself, I need to realize that God's love is unconditional and infinite. God has no other desire than to see his kingdom come into physical manifestation on planet earth." It truly is the Father's good pleasure to give all people his kingdom. He has no desire to see them die and go to heaven before they receive that kingdom, but he wants to give it to everybody right here on earth.

The current conditions on earth are very far away from God's kingdom. The current reality is so far from the highest vision of the Christ mind that it almost defies description. The reason current conditions are so far from God's vision is precisely that people have fallen into the duality consciousness. They are misusing their creative powers to ego-create a life of suffering rather than co-creating the kingdom of God. What will it take to change the situation? It is going to take that those who have a higher vision, such as yourself, will do everything in their power to spread that vision and awaken other people.

God wants you to multiply what you have received from him by giving it to other people. That is why Jesus said: "Inasmuch as ye have done it unto the least of these my brethren, ye have done it unto me" (Matthew 25:40). At the lower levels of Christ consciousness, you realize that you are one with God, but you cannot stop there. You need to transcend to the higher level and realize that you are one with God because God's Being is embedded in everything that was created. The Creator created everything out of its own Being. When you give of yourself to other people or to the Earth Mother, you are truly giving to God. Only, you are not giving to the God you perceive as a remote being in the sky. You are giving to the true, inner God who is within everything.

Take note of the subtle distinction here. I am not saying that there is no God in a higher realm, for truly there is a Being whose consciousness is focused as the Creator of this system of worlds. Part of the Creator's Being is embedded in everything ever created. There is an impersonal aspect of God, the Creator in a higher realm, and there is a personal aspect of God, the God who is in all. There is the God who is the All and the God who is in all. What the God who is the All wants you to do is to give light and love unconditionally to the God who is in all. The God in all is temporarily hiding behind a disguise of imperfect physical appearances. The Creator wants you to free that God, to free the Mother Light, to outpicture the perfection envisioned by the Creator. Thereby, the God who is in all will be one with the God who is the All. There will no longer be an artificial illusion of separation, created by the consciousness of anti-christ.

***

My beloved, what will make a decisive difference on this planet is that the more spiritually advanced people overcome all tendency to be focused on themselves and instead develop not only a global awareness but a universal awareness. You are here to be an emissary of God's light, an emissary of Christ vision. You are here to be a co-creator and bring the kingdom of God to earth. Only when you recognize the very reason your higher Being chose to come here, will you be able to experience and manifest the abundant life. The key to establishing the fig-ure-eight flow of the abundant life is to give out what you have, give out what you have received, give out what you have inter-nalized, give out what you have become. You must let the sun of your I AM Presence shine through your four lower bodies and let it shine upon the just and the unjust. This requires you to overcome the primary lie concerning love spread by the prince of this world.

The most insidious lie of all of the lies spread by the prince of this world, by the serpentine mind, is that you should – that you *must* – give love conditionally. This lie tries to make you believe that there are certain situations here on earth in which it is necessary, unavoidable and justified that you shut off the flow of God's unconditional love through your being. When you look at human beings today, you will see that almost everyone on this planet is trapped in the attitude that in order for them to give love to another human being, that person must live up to certain conditions—they must somehow deserve to receive love. This is an insidious lie, for true love comes from God, and God gives it to you unconditionally. He lets his light shine upon the evil and the good and lets his love rain upon the just and the unjust (Matthew 5:45). Who are *you* to set up conditions for giving it to others?

Not only does this lie prevent the manifestation of God's kingdom on a larger scale, but it prevents the manifestation of the abundant life for everyone who is trapped by this approach to life. The sun receives its joy from shining its light. If the sun was to set up conditions that caused it to shut off its light, it would hurt itself by turning off the source of its joy. When you allow any condition, in your mind or outside yourself, to stop the flow of God's light, God's love, through your being, you are cutting off the very source of your own joy, the very source of the abundant life—which is truly a state of consciousness.

So many people feel that they will only give love to someone else if that person lives up to a set of conditions that they have allowed to enter their beings. *All* of these conditions – and I am deliberately making an absolute statement here – are created by your mortal self and the prince of this world. *Any* condition that causes you to shut off the flow of God's love through your being springs directly from the mind of anti-christ and feeds the forces of darkness. There is no discussion about it; there is absolutely no exception to this rule. Once again, we have a subtle distinction that will confuse many people until they reach for the higher understanding of the Christ mind.

I am not saying that you need to go out and indiscriminately give away everything you own or give in the same way to everyone you meet. There is a fundamental difference between giving *conditionally* and giving with discrimination, with *discernment*. In order to understand that difference, you need to again consider the nature of love as a force that will not allow anything to stand still in a limited state. God's love always wants everything to become more than it is right now, to transcend its current state. I am not saying that you have to treat everybody with the same love or kindness. I am not saying you have to be soft-spoken or gentle to everyone you meet. What I *am* saying is that you need to let God's love flow through your being in every situation you encounter. You need to let love do its work freely and without stopping it, without imposing conditions on what God's love can and cannot do through you. What does God's light want to do through you? It wants to transform everyone you meet by helping them awaken to the need to come up higher, the need to self-transcend, the need to become more.

If you want an example of this, study the life of Jesus with a new awareness that goes beyond the false image built by so many Christian churches. Jesus has been portrayed as a touchy-feely spiritual teacher who was kind and loving to everybody, and when I say "kind and loving" I mean in a human, sympathetic way. Many people have gotten themselves into a state of consciousness in which they believe that love is always soft and gentle. If you are loving, you are always speaking gently to people, making them feel good about being in a bad situation or a limited state of mind. This is a misunderstanding of the nature of love, and it deteriorates into human sympathy, which might seek to help people feel good but does nothing to help them transcend their current state of misery and limitation.

Jesus was not that kind of a spiritual leader. He was not always soft-spoken and gentle, he was often very firm and very direct. Look at how he challenged the scribes and the Pharisees and how he threw the money changers out of the temple. Look at how many times he challenged his own disciples and told them they were without understanding or had too little faith. Jesus had true divine love, and therefore – in every situation he encountered, for every person he met – he wanted everything to become more. Jesus did not want to leave any situation or person the same as when he found them. He wanted to help and inspire them, or even challenge and impel them, to transcend themselves, to come up higher, to become more. This is true love. You will not leave anything the same, you will not allow the current misery and struggle on planet earth to remain. It is not loving to simply go around and extend sympathy to people. It is loving to do whatever is necessary to help them transcend their current state of consciousness, which is the real cause of their outer struggle.

In order to help people – who are stuck in selfishness and self-centeredness – transcend their current state of consciousness, it might be necessary to be very firm and very direct. It might be absolutely necessary to challenge and expose the dualistic beliefs to which they have become attached. It may be necessary to shake their belief that they know everything or challenge whatever excuse they use for not changing themselves. Some think this is unkind, but from a greater perspective, it is not unkind—it is the ultimate kindness. It is not kind to leave people in a state of consciousness which guarantees that the cosmic mirror will continue to return misery and struggle to them. It is kindness to do whatever is needed to shake them out of that state of consciousness and help them take responsibility for their lives so they can project something into the cosmic mirror that will be returned as more abundant conditions. This is true spiritual kindness, and it is a rare commodity on earth. You can help make it more common—if you will raise your understanding of the nature of love.

***

The master key to manifesting the abundant life for yourself is that you see yourself as a co-creator who is here to help the earth come closer to manifesting the kingdom of God. You are not here to simply accept conditions the way they are or to help people feel good about being in their current limitations. You are here to help them come up higher, to help all life come up higher.

What will it take for you to truly fulfill that role? It will take a shift in perception so that you overcome another of the insidious illusions created by the prince of this world. What the prince of this world wants you to believe is that the current limitations and imperfections you find on earth are real in an ultimate sense. The prince of this world wants you to believe that the current state of imperfection and struggle is unavoidable because God is not here on earth, and therefore God's kingdom cannot be manifest here on earth. This is the ultimate illusion presented by the prince of this world who is skillfully using the current state of the material universe to build this illusion.

The material universe is the latest sphere of God's creation. When God creates a new sphere in the void, that sphere only has enough light in it to set it apart from the void. Self-aware beings from a higher sphere descend into the new sphere in order to bring God's light and to superimpose the vision of the Christ mind upon the Ma-ter Light. The purpose is to make the latest sphere outpicture the Christ vision. As long as a new sphere has not yet been filled with a critical mass of light, it will inevitably seem as if God is not present in that sphere. This is so because God's light is not present in the intensity that makes it obvious to the grosser senses of the physical body. There is still not enough light in the material universe to make it possible for the physical senses to see the light behind outer manifestations. Your eyes cannot see that physical matter is truly made from the Mother Light that has taken on a temporary form. It is natural, at this point in the earth's evolution, that the physical senses of human beings cannot see God's light behind outer manifestations. The Conscious You is perfectly capable of seeing God's light. In order to see it, you have to stay outside of the veil of illusion created by the prince of this world.

This veil is based on the belief that what you see with the senses is real and what you do not see, namely God's light, does not exist. This is the illusion created by the prince of this world in an attempt to control this world and prevent God's co-creators, who are here to bring God's light, from fulfilling their missions. The prince of this world first managed to make these self-aware beings forget their true identity and identify with the physical body. He is now trying to use the limitations of the physical body to keep people trapped in this illusion. He wants you to believe in the illusion that God is not here and that the current imperfections are real, unavoidable and permanent. He wants you to believe in this so that you will not let your light shine and thereby displace the current conditions, raising them according to the perfect vision of the Christ mind. This is the plot perpetrated by the prince of this world and by your mortal self. How can you overcome this grand illusion of the ages, this illusion that entraps over 99 percent of the people on this earth? How can you free yourself from it? You can do so only by purifying your four lower bodies. By doing so, you will be able to grasp the higher vision that God holds for this planet, which is what we might call the immaculate concept. The immaculate concept is the true meaning of the immaculate conception.

I was the one who gave birth to Jesus through what orthodox Christian churches call the immaculate conception (Luke 1:35). This does not mean that Jesus was conceived in an unnatural or supernatural manner. It means that after I received the visitation of the angel, and accepted the dramatic change it was to bring forth a child, I was given the immaculate concept, the immaculate vision, for Jesus and his mission. I was given an inner vision of who Jesus was as a spiritual being, I was given a vision of why he came to earth and what he was meant to accomplish in that lifetime. Throughout his life, it was my duty and my challenge – and sometimes my struggle – to hold true to that immaculate concept. There were periods when Jesus was a very difficult child, a very difficult teenager and even sometimes a difficult adult. No matter what he did or what happened, it was my challenge to remain true to the immaculate vision that he would manifest his full Christhood and fulfill his mission.

There were many different scenarios for how Jesus' mission could have been outplayed in outer circumstances. It was indeed the highest potential that many of the people, and even some of the leaders of the Jewish religion, would have received him as the Messiah. Obviously, that did not come to pass, and we might even say that it was close to the lowest potential that took place in terms of outer events. From a higher perspective, Jesus' mission was a complete success because he attained the full Christ consciousness and thereby demonstrated the path to Christ-hood. The essence of that path is that you do not sit around and wait for ideal conditions on earth before you let your light shine and give of God's love. On the contrary, you take whatever conditions you face, no matter how difficult they might be, and you let God's light and love raise those conditions higher. Regardless of outer conditions and how imperfect they might seem, from a higher perspective Jesus' mission was a success. Likewise, your mission can be a success, even if your outer circumstances do not live up to some human standard. The key is that you must be willing to transcend your limitations.

It was my role and my challenge to see beyond the outer conditions and *always* see Jesus victorious, namely that he would win his resurrection. Even when I saw him standing trial, when I saw him struggling through the crowded streets of Jerusalem carrying his cross, and even when I saw him hanging on the cross, it was my challenge to see beyond these outer, very stressful and very imperfect conditions. I had to hold true to my vision of the immaculate concept and hold the firm vision that Jesus would rise above all human limitations and win his eternal freedom in the resurrection.

This is the challenge that you face in your personal life, and this is the challenge you face on a planetary scale in this age. The central challenge of life on earth is to *never* let any condition trick you into shutting off the flow of God's light and love through your four lower bodies. You must remain true to your highest vision, never accepting imperfections as real, permanent or insurmountable. You must realize that behind all outer conditions is the pure Ma-ter Light, and the Ma-ter Light has the potential to outpicture any vision projected upon it through self-aware minds. The matter light can as easily outpicture God's perfection as it can outpicture the current imperfections found on earth.

It is important that humankind is awakened to the connection between their consciousness and what happens on the physical planet in the form of natural disasters and human conflicts. Unless people are voluntarily awakened to this reality, you will see many forms of calamities and upheavals on this planet, caused by the fact that the cosmic mirror is reflecting back to humankind what has been sent out. This is not done to punish; it is done in the hope that people will one day awaken by seeing the consequences of their actions. Hopefully, they will begin to ponder whether there is a hidden cause and whether they need to change themselves in order to avoid these outer calamities. It is my great hope that people can be awakened through spiritual guidance rather than going through the School of Hard Knocks.

A realistic assessment is that there will indeed be many calamities before there is a large-scale awakening. I must prophesy to you that it is likely that there will be many calamities before the awakening reaches critical mass. What I need from the most spiritually awakened people on this planet is an uncompromising adherence to the task of holding the immaculate concept for humankind and planet earth. I need those who will look beyond outer conditions, no matter how dire these conditions might seem, and hold true to the immaculate concept that the earth is constantly coming closer to manifesting God's kingdom.

When you are looking at a woman giving birth, seeing how she goes through wave upon wave of pain, you could become so distraught that you forget she is simply going through a temporary pain in order to give birth to a beautiful new child. I need those who will look at the Earth Mother and see that even though she might be going through various pains and calamities, they are simply birth pains that are paving the way for a new and better age, a golden age. I am not saying God wants such calamities; I am simply saying that humankind does not seem willing to awaken without feeling the earth shake beneath their feet.

***

In order to hold true to the immaculate concept, you must be willing to look beyond the outer imperfections. Doing this consistently means knowing a very important truth. Many spiritual people have been inspired by the analogy that you cannot remove darkness from a room. Imagine that you have a room that is in total darkness. You cannot carry the darkness outside and dump it. Darkness has no substance, and what has no substance cannot be removed or destroyed. The duality consciousness, the consciousness of anti-christ, has no reality to it. It truly has no substance, it is nothing but the absence of light, the absence of Christ truth. There is currently an absence of light on planet earth, as there is in the entire material universe. This is meant to be a temporary condition that will be rapidly overcome as more and more people allow God's light to shine through their beings. What has happened on earth is that the prince of this world has managed to make most people believe in the lie that this absence of light is permanent and unavoidable. It supposedly shows that God is not here, that God does not want to be here and that God does not care about human beings. Some even believe it shows that God does not exist.

Throughout history, many people have been caught up in the fight against evil. They have been trapped in the belief that in order to remove evil, they have to destroy it and its manifestations on earth. In most cases they have identified a certain group of people as the cause of evil, and thus they have fallen prey to another satanic lie, namely that if only they kill all people who belong to that race, nationality or religion, they will have removed evil from the planet. This is the lie that it is necessary and justified to do evil so that good may come. This is truly a satanic lie because, as I have said, you cannot remove something that has no substance. If you commit evil in order to remove evil, you only add to the darkness – to the misqualified energy – and thereby you feed the forces of evil.

Let me give you another subtle distinction. In its essence, darkness has no substance. The consciousness of duality has no substance or reality, and it can continue to exist only as long as self-aware beings allow it to remain in their minds, in their spheres of self. On planet earth you have a phenomenon that adds to the power of darkness, and that phenomenon is the misqualified energies produced by humankind over the ages. This is a temporary substance that those who are trapped in the consciousness of anti-christ can use to further their control over human beings. I earlier called this misqualified psychic energy. Darkness, meaning the unreality of the consciousness of anti-christ, has no substance, no reality, and it truly can do nothing of itself. Once self-aware beings become trapped in the consciousness of duality, they can use misqualified psychic energy to attain power over others.

Because this misqualified energy has substance, it is possible to remove the misqualified energy and thereby take power away from the forces of darkness. You cannot overcome misqualified energy by removing or destroying it. Once energy has been brought into the matter realm, you cannot make it disappear, you cannot turn it into nothing. The only way to overcome misqualified energy is to transform it back into a state of purity by infusing it with high-frequency light that raises its vibration and by imposing the pure vision of the Christ mind to give it a more perfect form.

If you allow yourself to be drawn into a human conflict and think you have to kill other people in the name of God, you are only misqualifying more energy, thereby adding to the total sum of misqualified energy used by the forces of darkness. You cannot combat darkness through negative feelings or actions that violate God's law of love. You will only add to it, thereby becoming more enveloped in it and adding to the planetary force of darkness. Misqualified energy is ultimately unreal. It cannot exist forever because the contracting force of the Mother will eventually cause all structures made of misqualified energy to self-destruct. The imperfect conditions that are made from mis-qualified energy are also unreal. You cannot *remove* the imperfect conditions on earth. You cannot simply grab them and throw them into a black hole in order to make them disappear. The true key to removing darkness on earth is to infuse it with light, to *infuse it with love,* so that the darkness transcends its current state of limitation and becomes more.

Many people look at the imperfections on earth and become agitated. They become angry and feel they have to do some-thing to change this, to combat the darkness. As long as you are motivated by fear or anger, anything you do will only misqualify more energy and therefore add to the force of darkness. When you are in a state of consciousness that is based on fear, anger, hatred, pride or other negative emotions, you are allowing cer-tain conditions to cause you to cut off the flow of God's love through your being.

This should be obvious by looking at a person who is angry. Is that person expressing any love? Of course not! The person is saying that because someone has done something wrong, it is justified that the person becomes angry and therefore does not respond to the situation with love. People are saying that if someone does something wrong to them, they *must* shut off the flow of God's love through them and respond with nega-tive feelings instead of responding with love. Did not Jesus tell you to love your enemies and to turn the other cheek? In all of his teachings, Jesus was attempting to give one simple mes-sage. The essential message that Jesus gave was this: "No matter what happens, no matter what other people do to you, no matter what life throws at you, *always respond with love!"* The love with which you must respond is the divine love that does not accept any imperfections as ultimately real or as permanent. You are allowing God's love to flow through your being and infuse the imperfect conditions whereby they will transcend themselves and become more.

Most people are trapped in a reactionary pattern. Someone harms them and they become angry at that person. They now go into a mode dominated by the flight or fight response. They first try to get away from the other person, to run away from the problem. If that is not possible, they either seek revenge or they want the other person to be punished. What people do when they go into this state of consciousness is that they abandon the immaculate concept. They accept an imperfect image, an imperfect vision, of the other person. They accept that vision as permanent, and they say that this person is a bad person. This is only adding to the other person's burden and adding to the misqualified energy that hangs as a dark cloud around this planet. Through the energy they misqualify, due to their imperfect vision and negative feelings, they are reinforcing the imperfect image, making it even more difficult for the other person to escape it. This is precisely what has caused so many human conflicts to be turned into negative, self-reinforcing spirals that no one has the power to stop. The reason people do not have the power to stop such spirals is that they are not willing to use the key given by Jesus, namely to stop reinforcing the downward spiral by turning the other cheek (Matthew 5:39). Only when someone decides to forgive rather than seek revenge (Matthew 18:22), can a spiral of violence and counter-violence and counter-counter-violence be broken.

No self-aware being created by God is an inherently bad or evil being. Everyone was created in the immaculate concept and has the potential to get back to that higher reality. All people who violate the law of love do so because they are trapped in the duality consciousness. If you want to punish or destroy such a person, you are actually falling prey to the very same state of consciousness that caused the person to do whatever the person did to you. What you should be doing instead is to hold the immaculate concept for the other person and yourself. You should do everything you can to keep yourself from reacting to the situation in a dualistic manner. You should hold the vision that the other person will transcend his or her imperfect beliefs and once again discover his or her true identity as a God-free spiritual being.

Many people have been exposed to enormous atrocities at the hands of other people. I know it can be difficult to pull oneself out of the negative feelings that result from such experiences. The only way for you to become free of such negative events is to raise yourself above the dualistic consciousness of seeking an eye for an eye and a tooth for a tooth. Only when you focus all attention on raising both yourself and other people, will you truly be able to free yourself and manifest a more abundant life.

Jesus came to this earth 2,000 years ago to help humankind rise above the consciousness of wanting an eye for an eye. If his teachings had been internalized by all, the kingdom of God would already have been manifest on earth. It is not too late, but it will not happen unless the most spiritually aware people make a wholehearted effort to free themselves from the duality consciousness.

***

What I need you to do is to fundamentally change your outlook on life and your approach to life. I need you to make it the main priority of your life to remain true to the immaculate concept, the immaculate vision. I realize fully that at this point you might not have the ultimate vision that is stored in your I AM Presence and in the universal Christ mind. Because you have followed this course, you do have a much higher, a much more spiritual, vision than the vast majority of people on this planet. I need you to remain true to the highest vision you have right now, and no matter what happens on the outer – in your personal life or on a planetary scale – I need you to always focus your attention on the highest possible vision. I need you to never go below that vision and accept that some imperfection is ultimately real or is unchangeable. I need you to remain true to the highest vision you have right now while constantly seeking to attain a higher and clearer vision by going within. You do this by asking your Christ self and your spiritual teachers to guide you to a higher vision. I need you to be constantly transcending yourself and to be constantly visualizing that other people, outer conditions and the entire planet are transcending themselves and becoming more.

How do you remove darkness from the earth? You remove it by loving it with divine love whereby it becomes more, it transcends itself, it becomes turned into the light of God and the vision of Christ. I am not saying you actually love the darkness but that you love the Mother Light that has been trapped in an imperfect matrix. You love the light itself with such force that you set it free from the imperfect form and turn it back into the pure Mother Light. I am not here talking about the false light that can give even Satan the appearance of an angel of light (2Corinthians 11:14). I am not talking about the hypocrisy that the scribes and the Pharisees had, thinking they were holier than other people because of outer conditions. I am talking about the true light that sees beyond all material conditions and sees beyond the entire dualistic illusion. The consciousness of duality sets up two extremes, namely relative good and relative evil. There are many conditions on earth that might appear to be

332 ❦   *Your Life's Plan for Abundance*

good, but they are only *relatively* good. They are not the *undivided* good of the mind of Christ. I need you to sharpen your discernment so you can see beyond the appearances of both relative good and relative evil, even beyond the lie of absolute evil. I need you to remain true to the immaculate concept and to constantly strive for a higher vision by putting on the mind of Christ.

As a general rule for your outer behavior, you can take the admonishment of Jesus to love everything with divine love. Whatever situation you encounter, ask yourself this question: "Is my reaction to this situation based on the highest vision of love that I currently have?" You can also ask yourself: "Am I seeking to make this situation better, to help it become more, or have I fallen into the trap of affirming its current state of imperfection as unchangeable?" If you want a rule for how to deal with other people and outer situations, I can give you a very simple guideline, namely to bless everything. Bless everything by letting the very life force itself, namely God's unconditional love – what many Christians call the Holy Spirit – stream through your being. Blessing something means that you are seeking to make it better, to transform it, to help it become more, to accelerate it and help it transcend its current imperfection. Bless everyone and everything to the best capacity of your current vision. Then constantly bless yourself so you can enhance your vision.

Let me bring what we have just discussed together with something I talked about earlier. The essential principle here is that you do not seek to destroy something bad but that you transform it into something better. I have earlier talked in great detail about the need to let your mortal sense of identity die. I know these teachings can seem contradictory so let me help you rise above the dualistic view that projects a contradiction where no contradiction exists. I have just talked about two forms of darkness, namely that which has substance and that which has no substance. If we want to be truly thorough, we might say that there are three forms of darkness:

•   There is the original darkness that exists in the void. This is not evil and it is not in opposition to the light of the Creator. It is simply an absence of the light of the Creator and will willingly be replaced by light. This darkness is no concern to you because it is not actively opposing the manifestation of God's kingdom on earth.

•   There is the darkness that I have called the duality consciousness, the consciousness of anti-christ. This darkness is not passive because it was born out of an act of will, or rather an act of anti-will, that rebels against the will of the Creator. This darkness is ultimately unreal and has no substance to it whereby I mean that it has no material existence. It exists only in the minds of self-aware beings and can continue to exist only as long as these beings choose to see it as real. This is the kind of darkness that opposes your growth from inside your mind, and even through other people, seeking to take over and control your mind through dualistic lies and illusions.

It is this form of darkness that makes up your mortal self, and it has created a false image of the world, a graven image, an idol. This false image is what has given birth to your mortal self, your sense of identity as a mortal, limited and imperfect being. If you actively fight against this form of darkness and try to destroy or eradicate it, you will inevitably become more enveloped in the duality consciousness. You will misqualify energy, create karma and project imperfect images into the cosmic mirror. You can never actually destroy or eradicate this form of darkness, which is why Jesus told you not to resist evil (Matthew 5:39).

The only way to overcome this form of darkness is to transcend it, to rise above it, to refuse to accept it as real, thereby simply leaving it behind. That is why you have to allow your mortal sense of identity to die. When this mortal self dies, the consciousness of anti-christ, the prince of this world, will have nothing in you (John 14:30) whereby he can control, force or tempt you into a dualistic reaction to imperfect conditions. In order to fully do this, you need to realize that many dualistic conditions are perversions of Christ truth. In order to fully allow the dualistic sense of identity to die, you need to see beyond it and grasp your true identity. You cannot exist in a vacuum so you must see your true identity before you can let go of your mortal identity. We might say that you overcome this form of evil, which is based on a lie, by replacing it with Christ truth. You can let your mortal sense of self die and be reborn into your true spiritual identity. This form of darkness is like a filmstrip with imperfect images that exist in the minds of self-aware beings. The only way to overcome it is to replace it with another filmstrip based on the vision of Christ, the immaculate concept.

•   The third form of darkness is what I have called misqualified energy, and it is created by taking the pure Mother Light and lowering its vibration by imposing a dualistic image and feeling upon it. This darkness has an actual, material substance because it is made from the Mother Light. We might say that the consciousness of duality exists only in the mind of self-aware co-creators, and thus it does not have what scientists would call an objective existence, an existence that is independent of the mind. The Mother Light was created by the Creator, and once lowered in vibration it has an objective existence, meaning that it can exist independently of the minds of co-creators.

The misqualified Mother Light cannot be purified by ignoring it. It will not simply die by you transcending the illusions of anti-christ. It will be purified only when you transform its imperfect forms by replacing them with the perfect vision, the non-dualistic vision, of the Christ mind. This is what I have called spiritual alchemy, and my invocations are designed to help you invoke the high-frequency energy that will raise the vibration of misqualified energy. They are also designed to help you resolve the dualistic beliefs that prevent you from letting your mortal self die. They have a double function of helping you overcome the two forms of darkness that prevent you from being here below all that you already are Above. In order to overcome this form of darkness, you have to transform it into something higher.

Let me apply this to the issue of selfishness. One might say that the only problem on earth is selfishness, namely that God's co-creators have forgotten their true identity and have become focused on the physical body and the mortal self, thereby acting as if they are the only beings that matter. How do you escape selfishness? You do so by transforming the misqualified energies that pull you into egotistical patterns of thoughts, feelings and actions. You do so by transcending the sense of self that is so narrowly focused. As you transform the misqualified energies, you can expand your vision of self.

There truly is a form of divine selfishness, although it would be better to call it determination. The divine equivalent of selfishness is the uncompromising determination that will not let anything prevent you from carrying out your divine plan. This is a very necessary quality, and without it no progress could ever be made on earth because the anti-will of the duality consciousness would overpower all efforts to change, dragging everyone down to the lowest common denominator.

The real key to overcoming selfishness is to expand the sense of self, to transcend your sense of self. You begin by reclaiming your personal, inner connection to your own higher being. You see that you are more than the body, more than the mortal self and even more than the four lower bodies. You then go to the next level and realize that you are an extension of the Creator. From there, you go to the final level and see that everyone and everything is also made from the Creator's Being. Your ultimate sense of self encompasses everyone and everything. When you have established this correct sense of self, you will have fully overcome the human, dualistic form of selfishness. You will not have eradicated or destroyed it; you will have transformed it into its divine equivalent. In order to do this, you must let go of the sense of self based on human selfishness, you must be willing to let this self die.

***

Everything in the material universe is made from the Mother Light. The Mother Light cannot, by itself, take on form, but it must be acted upon by a self-aware being. All human beings on earth are constantly acting upon the Mother Light through the creative faculties they were given by God, namely their free will and imagination. Through the power of their imagination, they are envisioning imperfect, dualistic images. Through the power of their will, they are choosing to accept those images as real and unavoidable. Through the power of their vision, they are imposing those images upon the Ma-ter Light. That is why planet earth currently has so many imperfect conditions that it almost defies comprehension. What is needed in order to change the current struggle and suffering is a group of people who will take up the role of being guardians of the Mother Light. These people will recognize that everything is made from the Mother Light. They will recognize that all imperfect conditions on this planet are produced because dualistic images were projected onto the screen of the Mother Light. They will recognize that things will change only when a critical mass of people use their creative faculties to impose a higher, Christlike, image upon the Ma-ter Light, thereby transforming an imperfect planet into the kingdom of God. This is indeed the power of true, spiritual alchemy.

You might have heard about the alchemists and their futile attempts to turn lead into gold. You might have been given a somewhat scornful view of the alchemists, and indeed many alchemists *were* charlatans. Nevertheless, behind the commonly known movement of the alchemists was a deeper understanding of the reality of life. Certain people had understood that there is a spiritual alchemy which does not seek to turn base metals into gold but seeks to turn the "base metal" of the human consciousness, the consciousness of duality, into the spiritual gold of the Christ consciousness. You are not seeking to remove something that is imperfect, dark or evil. You are seeking to transform it into something that is more, something that is closer to the Christ vision. You are taking what is lower and transforming it into something higher. Instead of seeking to destroy what is lower, you are seeking to make it better, to help it transcend itself and outpicture the perfect vision of Christ. This is especially important when dealing with other people. A person will do evil only because he or she is trapped in the duality consciousness. Behind the outer appearances is the conscious self of that person, which was created in the immaculate concept and longs to be free to express that vision. You do not love the outer appearance – the mortal self – yet you don't seek to destroy it either. You see past it and seek to set the conscious self free to be who it really is.

There is an essential difference between seeking to destroy an imperfection and seeking to transform that imperfection into perfection. If you see this difference, then you are truly among the avant garde of the spiritual beings who came to earth to manifest God's kingdom. You are in a unique position to take up your rightful role as a guardian of the Mother Light.

The Mother Light itself has intelligence, has awareness. The Mother Light itself knows very well that it is not currently expressing God's perfection. The Mother Light can see the highest vision, the highest potential for planet earth and would love nothing more than to outpicture it in the form of perfect physical conditions. The Mother Light has vowed to take on the role of allowing God's co-creators, meaning the self-aware beings created by God, to do whatever they want with the Mother Light. The Mother Light has lovingly vowed to outpicture whatever images self-aware beings project upon it whereby these co-creators can have an opportunity to learn from their own choices, to learn by seeing the consequences of their choices outpictured in matter. This is truly an act of unconditional love because the Mother Light knows the highest potential for earth but is nevertheless allowing human beings to create imperfect conditions that are far below the highest potential. If this is not unconditional love, then I don't know what is. The Mother Light itself would love nothing more than to be set free from the current imperfect images and instead have the perfect images of the Christ mind projected upon it. The Mother Light wants to manifest God's kingdom on earth. The Mother Light wants to be obedient to the will of the Father and the vision of the Son.

The entire material universe is created from two basic elements, namely the expanding force of the Father and the contracting force of the Mother. The expanding force of the Father is God's unconditional love that wants everything to transcend itself. The contracting force is what makes it possible for a form to exist in time and space. The contracting force is also driven by unconditional love, which is why it will not allow a self-aware being to be trapped forever in an imperfect sense of identity. For a sustainable creation to occur, the expanding force of the Father and the contracting force of the Mother must be balanced through the vision of the Son, the universal Christ mind and the individualized Christ minds of God's co-creators. If planet earth is to manifest the kingdom of God, it can only happen when the perfect vision, held in the mind of Christ, is imposed upon the Mother Light. *That* vision can be imposed only when a critical mass of people in physical embodiment awaken to their true identity and their true role. It can happen only when these people decide to be the Christed ones on earth, to manifest the Christ consciousness, and through that Christ consciousness project the perfect images of God's kingdom onto the Mother Light that makes up planet earth.

This is the true meaning of the Son of God, the only begotten of the Father. That is why Jesus said that if you believe on him – to the point of being willing to follow in his footsteps and manifest the Christ consciousness – you can do the works that he did (John 14:12). You too can become a son or daughter of God, fulfilling your rightful role on this planet. When a critical mass of people begin to guard the Mother Light, this planet will truly manifest a golden age of such peace and prosperity that most people could not even imagine it in their current state of consciousness. They would immediately reject it as pure fantasy, as a Utopia that could not possibly come to pass. It *can* indeed come to pass, but it can only come to pass when people begin to accept it, when they see the vision and accept that vision as a very real potential. You must even transcend the point of accepting it as a *potential* and begin to use the power of your will, your imagination and your vision to affirm it as a *reality*.

I need all guardians of the Mother Light to use the power of your vision to let your eye be single so that you do not allow your vision to be pulled into any of the dualistic images created by the prince of this world. You need to focus your eye single-mindedly on the vision of Christ, and then you need to see that vision superimposed upon all outer conditions. I need you to see outer conditions as temporary and unreal, and then see them replaced by the vision of Christ.

I am not hereby saying that you need to ignore imperfections. I have gone to great length to explain to you the need to stop running away from responsibility. I need you to acknowledge the imperfections that are currently in existence and I need you to understand that they spring from the duality consciousness. You never allow yourself to see them as real, as permanent or as beyond being changed. You see them as temporary, unreal mirages projected onto the Mother Light, and then you see beyond them. You see the pure Mother Light that is the underlying reality behind all outer manifestations, and then you see the absolute reality that the Mother Light has the potential to outpicture any image projected upon it. It is like a movie screen that will reflect any image projected upon it through a filmstrip. You envision that it is possible that the Mother Light can quickly – in fact instantly – stop outpicturing an imperfect vision and start outpicturing a more perfect vision. You can then use the power of your vision to visualize how the imperfect condition is transformed and becomes more perfect.

There is an essential difference between running away from imperfections, thereby allowing them to continue to exist, and acknowledging the imperfections but seeing them as temporary and unreal, thereby projecting a real image upon the Mother Light. This is the difference between those who *think* they are spiritual, but have not brought their spirituality into the matter realm, and those who truly *are* spiritual and recognize that they are here to take dominion by seeing God behind everything and seeing God's perfect vision outpictured in all things. My challenge to you is this:

• Always remain true to the highest vision you can currently see.

• Constantly keep up the effort to expand your vision so that you can grasp a higher vision tomorrow than you can see today.

• Never allow yourself to be trapped in an attitude or belief system that makes you think you have the highest possible vision or the highest possible spiritual truth and understanding.

• Always keep transcending yourself and your vision of God's kingdom.

When should you stop seeking to transcend yourself and your vision? It is very simple, namely when you see God in everything, when you see God as the first cause behind all outer manifestations – no matter how imperfect they are – and when you see God's kingdom manifest in every situation you encounter. You will never stop transcending yourself because God is constantly transcending himself, your Creator is constantly transcending itself and becoming more. When you are in the River of Life, you are constantly transcending your vision. This is indeed the truly abundant life, namely that you are always in the process of becoming more. Abundance is not a static state of owning a certain amount of money or material possessions. Abundance is a living, dynamic state of always being in the process of becoming more.

Ah, my beloved, this is the abundant life, and it truly is the Father's good pleasure to give it to you. It has been my good pleasure to give you these teachings that truly contain the keys you need in order to manifest the abundant life—if you are willing to internalize my teachings and apply them in every aspect of your life. I have given you what you need, now the challenge is to apply it, to become it. Will you take the key, will you put it in the lock, will you turn it until your hear the click, which means that the truth has "clicked" in your mind. Will you let the famous light bulb turn on in your mind so you finally see that the door to the prison of your mortal self was never locked. You can fling that door wide open and walk out of the prison and into the sun of your I AM Presence.

When you walk out of that prison, I will be there to greet you. Your Christ self will be there to greet you. Your personal spiritual teachers will be there to greet you. We will take you into our arms, and we will share a moment – a cosmic interval – of oneness with you. In that oneness with each other, we will be one with all life and we will be one with our Creator. In that oneness we will discover an abundance that is beyond anything found on earth, anything that can be envisioned by the duality consciousness or described in words. We will know the true abundance that can be known only through the Christ mind. I leave you with a little play on words: "When you see all life as one, your victory will be won."

14 | I INVOKE IMMACULATE VISION

In the name I AM THAT I AM, Jesus Christ, I call to all representatives of the Divine Mother and the Divine Father, especially Sanat Kumara, Lady Master Venus and Mother Mary, to help me be the open door for unconditional love that superimposes the immaculate vision upon the Mother Light. Help me accept my creative powers and see the factors that block the flow of my God-given creativity, including...

[Make personal calls.]

1. I understand the nature of love

1. I am stepping up to knowing what I can do with my spiritual attainment in order to bring God's kingdom to earth. I am finding my place in the greater, timeless, work that is God's creation.

Sanat Kumara, Ruby Fire,
I seek my place in love's own choir,
with open hearts we sing your praise,
together we the earth do raise.

Sanat Kumara, Ruby Ray,
bring to earth a higher way,
light this planet with your fire,
clothe her in a new attire.

2. I am completing the circle so that the light flows back to God. I am completing the figure-eight flow so that God can multiply from Above what I have multiplied here below. I am giving freely what I have freely received.

Sanat Kumara, Ruby Fire,
initiations I desire,
I am for you an electrode,
Shamballa is my true abode.

Sanat Kumara, Ruby Ray,
bring to earth a higher way,
light this planet with your fire,
clothe her in a new attire.

3. I am developing a sense of oneness with God and oneness with all life. I am seeking to raise the consciousness of other people and even the collective consciousness. By giving of my light to help others, I am completing the figure-eight flow, helping to raise everyone to the Christ consciousness.

Sanat Kumara, Ruby Fire,
I follow path that you require,
initiate me with your love,
the open door for Holy Dove.

Sanat Kumara, Ruby Ray,
bring to earth a higher way,
light this planet with your fire,
clothe her in a new attire.

4. Love is the most powerful force in the universe. I am breaking through the opposition to the manifestation of the abundant life because I have a will power that is based entirely on love. I am giving of what I have and what I have learned.

Sanat Kumara, Ruby Fire,
your great example all inspire,
with non-attachment and great mirth,
we give the earth a true rebirth.

Sanat Kumara, Ruby Ray,
bring to earth a higher way,
light this planet with your fire,
clothe her in a new attire.

5. I am looking in the mirror to see where I have not transcended a certain level of understanding and attainment. I am taking the ultimate step to establishing the abundant life. I am freely giving what I have received, using it to help others by inspiring them to come up higher.

Sanat Kumara, Ruby Fire,
you are this planet's purifier,
consume on earth all spirits dark,
reveal the inner Spirit Spark.

Sanat Kumara, Ruby Ray,
bring to earth a higher way,
light this planet with your fire,
clothe her in a new attire.

6. I am transcending the insanity that seeks to prevent something from becoming more by holding it in a limited state. I accept God's unlimited abundance, and I say: "God, come into my life. I want to multiply what I have; I want it to become more."

Sanat Kumara, Ruby Fire,
you are a cosmic amplifier,
the lower forces can't withstand,
vibrations from venutian band.

Sanat Kumara, Ruby Ray,
bring to earth a higher way,
light this planet with your fire,
clothe her in a new attire.

7. Love is a constant flow, namely the River of Life which never stands still. The River of Life never seeks to own or possess anything; it is constantly giving, it is constantly flowing—changing, transcending itself and becoming more. It does not seek to own any one thing because it sees itself as one with every good and perfect thing.

Sanat Kumara, Ruby Fire,
I am on earth your magnifier,
the flow of love I do restore,
my chakras are your open door.

**Sanat Kumara, Ruby Ray,
bring to earth a higher way,
light this planet with your fire,
clothe her in a new attire.**

8. Only in becoming more – in being one with the River of Life – can I truly own anything. It is only in self-transcendence that I have true ownership because only when I transcend myself will I stay in the River of Life. Only when I stay in that river, can I have abundance, the true abundance that is constantly growing and becoming more.

Sanat Kumara, Ruby Fire,
venutian song the multiplier,
as we your love reverberate,
the densest minds we penetrate.

**Sanat Kumara, Ruby Ray,
bring to earth a higher way,
light this planet with your fire,
clothe her in a new attire.**

9. With all I know about God, as a completely self-contained Being who is constantly giving of himself, I realize that God's love is unconditional and infinite. God has no other desire than to see his kingdom come into physical manifestation on planet earth.

Sanat Kumara, Ruby Fire,
you are for all the sanctifier,
the earth is now a holy place,
purified by cosmic grace.

**Sanat Kumara, Ruby Ray,
bring to earth a higher way,
light this planet with your fire,
clothe her in a new attire.**

2. I am transforming current conditions

1. Current conditions on earth are far from God's vision because people have fallen into the duality consciousness. The only way to change the situation is that those who have a higher vision will spread that vision and awaken other people.

O Venus, show me how to serve,
your cosmic beauty I observe.
What love from Venus you now bring,
our planets do in tandem sing.

**O Venus, service so divine,
you are for earth a cosmic sign.
Your selfless service is now mine,
a life in service I define.**

2. There is the God who is the All and the God who is in all.
The God who is the All wants me to give light and love unconditionally to the God who is in all. The Creator wants me to free
that God, to free the Mother Light, to outpicture the perfection
envisioned by the Creator. Thereby, the God who is in all will be
one with the God who is the All.

O Venus, your love is the key,
the hardened hearts on earth are free.
Embracing future bright and bold,
our planet's story is retold.

O Venus, service so divine,
you are for earth a cosmic sign.
Your selfless service is now mine,
a life in service I define.

3. I am developing a global awareness, even a universal awareness. I am an emissary of God's light, an emissary of Christ
vision. I am a co-creator bringing the kingdom of God to earth.
I am experiencing and manifesting the abundant life.

O Venus, loving Mother mine,
my heart your love does now refine.
I am the open door for love,
descending like a Holy Dove.

O Venus, service so divine,
you are for earth a cosmic sign.
Your selfless service is now mine,
a life in service I define.

4. I am establishing the figure-eight flow of the abundant life by giving out what I have, giving out what I have received, giving out what I have internalized, giving out what I have become. I am letting the sun of my I AM Presence shine through my four lower bodies and letting it shine upon the just and the unjust.

O Venus, play the secret note,
that is for hatred antidote.
All poisoned hearts you gently heal,
as love's true story you reveal.

O Venus, service so divine,
you are for earth a cosmic sign.
Your selfless service is now mine,
a life in service I define.

5. I am shifting my perception and I see that the current limitations and imperfections on earth are truly unreal. I see that God is here on earth, and therefore God's kingdom can indeed be manifest here on earth.

O Venus, love fills every need,
for truly, love is God's first seed.
O let it blossom, let it grow,
sweep earth into your loving flow.

O Venus, service so divine,
you are for earth a cosmic sign.
Your selfless service is now mine,
a life in service I define.

6. I will no longer wait for ideal conditions on earth before I let my light shine and give of God's love. I am taking whatever conditions I face, no matter how difficult they might be, and I am letting God's light and love raise those conditions higher.

O Venus, music of the spheres,
heard by those who God reveres.
Our voices now as one we raise,
singing in adoring praise.

**O Venus, service so divine,
you are for earth a cosmic sign.
Your selfless service is now mine,
a life in service I define.**

7. I am true to my highest vision, never accepting imperfections as real, permanent or insurmountable. Behind all outer conditions is the pure Ma-ter Light, and the Ma-ter Light has the potential to outpicture any vision projected upon it through self-conscious minds. The Ma-ter light can as easily outpicture God's perfection as it can outpicture the current imperfections.

O Venus, we are joining ranks,
Sanat Kumara we give thanks.
Our planet has received new life,
to lift her out of war and strife.

**O Venus, service so divine,
you are for earth a cosmic sign.
Your selfless service is now mine,
a life in service I define.**

8. No matter what happens, no matter what other people do to me, no matter what life throws at me, I am always responding with love! I am responding with the divine love that does not accept any imperfections as ultimately real or as permanent. I am allowing God's love to flow through my being and infuse the imperfect conditions whereby they are transcending themselves and becoming more.

> O Venus, your sweet melody,
> consumes veil of duality.
> Absorbed in tones of Cosmic Love,
> all conflict we now rise above.

> **O Venus, service so divine,**
> **you are for earth a cosmic sign.**
> **Your selfless service is now mine,**
> **a life in service I define.**

9. I am holding the immaculate concept for any situation. I refuse to react to any situation in a dualistic manner. I am holding the vision that the situation will be accelerated. It is the main priority of my life to remain true to the immaculate concept, the immaculate vision.

> O Venus, shining Morning Star,
> a cosmic herald, that you are.
> The earth set free by sacred sound,
> our planet is now heaven-bound.

> **O Venus, service so divine,**
> **you are for earth a cosmic sign.**
> **Your selfless service is now mine,**
> **a life in service I define.**

3. I am blessing everything

1. I am remaining true to the highest vision I have right now. No matter what happens on the outer, I am always focusing my attention on the highest possible vision. I see that imperfections are ultimately unreal and that everything is changeable.

Sanat Kumara, Ruby Fire,
I seek my place in love's own choir,
with open hearts we sing your praise,
together we the earth do raise.

Sanat Kumara, Ruby Ray,
bring to earth a higher way,
light this planet with your fire,
clothe her in a new attire.

2. I am remaining true to the highest vision I have right now while constantly seeking to attain a higher and clearer vision by going within. I am asking my Christ self and my spiritual teachers to guide me to a higher vision.

Sanat Kumara, Ruby Fire,
initiations I desire,
I am for you an electrode,
Shamballa is my true abode.

Sanat Kumara, Ruby Ray,
bring to earth a higher way,
light this planet with your fire,
clothe her in a new attire.

3. I am constantly transcending myself and I am constantly visualizing that other people, outer conditions and the entire planet are transcending themselves and becoming more.

> Sanat Kumara, Ruby Fire,
> I follow path that you require,
> initiate me with your love,
> the open door for Holy Dove.

> **Sanat Kumara, Ruby Ray,**
> **bring to earth a higher way,**
> **light this planet with your fire,**
> **clothe her in a new attire.**

4. I am removing darkness from the earth by loving it with divine love whereby it becomes more, it transcends itself, it becomes turned into the light of God and the vision of Christ.

> Sanat Kumara, Ruby Fire,
> your great example all inspire,
> with non-attachment and great mirth,
> we give the earth a true rebirth.

> **Sanat Kumara, Ruby Ray,**
> **bring to earth a higher way,**
> **light this planet with your fire,**
> **clothe her in a new attire.**

5. I am not actually loving the darkness but I am loving the Mother Light that has been trapped in an imperfect matrix. I love the light itself with such force that I set it free from the imperfect form and turn it back into the pure Mother Light.

Sanat Kumara, Ruby Fire,
you are this planet's purifier,
consume on earth all spirits dark,
reveal the inner Spirit Spark.

Sanat Kumara, Ruby Ray,
bring to earth a higher way,
light this planet with your fire,
clothe her in a new attire.

6. I am sharpening my discernment. I am seeing beyond the appearances of both relative good and relative evil, even beyond the lie of absolute evil. I am remaining true to the immaculate concept and constantly striving for a higher vision by putting on the mind of Christ.

Sanat Kumara, Ruby Fire,
you are a cosmic amplifier,
the lower forces can't withstand,
vibrations from venutian band.

Sanat Kumara, Ruby Ray,
bring to earth a higher way,
light this planet with your fire,
clothe her in a new attire.

7. I am loving everything with divine love. Whatever situation I encounter, I ask myself: "Is my reaction to this situation based on the highest vision of love that I currently have?"

Sanat Kumara, Ruby Fire,
I am on earth your magnifier,
the flow of love I do restore,
my chakras are your open door.

Sanat Kumara, Ruby Ray,
bring to earth a higher way,
light this planet with your fire,
clothe her in a new attire.

8. "Am I seeking to make this situation better, to help it become more, or have I fallen into the trap of affirming its current state of imperfection as unchangeable?"

Sanat Kumara, Ruby Fire,
venutian song the multiplier,
as we your love reverberate,
the densest minds we penetrate.

Sanat Kumara, Ruby Ray,
bring to earth a higher way,
light this planet with your fire,
clothe her in a new attire.

9. I am blessing everything. I am letting the very life force itself, namely God's unconditional love, the Holy Spirit, stream through my being. I am blessing everyone and everything to the best capacity of my current vision. I am constantly blessing myself and enhancing my vision.

Sanat Kumara, Ruby Fire,
you are for all the sanctifier,
the earth is now a holy place,
purified by cosmic grace.

Sanat Kumara, Ruby Ray,
bring to earth a higher way,
light this planet with your fire,
clothe her in a new attire.

4. I am in cosmic oneness

1. I have uncompromising determination and will not let anything prevent me from carrying out my divine plan. I am overcoming selfishness by expanding my sense of self, by transcending my sense of self.

O Venus, show me how to serve,
your cosmic beauty I observe.
What love from Venus you now bring,
our planets do in tandem sing.

O Venus, service so divine,
you are for earth a cosmic sign.
Your selfless service is now mine,
a life in service I define.

2. I am an extension of the Creator. I see that everyone and everything is also made from the Creator's Being. My ultimate sense of self encompasses everyone and everything.

Your Life's Plan for Abundance

O Venus, your love is the key,
the hardened hearts on earth are free.
Embracing future bright and bold,
our planet's story is retold.

**O Venus, service so divine,
you are for earth a cosmic sign.
Your selfless service is now mine,
a life in service I define.**

3. I am a guardian of the Mother Light by using the power of my vision to let my eye be single. I do not allow my vision to be pulled into any of the dualistic images created by the prince of this world.

O Venus, loving Mother mine,
my heart your love does now refine.
I am the open door for love,
descending like a Holy Dove.

**O Venus, service so divine,
you are for earth a cosmic sign.
Your selfless service is now mine,
a life in service I define.**

4. I am focusing my eye single-mindedly on the vision of Christ, and I see that vision superimposed upon all outer conditions. I see outer conditions as temporary and unreal, and I see them replaced by the vision of Christ.

O Venus, play the secret note,
that is for hatred antidote.
All poisoned hearts you gently heal,
as love's true story you reveal.

**O Venus, service so divine,
you are for earth a cosmic sign.
Your selfless service is now mine,
a life in service I define.**

5. I acknowledge the imperfections that are currently in existence and I understand that they spring from the duality consciousness. I also see that they are unreal, impermanent and that they can indeed be changed.

O Venus, love fills every need,
for truly, love is God's first seed.
O let it blossom, let it grow,
sweep earth into your loving flow.

**O Venus, service so divine,
you are for earth a cosmic sign.
Your selfless service is now mine,
a life in service I define.**

6. I see that current conditions are temporary, unreal mirages projected onto the Mother Light. I see beyond them. I see the pure Mother Light that is the underlying reality behind all outer manifestations. I see the absolute reality that the Mother Light has the potential to outpicture any image projected upon it.

O Venus, music of the spheres,
heard by those who God reveres.
Our voices now as one we raise,
singing in adoring praise.

**O Venus, service so divine,
you are for earth a cosmic sign.
Your selfless service is now mine,
a life in service I define.**

7. I see that it is possible that the Mother Light can instantly stop outpicturing an imperfect vision and start outpicturing a more perfect vision. I am using the power of my vision to visualize how the imperfect condition is transformed and becomes more perfect.

O Venus, we are joining ranks,
Sanat Kumara we give thanks.
Our planet has received new life,
to lift her out of war and strife.

**O Venus, service so divine,
you are for earth a cosmic sign.
Your selfless service is now mine,
a life in service I define.**

8. I am walking out of the mortal prison, and Mother Mary is there to greet me. My Christ self is there to greet me. My personal spiritual teachers are there to greet me. I am in the arms of my ascended teachers and we are sharing a cosmic interval of oneness.

O Venus, your sweet melody,
consumes veil of duality.
Absorbed in tones of Cosmic Love,
all conflict we now rise above.

**O Venus, service so divine,
you are for earth a cosmic sign.
Your selfless service is now mine,
a life in service I define.**

9. In that oneness with each other, we are one with all life and are
one with our Creator. In that oneness we discover an abundance
that is beyond anything found on earth, anything that can be
envisioned by the duality consciousness or described in words.
We know the true abundance that can be known only through
the Christ mind. I see all life as one, and thus my victory is won.

O Venus, shining Morning Star,
a cosmic herald, that you are.
The earth set free by sacred sound,
our planet is now heaven-bound.

**O Venus, service so divine,
you are for earth a cosmic sign.
Your selfless service is now mine,
a life in service I define.**

Sealing

In the name of the Divine Mother, I call to Sanat Kumara, Venus and Mother Mary for the sealing of myself and all people in my circle of influence in the creative flow of the Divine Mother, the River of Life. I call for the multiplication of my calls by all representatives of the Divine Mother, so that we form the perfect figure-eight flow of "As Above, so below." Thus, I accept that this is fully manifest, because the mouth of the Lord, the Divine Mother that I AM, has spoken it. Amen.

15 | FLOWING WITH THE
RIVER OF LIFE

Allow me to make one more attempt to explain to you the essence of the mortal self, or what many people call the human ego. The most important point you can understand about the mortal self is that it is engaged in an impossible quest. The quest is impossible because the mortal self is born of duality. The mortal self has a built-in conflict, a built-in contradiction, that can never – and I truly mean *never* – be resolved. The mortal self was born when the Conscious You decided that it would no longer make decisions. The real problem with this decision was that the Conscious You denied its true identity, its true nature. The Conscious You denied that it is a co-creator with God, and therefore it denied the fact that – by your very nature – you are worthy and acceptable in the eyes of God. The Conscious You has come to accept the dualistic lie that you are separated from God and that you are not worthy to come back to God because you have made some kind of mistake. In reality, you have only temporarily departed from the immaculate concept by accepting a lower sense of identity, but you can always come back to that pure vision.

When you accepted the sense of unworthiness, the Conscious You withdrew into a little cage. The Conscious You can never fully withdraw from being conscious. The Conscious You can withdraw from making decisions, but it cannot withdraw from having conscious experiences. The Conscious You can stop making decisions, but it cannot choose to stop experiencing the consequences of its decisions or lack of decisions. Because self-awareness comes before will, the Conscious You cannot choose to stop being conscious, although it can try to numb itself so that it is barely conscious. The Conscious You can never completely lose its longing for wholeness, its longing to come back to God's kingdom, to once again be in the River of Life and experience the abundant life. This is a safety mechanism that can never be completely turned off. No matter what the Conscious You does, it will always have an inner longing for wholeness, a longing for something more.

When the mortal self was born, it attempted to fill the void that had been created because the Conscious You no longer had a direct experience of its I AM Presence. The mortal self is always engaged in a quest to set itself up as a worthy replacement for your I AM Presence, for the true identity that is still stored in the universal Christ mind. Your inner quest for wholeness can be filled only through oneness with your I AM Presence, the oneness that releases the flow of God's light through your lower being. That oneness can be attained only when you accept and recognize that you are worthy to face God, to be one with God. The Conscious You has simply forgotten its worthiness, and it can come back to it by recognizing the eternal truth that because you were created as an extension of God, you are inherently worthy to be one with God. In fact, you were never separated from God, you never lost your worthiness.

In contrast to this, the mortal self was not created by God, and thus it never has been, and it never will be, worthy in the eyes of God. The Conscious You has a built-in worthiness because it has an immaculate concept in the universal Christ mind. It is not a matter of *earning* worthiness by doing things in the matter realm; it is simply a matter of *accepting* it. The mortal self does not have this built-in worthiness, and therefore it can never earn it. The universal Christ mind does not contain an immaculate concept for the mortal self, and thus this self has nothing, no reality, to which it can return. The mortal self is constantly trying to build a false sense of worthiness, an image of being worthy, which it then builds up to the point where it believes it is acceptable in the eyes of God because of all these outer conditions. It thinks that by doing outer things for God, God will have to let it into the kingdom.

The mortal self is born from the illusion of separation, and therefore it uses the consciousness of separation in an attempt to create an illusion of oneness with God. Of course, that which is born of separation can never come back to oneness. The mortal self is trying to build an image, a golden calf, that is worthy in the eyes of God, and it uses the things of this world to build up that image. It is attempting to say that if it adds together enough "things" built from the duality consciousness, it will be worthy, it can build a tower that reaches into the heavens. No matter how many zeros you add together, they will never add up to one—the oneness with God.

This is an essential key to freeing yourself from the prison of the mortal self. The Conscious You can become whole by accepting its oneness with God whereas the mortal self can never do this. It is seeking to please the remote god, the idol of its own making. The Conscious You simply needs to stop dancing around this golden calf and climb the mountain of God, the mountain of self-transcendence.

***

The basic frame of mind of the mortal self is that it constantly feels threatened. It feels threatened because it is trying to uphold an illusion, an illusion of worthiness and authority that gives it a sense of security. The mortal self feels that as long as it can convince the Conscious You to believe in its illusion, it will be in control, it will survive. Your mortal self knows that if you were to separate yourself from its illusion, you would stop feeding it energy and thus it would die. To the mortal self, upholding its illusion is literally a matter of life and death. Unfortunately for the mortal self – and fortunately for you – everything in the material world is constantly seeking to tear down its illusion, its false sense of security. To understand the basic dilemma of the mortal self, consider the following:

• The Creator is constantly transcending itself. God is the River of Life that is constantly in the process of becoming more.

• The duality consciousness is separated from God, and it is not part of the River of Life.

• The duality consciousness and your mortal self cannot fathom that God is constantly transcending itself. It cannot experience God's Being directly. It can know God only by creating a mental image of God.

• The mortal self believes God is perfect, and it interprets perfection as something that could not and would not need to change. It believes God is static and it is seeking to create a non-changing image of God. This image inevitably becomes a graven image that will trap you in a limited view of God.

• God has given you free will so you have a right to adopt a graven image of God. Such an unchanging image automatically sets you outside the River of Life, and as long as you hold on to that image, you cannot inherit your Father's kingdom. You cannot have the abundant life.

• Because God loves you unconditionally, he does not want you to remain outside his abundance forever. He has designed the material universe in such a way that it always seeks to break down the illusion that you are separated from God. Every aspect of the material universe is designed to challenge the dualistic illusions created by the mortal self.

• The primary challenge to a dualistic world view comes from the duality consciousness itself. This state of consciousness is based on two relative opposites that seek to cancel out each other. If your mortal self goes too far into one relative extreme, its world view will inevitably be challenged by the opposite extreme.

Once again, there is a subtle distinction that cannot be grasped by the intellect but can be understood by the heart. When the Conscious You sees itself as one with the River of Life, you know with absolute certainty that God is the ultimate reality behind all surface appearances. You know that the Mother Light can take on any form, but only the forms that express the immaculate concept are ultimately real. Imperfect forms have only a temporary existence, and they have no actual power over you. They are based on an illusion, and if you do not accept the reality of this illusion, it cannot influence you. The prince of this world will come and have nothing in you—because you know that the prince of this world is not real.

When you are in the reality of God, you know there are no opposites, you know that nothing could ever oppose the reality of God. Only God has ultimate reality, and in God there are no divisions, no contradictions. When you partake of the duality consciousness – the knowledge of good and evil – you lose the direct experience of God's Being, of God's reality. You now enter a world – a house of mirrors – in which everything is defined by two relative opposites, such as good and evil. Your mortal self is born of separation from the River of Life, and – by its very nature – it has an absolute belief in the reality of relative good and evil. It believes both are real but that one can destroy the other.

The inevitable consequence is that if you believe relative good is real, you will also believe that relative evil is real. If you create a graven image of God, you will inevitably have to create a graven image of the opposite of your relative god, namely the devil. In the world of duality, nothing can exist without an opposite. As long as you believe your relative image of God is real, you will also believe your image of the devil is real. You believe the devil is as real as God, that evil is as real as good. In a sense, it is true that relative evil is as "real" as relative good, but when you step outside the duality consciousness, you see that only God is real and all that is less than God's absolute good is unreal. It has no objective existence but exists only in the minds of self-aware beings who are trapped in the duality consciousness. It has power over you only if you give it power, if you give it "reality" in your world view.

Consider the consequences of this. When you step into the world of duality, you automatically encounter a threat to everything you believe. This is inevitable because everything has an opposite. You cannot define an idea, a belief system, that will not be instantly opposed by its opposite. If you define something as good, there will instantly be an opposite that you then see as evil. Because you believe both relative opposites are real, you think it is possible for something to oppose and destroy your world view. You believe the devil is real and has the power to threaten you, and therefore you will feel threatened by anything that opposes your world view. This is why the mortal self constantly feels threatened, and this is why many religious people feel threatened by the devil.

My beloved, it is a great burden to my heart that so many people are afraid of the devil, are afraid of evil. Consider how different people deal with this threat. Many Christians fear the devil to such an extent that they dare not even consider ideas that are beyond their literal interpretation of the Bible. They would not even dare to read this course, fearing it is of the devil. Many New Age people are open to new ideas, but they deal with the threat of evil by ignoring it, by refusing to even consider it. Both types of people are trapped in the pattern of running away from something that seems threatening to their sense of security. They both fear evil, and their fear prevents them from taking a closer look at it. If they were willing to overcome their fear and take a closer look, they would realize that evil only exists in the realm of duality. The ultimate way to overcome evil is to separate the Conscious You from the mortal self. When you clear your four lower bodies of dualistic beliefs, the prince of this world will have nothing in you and thus you need not fear anything in this world.

Jesus, the Buddha and other spiritual leaders had no fear of the devil because they had internalized what I have just told you. They had become enlightened to the reality that there is no opposite to God, there is no opposite to Christ truth, to the Buddha nature. The mind of anti-christ thinks it is in opposition to the truth of Christ, but it is simply outside of, disconnected from, the reality of Christ. Anti-christ is trapped in its own world, a world that is inescapably dominated by two relative opposites. Anti-christ is not in opposition to Christ, but in opposition to its own relative version of Christ truth. Evil is not in opposition to the absolute good of God. Evil is a relative force that is in opposition to relative good. The reality of God and the truth of Christ are above all relative opposites. A Christed being is never pulled into the ongoing, dualistic struggle between two relative opposites. A Christed being never takes sides in the human power struggle, which is why the devil could not tempt Jesus. A Christed being stays true to the one vision, the single-eyed vision, of the Christ mind. He or she realizes that the kingdom of God will not be manifest by having relative good replace or eradicate relative evil. The kingdom of God will be manifest only when a critical mass of people rise above the entire dualistic struggle.

***

There is only one way for you to free yourself from the mortal self, and that is by transcending its dualistic mindset. In order to do this, it is helpful to realize that the mortal self will never see or admit that its graven image, its basic world view, is an illusion. If its belief system was proven wrong, the mortal self believes it would die—which is true. The very essence of the mortal self, the very modus operandi of the mortal self, is that its dualistic world view, its basic paradigm, can never be proven wrong. You will never convince the mortal self that it is living a lie, you will never make it see through the duality consciousness out of which it is born. The mortal self will forever be engaged in the impossible quest to prove the infallibility of its dualistic beliefs by defending them against the dualistic opposite of its beliefs.

The problem is that the mortal self has no reality. The Conscious You has a reality that is beyond its sense of identity, that is beyond the contents of the sphere of self. The Conscious You can exist independently of any ideas defined in this world. The mortal self has no independent reality. It simply cannot exist independently of the dualistic beliefs from which it was born. If those beliefs were proven wrong, the mortal self would cease to exist. Don't expect to have the mortal self voluntarily give up its attempts to maintain its existence. The bottom line is that the Conscious You created the mortal self and the Conscious You needs to "uncreate" that self by separating itself from it and letting it die.

The basic strategy of the mortal self is that it is trying to set itself up as a replacement for the immaculate concept for your Being, the immaculate concept stored in the universal Christ mind. This blueprint is meant to be the lodestone for your exercise of free will in the material realm, the rock of Christ that gives you a firm foundation for making decisions in alignment with God's laws. The mortal self is trying to use the consciousness of anti-christ to set itself up as the ultimate authority, as the representative of God, as the only begotten Son of the Father, as the Christ. It is trying to set itself up as a replacement for Christ truth, and it becomes an impostor of Christ that perverts Christ truth through the dualistic mind. It takes Christ truth and makes it relative, thereby turning it into the consciousness of death instead of the consciousness of life.

Your mortal self has set itself up as a false authority, and it claims that it knows better than anyone else how to run your life. You should allow the mortal self to run your life. If you do so, you are guaranteed to be saved; if you do not, you are guaranteed to go to hell. The mortal self's claim to a position of authority is a house built on sand. Consequently, the mortal self can maintain its position only by using fear, the fear that makes you afraid to take a closer look at its claim to authority. If you did take such a look, while asking for the guidance of your Christ self, you would see through the claims of the mortal self.

Instead of transcending itself and becoming more, the mortal self is trying to hold on to the dualistic image, the graven image, it has built. The graven image is being threatened by its very nature because it is disconnected from the River of Life. Nothing static can survive; it will constantly be threatened by the forward moving river of God's creation. How are the actual threats formed? The consciousness of duality is based on the creation of two relative extremes, two opposites. You may call them good or evil, black or white or anything else you desire. Regardless of the name, these polarities are opposites, yet both are outside of Christ truth. As long as you are trapped in duality, you cannot escape the contradiction and the conflict built into this frame of mind.

The mortal self has a desire to create the ultimate illusion of wholeness, the ultimate illusion of security, and it attempts to do this by defining an infallible belief system. Throughout history, various civilizations have defined a religious or political belief system and have declared it to be the ultimate system, meaning that it is based on an infallible or absolute truth. Any idea defined in the realm of duality has an opposite, and thus any "ultimate" belief system will, by its very nature, be threatened by an opposite idea. The people who adhere to such a belief system will feel threatened by those who are not "true believers." This gives rise to the need to convert other people or to force them to accept your beliefs. Carried to the extreme, you see the belief that it is justified by some ultimate authority, such as God or the forces of nature, that you kill all those who refuse to accept the only true belief system. Obviously, other people will want to survive so they will seek to destroy your absolute belief system, possibly by replacing it with their own infallible religion. If the mortal self moves too far into one dualistic extreme in order to build or defend its graven image, it will automatically generate an opposite reaction that seeks to break down its false image. Everything the mortal self does will generate a force that threatens its illusion, turning the life of the mortal self into an ongoing struggle to do what cannot be done.

The mortal self will never see that this struggle is created by itself because it can never see beyond the duality consciousness. The mortal self is completely convinced that its image is right, but that external forces are trying to destroy its true belief system. Because its image is absolutely right, everything else must be false, and the forces who believe in this false image are trying to destroy the mortal self and its true image. The universe is a mirror so if you send out the belief that you are threatened, the cosmic mirror will reflect back circumstances that do threaten your belief system. The purpose is to help you transcend your current beliefs by reaching for a higher understanding.

If you send out an impulse based on duality, the cosmic mirror reflects back conditions that outpicture duality, which inevitably causes your life to become a struggle. The message is that you need to transcend duality and reach for the Christ mind so the universe can reflect back the abundant life. The mortal self cannot fathom this concept, and thus it will simply dig its heels in the ground, doing everything possible to defend its graven image. The more your mortal self experiences a threatening reaction from the cosmic mirror, the more it thinks it needs to defend its image.

History shows many situations in which two groups of people were engaged in a conflict or even an outright war based on absolute belief systems. Each group claimed to have the absolute belief system and the absolute authority to eradicate all opposition to its beliefs. In many cases, each group believed that the survival of the entire world depended on the survival of its belief system. In reality, each group was defending a relative, dualistic belief system, which is clearly proven by the fact that each group was willing to use violence. When you depart from the way of love, you have set yourself outside the River of Life, and thus you simply cannot be representing the reality of God or the truth of Christ. When you resist evil, you have entered the realm of duality, and thus you have become part of evil. You are now part of the problem instead of being part of the solution.

The cosmic mirror is set up to reflect back what co-creators send out, in the hope that they can rise above any imperfect images by seeing an imperfect manifestation. Again, the message is simple, but the mortal self can never fathom it: "If I don't like what comes back, I must change what I send out." Or as Jesus put it 2,000 years ago: "Do unto others what you want them to do to you."

The cosmic mirror is designed to help you overcome any dualistic illusions in which you are trapped. When you confine your mind to a dualistic belief system, you inevitably begin to fear what opposes your beliefs. When you send fear into the cosmic mirror, you attract to you exactly what you fear. This gives you an opportunity to confront your fear and rise above it. If you let your mortal self run your life, you will only seek to destroy what seeks to threaten your beliefs. This traps you in an endless struggle to defend an illusion that is threatened by its own dualistic nature. The mortal self simply cannot realize that it is being threatened by the images it is sending into the cosmic mirror. It cannot see that the threat comes from itself. It can never escape this cycle of defending itself against self-created threats, and if you allow the mortal self to run your life, your life will be one long struggle. The only way out is that the Conscious You separates itself from the dualistic illusion of the mortal self and refuses to engage in its never-ending struggle.

***

The mortal self, by its very nature, creates the condition that threatens its world view. When the reflection comes back from the cosmic mirror, the mortal self is forced to deal with that condition. How does the mortal self deal with a threat to its belief system? It was God's hope for designing this universe that when people received unpleasant reactions from the cosmic mirror, they would realize that they need to change what they are sending out. Thereby, they can rise above their dualistic beliefs and return to the abundant life. This system can break down if the Conscious You refuses to make decisions and seeks to run away from challenging circumstances, allowing its reaction to be determined by the mortal self. The mortal self is completely focused on making it seem like its illusion is right, and therefore the mortal self does not ever have the thought that perhaps it needs to revise its belief system. Instead, it is focused on avoiding the threat, avoiding the unpleasant response from the universe. In order to avoid this, it goes into what psychologists call the flight or fight response.

The first impulse of the mortal self is to run away from the threat, to avoid it, to ignore it, to deny it or to explain it away by its dualistic reasoning. The duality consciousness can always come up with arguments that support what it wants to believe. To a large extent, the mortal self can be successful in deflecting the threat by explaining it away. In the matter realm, you cannot always avoid a threat, you cannot always run away from or deny physical circumstances. When the mortal self cannot flee a threat, it goes into the fight response, and now it seeks to destroy the threat. In many cases, that means seeking to destroy the people who represent the threat. This can mean physically destroying, as in actually killing these people, or it can mean destroying them through psychic means by forcing them into submission or by silencing them through physical or psychic violence.

In many cases, the mortal self can be successful in avoiding a threat through the flight or fight response. It is inevitable that by doing so the mortal self sends out another impulse. When that impulse is reflected back by the cosmic mirror, it will take the form of an even more severe threat to the illusion of the mortal self. This is what turns your life into a continuous struggle, and it is the mortal self which is responsible for accelerating this struggle. The mortal self is sending out an action that generates a reaction from the cosmic mirror, and the stronger the action, the stronger the reaction. This can accelerate to the point where your entire life feels like one big deficit, and you are constantly running to put out fires or deal with this or that crisis. The Conscious You cannot escape experiencing at least some of this struggle. You simply have to decide how long you will let it go on before you decide to take back responsibility for your life and take dominion over your sphere of self.

There are people whose lives are completely consumed by the impossible quest of the mortal self. If you had been one of these people, you would not have had the awareness or the desire to follow this course. Neither would you have been willing to spend the time and effort to read such long books. Yet, your mortal self will never give up its impossible quest. It will never be able to escape the flight or fight response. It will never be able to stop the attempts to prove that its image of the world is correct.

People who have some degree of spiritual awareness have managed to separate themselves somewhat from the mortal self. They have risen above the more obvious games played by the mortal self. For example, they would never think to kill members of a different religion. There are, however, many more subtle games played by the mortal self. The spiritual path is a process during which the Conscious You must be constantly reaching for a clearer vision of the truth of Christ. Only by doing so can you see through and transcend the dualistic beliefs that the mortal self and the prince of this world are using to keep you trapped behind the veil of illusions. No matter how advanced you might consider yourself to be, it is wise to keep in mind that as long as you are in the matter universe, it is necessary to look in the mirror and consider whether you need to pull another beam from your own eye.

The mortal self is subtle, and the only way to escape it is to transcend it—and transcendence never stops. If you are not constantly transcending yourself, your mortal self will find a way to adapt its world view to your current knowledge and beliefs. It will use those beliefs, even a particular religion or spiritual belief system, to build the image that you don't need to rise any higher, that you don't need to transcend your present level. This is precisely what causes many spiritual people to go into a blind alley that prevents them from making further progress, even though they are very close to breaking through and manifesting the Christ consciousness.

The only true escape from the treadmill of the mortal self is to separate the Conscious You completely from that self. In order to accomplish this, you need to accept that you are worthy to face God, you are worthy to come back to God's kingdom, which is an inner sense of oneness with God. You are worthy to be one with your Creator and serve as a co-creator in this realm. The mortal self has, at its very core, a black hole. You can never fill a black hole. The mortal self is attempting to use the things of this world in order to fill its black hole—it is taking the way that seems right onto a human. It attempts to build the image that if you belong to the only true religion, if you believe in the only true teaching, if you follow the only true teacher and if you do this or that outer action, then you will be worthy in the eyes of

God. This is a subtle and persuasive danger for many religious and spiritual people, especially when they have been on the path for a number of years.

Many people have been engaged in the spiritual quest for decades, and when they look back at their lives, they feel they have studied so much, they have understood so much, they have done so many outer things. They see that they truly have come up so much higher than they were ten, twenty or more years ago. The mortal self whispers in their ears: "You have done enough, you have climbed high enough up the mountain. You can stop here and enjoy the view and you don't need to continue all the way to the summit." This is a very subtle temptation, and unfortunately it has stopped many sincere seekers just before they were ready to break through and manifest the Christ consciousness. You must make a sincere effort to see through it and rise above it.

The key to rising above the golden calf of thinking that your outer accomplishments make you worthy in the eyes of God is to realize that you are worthy by the very fact that God created you. The Conscious You is created worthy, and at the core of your being is not a black hole but the sun of your I AM Presence. You might currently have a sense of unworthiness or a doubt about your worthiness. That sense is the darkness that is the absence of the light of your I AM Presence. When you let that light shine, it will replace the darkness and you will know that you are worthy. Your life will be transformed so that the quest to fill the black hole of the mortal self is turned into a life of abundance, so that the deficit is turned into a surplus. As you feel the unlimited light of God stream through your being, you will spontaneously focus on giving to others rather than getting from others.

***

Because of the nature of the dualistic mind, there is always a dichotomy which makes it difficult to reach many people on earth. The consciousness of duality presents a peculiar challenge for a spiritual teacher. Consider the difficulty I face. I want you to recognize who you are and to know, with an inner knowing, that the Conscious You is fully worthy in the eyes of God. In order to help you overcome the illusion that you are not worthy, I must present you with the truth of who you are. I must describe your highest potential so that you know what the summit of the mountain of God looks like. If you do not know where you are going, how can you avoid stopping before you get there?

The mortal self has at least two ways of preventing you from accepting my teaching, namely each of the dualistic extremes. I have to give you the highest goal, yet at your current level of consciousness this goal might seem far above you, it might seem beyond your reach. If you have a sense of unworthiness or if you doubt your ability to rise higher, the mortal self will attempt to use my teaching to discourage you from making a sincere effort. It will try to make you focus on the mistakes you have made and use them to say that you are not worthy to follow the spiritual path, you are not a truly spiritual person. Why even try, when the goal is so far beyond you? The spiritual path is all about self-transcendence, and how could you ever be unworthy to transcend yourself? No matter how low you might be on the spiral staircase, you are always worthy to take a step higher.

Another aspect of the duality consciousness is the sense of pride, the sense that because of this or that outer condition you are better than others and you don't need to rise higher. The mortal self will use my teaching to reinforce the pride of thinking that because you have done so much in the past and because you already understand so much, you don't have to worry about overcoming the remaining illusions of your mortal self. If you are still on earth, there is obviously something you have not transcended, some step you have not taken. As long as you are in this world, it is always necessary to be willing to take the next step. The spiritual path is all about self-transcendence and how could you ever reach a point from which you cannot transcend yourself? You can reach a point from which you are not willing to go higher, but at that moment you have set yourself outside the River of Life. You are no longer a truly spiritual person, even if your mortal self has built an illusion that you are an advanced soul because of everything you have done in the past. What you have done in the past counts for nothing if it prevents you from taking the very next step.

There is nothing I can say that cannot be used by your mortal self in its attempts to reinforce its dualistic illusion and that illusion's hold over you. If you allow your mortal self to use my teachings to reinforce its illusions, you will only become more trapped in these illusions. This, of course, is not what I want to see happen. That is why I need you, meaning the Conscious You, to take a step back and use the teachings in this course to reach beyond the reasoning of your mortal self. I need you to reach up for the higher truth, the single-eyed vision, of the Christ mind.

The consciousness of anti-christ defines two extremes, and I have talked about the middle way. I am not saying that in order to be free of the extremes you have to go to the midpoint between the two extremes, which would only be a compromise between the extremes. A compromise between two dualistic extremes is still in the realm of duality. If one extreme is white and one extreme is black, the midpoint between them would be gray. If you mix relative black and white, you are not any closer to seeing the truth of Christ; you only see grayness. Imagine the old days when photographers only had black and white film. Everything shown on a black and white photograph is completely accurate, except for the fact that it does not show color. A flower is depicted in every detail, except nature has no gray flowers. If you overexpose a photograph, it will be all white. If you underexpose it, it will be all black. If you expose it somewhere in the middle, it will have a correct and lifelike distribution of light and dark areas but it will still not show color. I need you to reach beyond the black and white and the gray of the duality consciousness. I need you to put a color film in the camera of your mind so that you can see the true colors of the Christ mind.

I know this might seem beyond you or it might seem like you already have Christ truth in an outer teaching. I am asking you to avoid being trapped in either extreme. Do not be discouraged and do not ignore the need to look for a higher understanding. I ask you to begin where you are – no matter where you think you are – and take small steps towards expanding your understanding. I ask you to keep in mind that in order to reach the ultimate goal, you must keep taking small steps, you must keep transcending your present level of awareness, for as long as you are in the matter realm—and beyond.

There are two reactions that can stop your progress. One is the belief that you are not worthy because you have so many flaws and you are currently so far below the ideal. If you believe this, you will not even try to escape the duality consciousness. The other reaction is that you are already worthy because you have done so many outer things. If you believe this, you will think you don't need to do anything (more) to escape the duality consciousness because you are already saved. Both reactions are equally flawed.

It is actually easier to escape the sense of being unworthy because such people realize they are lacking something. As long as they are willing to try, they will rise higher. The most difficult challenge for a spiritual teacher is to reach the people who think they are worthy because they have fallen prey to the illusion of the mortal self that their outer deeds make them worthy. Such people are almost impossible to reach, as it was impossible for Jesus to reach the scribes and Pharisees. The irony is that many of these people do have a higher spiritual attainment, but they have been tricked into stopping their growth just before they could have broken through to the Christ consciousness. This is a trap that I would like to see all students of this course avoid.

***

As an intermediate step towards accepting your true worthiness, I ask you to contemplate what I have said about the mortal self being engaged in an impossible quest to fill a black hole and that it is doing so by using the "things" of this world. The key to the abundant life is to stop thinking that you need anything from this world, anything from outside your higher self, your I AM Presence, in order to manifest the abundant life, in order to regain your wholeness.

You lost your sense of wholeness because you separated yourself from God whereby you became trapped in the duality consciousness. There is nothing you could do with the duality consciousness that will make you worthy, that will help you reclaim your sense of worthiness. You never lost your worthiness; you simply believed the illusion that you had lost it. The blueprint of your true identity is stored in the universal Christ mind and can never be lost or destroyed by anything that happens in the material universe, it can never be touched by the duality consciousness. When you take a black and white photograph of a sunset, you cannot see the beautiful colors on the photograph, but that has not removed the colors from the actual sunset. The fact that you have now replaced your sense of identity, your sense of worthiness, with a black and white image has done nothing to eradicate who you really are. You do not need to earn your worthiness. You don't have to do anything in this world in order to reclaim your worthiness. You need to come to the point where you realize that you never lost your worthiness, and in order to reclaim it, you simply have to accept it. You have to accept that you – meaning the Conscious You – is, always has been and always will be worthy in the eyes of God. You are worthy to face God, worthy to be one with God, worthy to be an extension of God in this realm. The Conscious You has the capacity to identify itself *with*, to identify itself *as*, anything it can conceive and believe, anything it can accept as reality. If you identify yourself as worthy, you *are* worthy.

The true key to manifesting abundance is to stop thinking that you need anything from this world in order to have abundance. You are designed to be a co-creator with God. As Jesus said: "My Father worketh hitherto; and I work" (John 5:17). This statement describes the essence of your relationship with God. You are here to bring God's light into this world and to superimpose the vision of Christ upon the Mother Light. You are here to be God in action, to be God in manifestation. This is what God designed you to do, and God designed you so that you have everything – within yourself – that you need in order to fulfill this task. It truly is the Father's good pleasure to give you his kingdom, meaning that God wants his kingdom to be manifest on earth. You need to develop a firm acceptance of the fact that God will give you everything you need in order to manifest the abundant life for yourself and make your contribution to manifesting the kingdom of God on earth.

In reality, everything you need in order to manifest the abundant life and fulfill your mission can and will be given to you by God. You are designed with the capacity to fathom the vision of Christ and to let the light of God flow through your four lower bodies. The key to manifesting the abundant life is to separate the Conscious You from the mortal self and its belief that it needs something from this world in order to build a sense of wholeness, of worthiness, of security. Wholeness can be found only by being who you truly are. When you know who you are, you will trust – you will know – that God will give you everything you need.

The mortal self and the prince of this world are constantly trying to prevent you from fulfilling your spiritual mission, they are constantly trying to prevent the kingdom of God from becoming a manifest reality on this planet. Their primary weapon is the belief that you need something from this world in order to be who you are, in order to fulfill your mission. What you need in order to manifest the abundant life is the light of God and the vision of Christ, both of which can and will be given to you from your I AM Presence and Christ self, which are already within your sphere of self.

The third ingredient needed is that the Conscious You must have the will power to bring the light and the vision down through the four lower bodies so that it can become a manifest reality in the matter realm. The only thing that God cannot give you is this will power. God supplies the light, and the universal Christ mind supplies the vision. What you have to supply is the will, and that is precisely why your mortal self and the prince of this world are doing everything in their power to undermine your will.

The God who will give you everything you need is *not* the external God, the remote being in the sky. Many religious people have come to the recognition that they need to look to God for everything they need. They are still looking to the external God, and this is an impossible quest. The true key is to recognize that the God who can and will give you everything you need is the internal God. God is not doing things *for* you; God is doing things *through* you. If you passively wait for God to do the work for you, how could you ever take up your intended role as a co-creator with God?

***

This requires a change in your outlook on life. In the modern world you obviously need to make money in order to survive. Many people believe that in order to have abundance, they need to have a job, which makes them dependent upon an employer for their livelihood. If you step back from this approach, you can develop a higher view. You can come to the understanding and the acceptance that you are not working for a particular company, organization or government. You are truly working for God. At this very moment, God is providing for your material needs through a particular employer, but your employer is just an intermediary. If you were no longer working for that particular employer, then surely God is fully capable of finding another way for you to manifest the material supply you need. You obviously need to do your part in order to find or manifest the right livelihood.

If you allow yourself to believe that your livelihood depends on an employer, depends on anything in this world, your sense of abundance will always be vulnerable. You could lose a job in a variety of ways. If you think your abundance depends on having that job, then if the job is lost so is your sense of abundance. If you accept that you truly *are* working for God, you realize that the source of your abundance is beyond this world and thus it can never be lost. If God does not give you abundance through one particular employer, then surely the infinite resourcefulness of God can find other ways to give you what you need. You can depend on God for everything, yet this must never become co-dependency that makes you think God will do all the work for you. There is a fundamental difference between co-dependency and co-creation.

Building this sense that God will provide for all your needs will require that you are willing to trust, even though you do not have a full understanding of your situation or a tangible proof of what will happen in the future. For example, you need to trust that if you do not have abundant supply right now, there is a reason for this. This could be caused by your past karma, by the need to learn a lesson or by some aspect of your divine plan. You cannot let a lack of supply destroy your faith that God will give you everything you need. In order to develop this faith, you need to realize that God will not give you everything your mortal self thinks it needs.

God will not satisfy the false desires that can never be filled. Your mortal self is trying to build a sense of security by using the things of this world, and thus it will never think it has enough material things or money. The reality is that you always have the supply you need in order to transcend your current limitations and take the next step up the spiral staircase.

You need to escape the illusion that you need a certain amount of money in order to fulfill your divine plan. What you need to do – at this very moment – in order to fulfill your divine plan is to take the very next step up the spiral staircase. You have exactly what you need in order to take that step, you have exactly what you need to transcend your current sense of limitation. Not having an abundance of money may be exactly what you need in order to overcome a particular dualistic belief. You need to trust that if you do not have something, the larger reason is that you do not need it. You don't need it in order to take the next step on the spiritual path. You can stop worrying about what you don't have and focus all attention on getting the higher understanding that will empower you to make the best possible use of what you do have. When you prove yourself faithful over the few things you currently have, then surely God will make you ruler over many things.

***

There is a fundamental difference between *doing* and *being*. Your mortal self is absorbed in the quest of trying to do its way into heaven. It thinks you are here to do something for God, and if you do enough and do the right things, God will have to accept the mortal self. If the Conscious You believes in this illusion, you will become absorbed in the quest of trying to do your way back to heaven. There is nothing you could *do* that will bring you into heaven. There is only one way for you to inherit the kingdom of God, and that is to simply *be* who you are. The Conscious You must come to the point of accepting its true identity as a co-creator with God. When you fully accept that identity, you will *be* in heaven. You have not *done* your way into heaven, you are simply *being* in heaven right where you are, right in the present moment. You have overcome the illusion that you are separated from God and thus outside God's kingdom. Everything was created out of the Being of the Creator and God is within everything that was made. You *are* in God's kingdom right now, you simply need to overcome the illusion that you are separated from that kingdom. Only when you overcome that illusion, will you be in God's kingdom.

Consider one of the problems that the dualistic state of consciousness presents to a spiritual teacher. I have given you the concept of a path or a spiral staircase. In order to get back to heaven, you are taking one step at a time up that spiral staircase. There is nothing wrong with this image, and at a certain stage of your spiritual path, it is truly a very useful and very helpful image. There will come a point when the image of a path is no longer helpful. It can become a blind alley because the essence of walking a path implies distance. You are "here," you are going somewhere else, and in order to get "there" you have to keep taking one step at a time. The concept of a path implies that you have not yet arrived, that you are on your way. As long as you have to take another step, you have not arrived at the ultimate destination. There will come a point when you have reached the top of the spiral staircase, and at that point you must give up the idea that you still have a distance to travel. You must stop believing that you have many more steps to take. You must stop focusing on taking the next step. There comes a point where you have to take the final step, which is to realize and accept that there are no more steps; that you have arrived. At a certain level of the path, you are separated in consciousness from the kingdom of God. That separation is built from a number of dualistic illusions that you have allowed into your sphere of self. The Conscious You is so absorbed in, identified with, these illusions that it cannot instantly separate itself from all of them. If it were to do so, it would lose all sense of continuity, all sense of who it is. You throw out one illusion at a time, and you gradually reclaim your true identity as the God-free, spiritual being that you are.

There comes a point when you need to throw away the final illusion, the illusion that caused you to separate yourself from God in the first place. You need to accept that you are now in God's kingdom, that you are no longer on the way to a remote destination, but that you have actually arrived. If your mind is still focused on the image of a path, you might be thinking that you have to continue to take one step at a time. You maintain the sense of distance. You think there is an actual distance to travel instead of realizing that the real problem is the *sense* of distance. This sense of distance is an illusion that only exists in your mind. You have all along been inside God's kingdom without realizing where you are.

The final step on the spiral staircase is to step away from the staircase and accept that you always have been in the kingdom of God because there is no place else. In reality, the kingdom of God is where you are. In order to get to the kingdom of God, you have to travel along a path. But you will not arrive in the kingdom of God until you leave behind the path and accept that you *are* in the kingdom—*right now, right here.*

Being in the kingdom of God does not mean that self-transcendence stops. The kingdom of God is the River of Life that is always in the process of becoming more. Again, this is a subtle distinction that the mortal self cannot fathom. The goal of walking the spiritual path is not to arrive at an ultimate destination at which all progress stops. The problem you face is that you have descended into the duality consciousness, which means that you have become separated from the River of Life. Your growth has stopped or slowed down, but the River of Life has moved on without you because its progress never stops. The goal of the spiritual path is to traverse the steps that will bring you back to the River of Life. You are trying to get back to the place in the river where you would have been if you had not descended into the duality consciousness. When you reach the final step of the spiritual path, you immerse yourself in the River of Life. You are now moving with and in the River of Life instead of being behind trying to catch up. The River of Life is not a path because there are no distinct steps, just the smooth, never-ending flow of God's Being in which all life is one undivided whole.

***

While you are still traveling along the path, it is necessary for you to *do* certain things in order to rise higher, in order to expose the dualistic illusions. There comes a point when you have to stop *doing,* you have to stop thinking that you need something from outside yourself, that you need to do something in this world. You have to focus within and focus on receiving what God gives you freely. What is the key to receiving what God gives you freely? The first step towards receiving is to start giving. There may be people who are still so trapped in duality and separation that they are not capable of giving of themselves. When you reach a certain level on the spiritual path, you cannot progress any further until you start giving. This is precisely where many spiritual seekers get stuck. It is not enough to give with outer motives, with the dualistic motives of the mortal self. The mortal self is quite capable of giving, but it does so only to get something for itself. It does so from the limited vision of its own dualistic world view. In order to truly give, you need to separate the Conscious You from this vision so that you can give from the greater vision of the Christ mind that considers the need to raise all life.

When you give this way, you give selflessly, meaning that you are giving to raise the whole rather than to benefit only one part—yourself. You give without expecting a particular reward, even without expecting any return. This is the kind of giving that will multiply your talents, and it will inevitably cause the cosmic mirror to reflect back a more abundant life. True giving means that the act of giving is separated from any consideration of a return. You give because you know you are a sun, a flame, of God's light and it is your nature to give, to radiate light. You do not give in order to get something back. You give because it is your nature to share who you are. Pure giving carries its own reward. It is in the act of giving that you feel the reward of inner fulfillment. This is the inner sense of wholeness, of knowing you have more than enough to give, that is the truly abundant life.

You receive freely from God because God expects no return from you. Giving freely means giving without expecting a return. The key to getting out of the sense of lack that prevents you from giving freely is to realize that you are here to bring God's kingdom by magnifying everything whereby the imperfections around you are transformed and become more. I talked about the flight or fight response of the mortal self. I talked about how the mortal self can become very subtle at the higher stages of the path. Many spiritual seekers, many people who have sincerely walked the spiritual path for decades, are still stuck in a very subtle version of the flight or fight response. They seek to run away from what seems to threaten their sense of security, anything that demands that they transcend themselves. If they cannot run away from it, they seek to stop it from disturbing them. These people are not trying to kill other people, but they are trying to prevent others from shaking their world view. When you are caught in this flight or fight response, you will inevitably shut off the flow of God's love through you.

When someone or something threatens your sense of equilibrium, your sense of being in control, your sense of security, you try to run away from it or fight it. This automatically shuts off the flow of God's light and love through your being. You are accepting the lie presented by the prince of this world, namely that this imperfect condition cannot be changed by God's light and love. You are refusing to let the light and love flow through your being and magnify that condition, thereby transforming it into a higher state. In refusing to let the light and love flow through you, you are shutting off the flow of life and thereby taking away your own sense of joy, your sense of abundance. The same happens when you attempt to fight a threat. You are again shutting off the flow of God's light, refusing to transform the imperfect condition into something higher. You are seeking to stop other people from bothering you rather than holding the immaculate concept that the people will be set free from the dualistic beliefs that caused them to do what they are doing.

Abundance is the opposite of lack. If you are in a state of abundance, you have more than you need for yourself, and the natural reaction is to give of your abundance to others. That is why God is giving of himself to you. If you refuse to give, you will shut off the sense of abundance and thus set yourself outside the River of Life. You will project an image of lack into the cosmic mirror, and guess what the mirror must inevitably reflect back to you?

There are people on earth who are trapped in the lower versions of this flight or fight response, and you see this outplayed in wars or feuds going on all over this planet. Most spiritual people have risen above this more obvious ego-game and would never even consider killing other people to seek revenge. They are still trapped in a more subtle version, which causes them to allow the imperfections on earth or the faults of other people to shut off the flow of God's light and love through their beings. If you are to have the abundant life, you must rise above the tendency to let anything in this world cause you to shut off the flow of light through your being. You must be the sun that always shines. You must see all imperfect appearances as being something real that has been trapped in an imperfect matrix, trapped by a graven image. It is either the conscious selves of other people that are trapped in the duality consciousness or the Mother Light that is trapped in an imperfect form. Your goal is to set both other people and the Mother Light free from all imperfections. You can do this in only one way, namely by helping them transcend their current imperfections and become more, thereby coming closer to the immaculate concept.

***

You have a choice to make. You can continue for the rest of your life to be trapped in this flight or fight response. Or you can make a very sincere and determined effort to rise above it. Everything I have given you in this course represents a key, a step, that allows you to rise above this endless game of the mortal self. As you apply these tools, you will indeed rise higher, but I will give you one more tool that can be a very effective intermediate step for anchoring yourself on the path to abundance.

This tool is based on the recognition that you are here to transform everything so that it will outpicture a more perfect image. You are not here to run away from imperfections or to destroy any imperfect form.

You are here to transform imperfections into the perfection of the kingdom of God. The essential tool that you can adopt right now is the practice that in every situation you encounter, you seek to bless everyone involved and you seek to bless the outer conditions. No matter how challenging the situation might be, no matter what other people do to you or don't do for you, always seek to bless them so that they can get to know better and thereby do better.

Be very alert to the tendency of your mortal self to trap you in a flight or fight response. When you feel this temptation from the mortal self and the prince of this world, go within your heart and focus on allowing the unconditional love of God to flow into the situation. Visualize the immaculate concept for how the situation could be transformed. Then, deliberately bless everything and everyone—with no desire for revenge or punishment but with a pure desire to see everything come closer to the perfect vision of the Christ mind. You can make up your own affirmations and visualizations if you like, but here are some suggestions:

I AM blessing this situation with the unconditional love of God that restores all to the immaculate concept, now and forever.

I AM blessing the Mother Light behind these appearances and I see it outpicture the perfect vision of Christ, now and forever.

Affirmation for when you are in a conflict with other people:

I AM blessing you with the unconditional love of God and I hold the immaculate concept for you.

I AM THAT I AM takes dominion here, now and forever!

I AM the River of Life, flooding this situation with unconditional love.

I AM being the Christ in action in this situation.

Visualization: Visualize your preferred image of me, Jesus or another spiritual master over the situation.

Visualization: Visualize that a person or situation is enveloped in tongues of living fire, a spiritual fire:

• Blue fire has the function of protection and realigning everything with the will of God.

• Golden yellow fire releases the wisdom of the Christ mind.

• Pink fire releases the unconditional love of God.

• White fire has the function of purification.

• Emerald green fire releases the immaculate concept and heals all imbalances.

• Purple and golden fire releases the peace of God.

- Violet fire transforms all imperfect energies and sets the Mother Light free to manifest a more perfect image.

Visualization: Look beyond the outer situation, person or manifestation. Visualize that behind outer appearances are infinite numbers of scintillating points of brilliant white light. It is almost like infinitely small particles of light that are vibrating, pulsing and radiating white light. Visualize that the outer appearances dissolve into a sea of these white, pulsating particles of the pure Mother Light. Then see how the particles form a holy image. This can be myself, Jesus, any other spiritual figure or even a beautiful sunset. Then see how the holy image is superimposed upon the outer situation and transforms it into the immaculate concept. If you cannot grasp a higher vision for the actual situation, allow the holy image to replace the imperfect conditions and accept that your higher being will visualize the perfect outcome of the situation. Use this visualization for any imperfect condition, including diseases. For example, you can visualize the diseased organ or body part dissolved into the pure Mother Light and then replaced by a more perfect vision. You can also combine this visualization with one or more affirmations.

Pick an affirmation or visualization that has a deeper meaning to you. Whenever you encounter an imperfect situation, use the affirmation (silently or aloud) or the visualization to avoid being trapped in a dualistic reaction, especially the reaction of thinking the situation is beyond change. If you take only one thing away from this course, the most important thing you can take with you is this:

- Bless everything and everyone you encounter.

Your Life's Plan for Abundance

- Bless every situation, bless every condition, bless every person and don't forget to bless yourself.

- Never accept any limitation as permanent or unchangeable.

- Always look beyond the outer conditions and reach for the higher vision of the Christ mind.

- Wherever you are, always take the next step.

- Whatever you know, always reach for a higher understanding.

I have told you many times that the universe is a mirror. If you bless everyone and everything you encounter – even if your outer mind thinks they don't deserve it – what do you think the cosmic mirror will reflect back to you? Can it do anything but bless you? What you do onto others, the universe will surely do onto you.

Never forget that God is not an angry God. He does not want to punish anyone, no matter what they have done; he wants to set them free from imperfections. God knows that he created perfect co-creators and thus there are no bad co-creators. All mistakes and imperfections arise from the duality consciousness so the only solution is to raise everything beyond duality. One of the most common problems on earth is that when someone does something to you, you react with negative feelings. You form a negative image of the other person, and you think it is permanent and infallible. You think the person is "bad" and thus deserves to be punished by remaining in a state of limitation and imperfection. You reason that the other person does not deserve to receive God's love through you, and you shut off the flow of light through your being. God wants all of his sons and daughters to become free of the duality consciousness, to become more and thus come home to his kingdom. God doesn't want to hold anyone in a state of limitation. When you hold on to any limited image, any graven image, or seek to punish others, you are setting yourself apart from the basic force of the universe, from the River of Life. If you are not seeking to help others become more, how can *you* become more? If you send into the cosmic mirror the desire to keep other people trapped in limitations, what must the mirror reflect back to you? How can you be truly free until you have a genuine desire to set others free? The Conscious You does have this desire, whereas the mortal self does not. Always bless everyone and everything. Cultivate a pure desire to see all imperfections rise above their current limitations. If you do this, how can the universe fail to reflect back to you conditions that raise you above all limitations?

***

I am not trying to say that you should shut off your creative abilities. The main problem you face is that you did shut off these abilities because you no longer wanted to make decisions. You can never stop co-creating so if you give away your power to make decisions, you are still co-creating. Only, you are now co-creating through the dualistic images created by your mortal self. I am not saying that you need to destroy these images so you have no images in your mind. Because your dualistic images have created imperfect consequences, it might seem safer to have no images in your mind, yet that simply isn't constructive. As long as you are in a physical body on earth, your mind – meaning all of your four lower bodies – can never be truly empty and you will always be co-creating. Instead of seeking to empty your mind of all images, it is far more constructive to empty it of dualistic images and fill it with the images of the Christ mind. Only dualistic images will create imperfect consequences. If you co-create through the perfect images of the Christ mind, you will indeed have the abundant life reflected back to you from the cosmic mirror.

You are here to bring the kingdom of God into manifestation on earth. That kingdom is not presently in manifestation. The way to bring it into manifestation is to envision an image that is not yet manifest in the matter realm. As you bring that image down through your four lower bodies, you superimpose it upon the Mother Light, making the light outpicture your image. This is the basic process of creation, and God has no desire to see you shut off your creative abilities. God wants you to use them by co-creating based on the true vision of the Christ mind instead of ego-creating through the dualistic vision of the mortal self. Seek to raise your vision so you can focus on the pure images of the Christ mind. This is what will inevitably happen as you purify your four lower bodies. If you will use the tools I have given you in this course, you will gradually move towards that goal.

Your life can be seen as a constant game, a constant contest or even a battle, between the Conscious You on one side and your mortal self and the prince of this world on the other side. The enemy within and the enemy without are constantly seeking to trap you in the illusion that because of this or that imperfection – in your own consciousness or in the material world – you have to shut off the flow of God's light and love through your being. They are trying to make you accept conditions for shutting off the flow of light that can transform all imperfections. This is one of the reasons Jesus told people not to judge (Matthew 7:1). When you judge with the outer mind, with the analytical mind, you are defining conditions. You are taking the approach that if people or situations do not live up to your conditions, your expectations, you will not give them love. Don't engage in this age-old battle between the false gods of the duality consciousness. Don't allow yourself to be pulled into seeing your mortal self, other people or the prince of this world as enemies. Don't resist evil (Matthew 5:39), simply transcend it and all of its dualistic games.

For a very long time, people on earth have been programmed to believe that there is an epic battle between good and evil. You find this theme in many older religions, but those religions were given when the collective consciousness was at a lower level than today. You will also see it in mythology and even in the modern entertainment industry. It is a common theme in books and movies that a group of "bad guys" start terrorizing innocent people. In the beginning, the hero tries to stay away from confrontation, but eventually things get so bad that he can no longer ignore the forces of evil. He then engages in violence to destroy the bad guys and overcome evil. This is a very persuasive image that has been programmed into people's minds from many sources. Although it may sound right, I can assure you that it springs from the consciousness of anti-christ. The prince of this world knows that the duality consciousness is based on two extremes, and he is skillfully using them to control people. The plot is very simple, and very effective. The prince of this world is trying to make all people believe that there truly is a battle between good and evil on this planet, that the forces of evil truly are in opposition to God and that they have real power. The purpose is to get everyone to engage in a battle against what they perceive as evil. Thereby, they will respond to situations with negative feelings and generate huge amounts of misqualified energy that will feed the forces of darkness.

Many spiritual people have been pulled into this battle, and their lives have been swallowed up by a struggle that truly has

Your Life's Plan for Abundance

done nothing to raise the collective consciousness and bring the kingdom of God closer to physical manifestation. This is the main force behind all religious conflicts, and such conflicts have created incredible atrocities. If you are to take up your role as a co-creator with God, as a guardian of the Mother Light, you need to stay away from this age-old, never-ending battle between the forces of relative good and relative evil. In order to avoid being pulled into this trap, you need to fully internalize the deeper meaning behind Jesus' statement: "Ye have heard that it hath been said, An eye for an eye, and a tooth for a tooth: But I say unto you, That ye resist not evil: but whosoever shall smite thee on thy right cheek, turn to him the other also" (Matthew 5:38-39). What Jesus gave people in this seemingly simple teaching is a way out of the duality consciousness—the *only* way out of the duality consciousness.

The entire plot of the prince of this world is to draw you into a conflict between two relative opposites so that you respond to life with negative feelings and thus bind yourself more firmly to the dualistic struggle. The only way to avoid being pulled into this downward spiral, this black hole, is to respond to every situation with divine love. You never allow anything to cause you to shut off the flow of divine love through your being. You seek to bless everything so that it will be accelerated beyond its current state of imperfection. You seek to bless people so they will transcend the duality consciousness that causes them to violate others. Evil has no ultimate reality. It is not in opposition to God. There truly is no battle between God and the devil because God recognizes no opposition, his eyes are too pure to behold evil (Habakkuk 1:13) because he sees only the immaculate concept. The battle between good and evil can exist only in the realm of duality, and it can continue to exist only as long as people remain trapped in the duality consciousness and therefore continue to throw wood on the fire. The ultimate planetary solution is that a

critical mass of people separate themselves from the consciousness of duality by separating their conscious selves from their
mortal selves. When a critical mass of people manifest the Christ
consciousness, you will see a shift in the collective consciousness. Many more people will then be able to grasp the truth I
have told you here, a truth that is currently beyond most people.

In order to make a personal contribution to this planetary
transformation, start by adopting the attitude that you are here
to bless and magnify everything. You are not here to preserve
things the way they are or to reinforce imperfections. You do
not give your light indiscriminately. You are here to raise up
everything so that it can transcend imperfections. You do this
by letting the light of God flow unconditionally whereby the
light can do its work according to a higher vision, perhaps even
a higher vision than you can grasp with your outer mind. You
do not need to judge with the outer mind what the light and
the love should be doing. You need to let if flow and let it do
its work. In some cases it will be supportive of people, in other
cases it will challenge people's illusions. In each case, the love
of God, the light of God, will magnify the situation and raise it
higher according to the vision of Christ. This vision will always
be very different from the dualistic vision that your mortal self
and the prince of this world want you to accept. That is why you
need to be independent of the forces of this world and let your
light shine no matter what other people do to stop you. You
are not here to adapt to the ways of the world; you are here to
transform the ways of the world by being true to who you are.
As the poet said: "To thine own self be true ..."

***

The true key to happiness, the true key to peace of mind,
is to overcome the tendency to judge everything according to

a dualistic standard. You need to escape the trap of constantly seeking to force the universe to live up to a set of dualistic expectations, expectations that can never be fulfilled because they are out of alignment with the truth of the Christ mind. If you want peace of mind, if you want true happiness, allow your dualistic expectations to die one by one. After all, do you remember signing a contract before coming into embodiment, a contract that would guarantee you anything in this world? There is no such contract, even though your mortal self believes there is. The contract you have with God is that he gave you free will and that you resumed full responsibility for the consequences of your choices. If you do not like the consequences that are currently being mirrored back to you by the universe, you only need to change what you are sending out. In order to do that, you need to let go of the dualistic expectations that cause you to send out imperfect images. Simply let them go and reach for the higher vision of the Christ mind. When you do so, you will overcome the sense that you can be threatened by anything in this world. You will overcome the sense of struggle.

When you know who you really are and see the greater purpose for which you came into the material universe, the petty, self-centered expectations and desires of your mortal self will seem so insignificant that you will spontaneously let them pass into the all-consuming fire of God's love. You will truly say with Paul: "When I was a child, I spake as a child, I understood as a child, I thought as a child: but when I became a man, I put away childish things" (1Corinthians 13:11). If you have been able to follow this long course, you are no longer a child, spiritually speaking. It is time to put away the childish expectations and beliefs of your mortal self and reach for the higher vision for why you are on planet earth in this crucial age. It is time to put away the dualistic beliefs and the selfishness that spring from the mortal self. It is time to look beyond yourself and realize that you are here as part of a large group of spiritual beings who volunteered to take embodiment at this time in order to help bring God's kingdom to earth. You are here for a purpose that is far grander than any of the desires of your mortal self.

You will find ultimate fulfillment, the ultimate sense of abundance, only when you plunge yourself into the River of Life and feel that you are now fulfilling your reason for being. There comes a point on the spiritual path when it is time to make a very serious decision and step up to an entirely different approach to life, an approach that is not centered around the little self but around the greater Self that you truly are. If you have read everything I have said up until this point, it is time for you to make that decision. It is time to accept that you are not a human being, it is time to start living like the spiritual being you truly are.

How can you do this? You can ultimately do so in only one way, namely by plunging yourself unconditionally into the River of Life and allowing that river to flow through you and take you where you need to go—regardless of where the dualistic, ego-centered expectations of your mortal self say you *should* go. This is truly the ultimate challenge, and I know it is not an easy task to let go of all expectations of how your life should unfold.

Even Jesus found this difficult, as evidenced by the struggle he endured in the Garden at Gethsemane the day before his trial. He was sweating drops of blood because he was fighting against the entire anti-will of the collective consciousness of humankind, the anti-will that did not want to see Jesus fulfill his mission of demonstrating the path to Christhood for all people. What made him vulnerable to that collective anti-will was the anti-will of his mortal self that still had some hold over him. After struggling with this for an hour, he finally realized that the only way out was full and unconditional surrender, and that is when he said: "Nevertheless, not as I will, but as thou

Your Life's Plan for Abundance

wilt" (Matthew 26:39). It was this unconditional surrender to the higher will that set Jesus fully free from the anti-will on both the personal and the planetary level. You too can come to that surrender by realizing that the higher will to which you need to surrender is not the will of an external being. It is the will of your own higher Being, the will that the Conscious You used when you created your divine plan. What you need to surrender is not your own will but the dualistic, ego-crazed will of your mortal self that truly is alien to your own will.

Only when you fully surrender to your highest will, can you let go of all of the graven images of your mortal self. Once again, a graven image is an image that stands still, that does not flow with the River of Life. Be aware of a very subtle distinction here. It is possible that your mortal self can have a correct image of God, the world and yourself. Many religious people adhere to doctrines that are not technically incorrect, meaning that they do not spring from the mind of anti-christ. Once you believe the doctrine is infallible and that an infallible doctrine could never change, could never be replaced by a higher understanding, you have turned a true spiritual teaching into a graven image. Imagine that you had never seen a river and someone showed you a still photo of a raging stream. You would think a river was made from ice that never moves. In reality, the river is constantly moving so a still photo can never give you a correct image of a river. The photo does give an accurate depiction of what the river looked like at the exact moment the picture was taken. Yet the river has now moved on and the image has changed. To fully know what a river is like, you need to experience its perpetual movement. Only when you realize that a river never stands still, can you truly appreciate the nature of a river.

It is possible to give a spiritual teaching that gives a correct understanding of what God was like at the moment the teaching was given. Only when you experience the self-transcending

River of Life, can you fully appreciate the nature of God. You can experience that River of Life only when you are fully submerged in it, flowing with it and thus experiencing the abundant life that will forever become more in a cosmic dance of such beauty and joy that the mortal self can never comprehend it. Leave the desert of the mortal self behind and dare to plunge yourself into the Living Waters of the River of Life. Dare to let your mortal self die so that the real you can be reborn into your true identity as an integral part of God's magnificent creation. Join me as we move forwards towards the infinite horizon of God's self-awareness that truly can become *your* self-awareness. God is All and in all. Dare to be more than the mortal self and you too can be All and in all. Dare to let your light so shine before people, that they may see your good works and glorify your Father – their Father – which is in all life.

16 | I INVOKE THE MANIFESTATION OF THE ABUNDANT LIFE

In the name I AM THAT I AM, Jesus Christ, I call to all representatives of the Divine Mother and the Divine Father, especially Alpha, Omega and Mother Mary, to help me attune to both my greater purpose for bringing my God Flame into the material world and my specific purpose for this lifetime. Help me accept my creative powers and see the factors that block the flow of my God-given creativity, including...

[Make personal calls.]

1. I am inherently worthy

1. I need nothing from this world, nothing from outside my I AM Presence, in order to manifest the abundant life, in order to regain my wholeness.

Beloved Alpha, God's great plan,
in Central Sun it all began,
what wondrous vision of a world,
the cosmic spheres were then unfurled.

**Beloved Alpha, in your light,
I now see God with inner sight,
as man I will no longer live,
my life to God I fully give.**

2. I never lost my worthiness; I simply believed the illusion that I had lost it. The blueprint of my true identity is stored in the universal Christ mind and can never be lost or destroyed by anything that happens in the material universe, it can never be touched by the duality consciousness.

Beloved Alpha, serve the All,
this is Creator's timeless call,
from out Creator's perfect whole,
sprang lifestreams with a sacred goal.

**Beloved Alpha, in your light,
I now see God with inner sight,
as man I will no longer live,
my life to God I fully give.**

3. I don't need to earn my worthiness. I don't have to do anything in this world in order to reclaim my worthiness.

Beloved Alpha, all was one,
as we were sent from Central Sun,
to you we shall in time return,
for cosmic union we do yearn.

**Beloved Alpha, in your light,
I now see God with inner sight,
as man I will no longer live,
my life to God I fully give.**

4. I realize that I never lost my worthiness, and in order to reclaim it, I simply have to accept it. I accept that I always have been and always will be worthy in the eyes of God. I am worthy to face God, worthy to be one with God, worthy to be an extension of God in this realm.

Beloved Alpha, I now see,
you with Omega form the key,
it was from your polarity,
that I received identity.

**Beloved Alpha, in your light,
I now see God with inner sight,
as man I will no longer live,
my life to God I fully give.**

5. I am designed to be a co-creator with God. God designed me so that I have everything within myself that I need in order to fulfill this task. It truly is the Father's good pleasure to give me his kingdom, meaning that God wants his kingdom to be manifest on earth.

Beloved Alpha, cosmic gate,
the nexus of your figure-eight,
I sprang from Cosmic Cube so bright,
I am at heart a spark of light.

Beloved Alpha, in your light,
I now see God with inner sight,
as man I will no longer live,
my life to God I fully give.

6. I have a firm acceptance of the fact that God will give me everything I need in order to manifest the abundant life for myself and make my contribution to manifesting the kingdom of God on earth. Everything I need in order to manifest the abundant life and fulfill my mission can and will be given to me by God.

Beloved Alpha, from your womb,
I did descend to matter's tomb,
but buried I will be no more,
my inner vision you restore.

Beloved Alpha, in your light,
I now see God with inner sight,
as man I will no longer live,
my life to God I fully give.

7. I am designed with the capacity to fathom the vision of Christ and to let the light of God flow through my four lower bodies. I am separating the Conscious You from the mortal self and I know I need nothing from this world in order to build a sense of wholeness, of worthiness, of security.

Beloved Alpha, I now know,
the love you did on me bestow,
a co-creator, I will bring,
the light to make all matter sing.

Beloved Alpha, in your light,
I now see God with inner sight,
as man I will no longer live,
my life to God I fully give.

8. Wholeness can be found only by being who I truly am. I know who I am and I trust – I know – that God will give me everything I need. What I truly need in order to manifest the abundant life is the light of God and the vision of Christ, which are already within my sphere of self.

Beloved Alpha, on this earth,
a new age we are giving birth,
for we are here to bring the love,
that you are sending from Above.

Beloved Alpha, in your light,
I now see God with inner sight,
as man I will no longer live,
my life to God I fully give.

9. I have the will power to bring the light and the vision down through my four lower bodies so that it can become a manifest reality in the matter realm. I am choosing to provide this will power.

Beloved Alpha, you and me,
we form a true polarity,
as up Above, so here below,
with life's own river I do flow.

Beloved Alpha, in your light,
I now see God with inner sight,
as man I will no longer live,
my life to God I fully give.

2. God gives me everything I need

1. The God who will give me everything I need is not the external God, the remote being in the sky. The God who *can* and *will* give me everything I need is the internal God.

Omega, I now meditate,
upon your throne in cosmic gate.
I'm born out of the figure-eight,
that Alpha and you co-create.

O Song of Life, you vitalize,
all hearts you truly synchronize.
O Sacred Sound, you alchemize,
turn earth into a paradise.

2. God is not doing things *for* me; God is doing things *through* me. I am truly working for God. God is fully capable of finding a way for me to manifest the material supply I need. I am doing my part in order to find or manifest the right livelihood.

Omega, in your sacred space,
my cosmic parents I embrace.
I see that it is such a grace,
that I take part in cosmic race.

O Song of Life, you vitalize,
all hearts you truly synchronize.
O Sacred Sound, you alchemize,
turn earth into a paradise.

3. I know God will provide for all my needs, even though I do not have a full understanding of my situation. I trust that if I do not have abundant supply right now, there is a lesson I need to learn. I am asking my Christ self to help me learn this lesson.

Omega in the Central Sun,
you show me life is cosmic fun.
And thus a victory is won,
my homeward journey has begun.

O Song of Life, you vitalize,
all hearts you truly synchronize.
O Sacred Sound, you alchemize,
turn earth into a paradise.

4. I always have what I need in order to transcend my current limitations and take the next step up the spiral staircase. I surrender the illusion that I need a certain amount of money in order to fulfill my divine plan.

Omega, femininity
is doorway to infinity.
With you I have affinity,
to know my own divinity.

**O Song of Life, you vitalize,
all hearts you truly synchronize.
O Sacred Sound, you alchemize,
turn earth into a paradise.**

5. At this moment, I am focused on taking the very next step up the spiral staircase of consciousness. I have exactly what I need to take that step, I have exactly what I need to transcend my current sense of limitation.

Omega, in your cosmic flow,
my plan divine I clearly know.
My heart is now a lamp aglow,
as love on all I do bestow.

**O Song of Life, you vitalize,
all hearts you truly synchronize.
O Sacred Sound, you alchemize,
turn earth into a paradise.**

6. I choose to stop worrying about what I don't have. I focus all attention on getting the higher understanding that will empower me to make the best possible use of what I do have. When I prove myself faithful over what I currently have, God *will* make me ruler over many things.

Omega, cosmic Mother Flame,
this is the light from which I came.
As I take part in cosmic game,
Christ victory I do proclaim.

O Song of Life, you vitalize,
all hearts you truly synchronize.
O Sacred Sound, you alchemize,
turn earth into a paradise.

7. There is nothing I could do that will bring me into Heaven. There is only one way for me to inherit the kingdom of God, and that is to simply be who I am. I am *being* in Heaven right where I am, right in the present moment.

Omega, I now comprehend,
why I did to earth descend.
And thus I fully do intend,
to help this planet to ascend.

O Song of Life, you vitalize,
all hearts you truly synchronize.
O Sacred Sound, you alchemize,
turn earth into a paradise.

8. I surrender the final illusion, the illusion that caused me to separate myself from God in the first place. I accept that I am now in God's kingdom, that I am no longer on the way to a remote destination, but that I have actually arrived. The kingdom of God is where I AM.

Omega, I do now aspire,
to join the ranks of cosmic choir.
My heart burns with a Christic fire,
that is this planet's sanctifier.

**O Song of Life, you vitalize,
all hearts you truly synchronize.
O Sacred Sound, you alchemize,
turn earth into a paradise.**

9. I immerse myself in the River of Life. I am now moving with
and in the River of Life instead of being behind trying to catch
up. The River of Life is not a path because there are no distinct steps, just the smooth, never-ending flow of God's Being
in which all life is one undivided whole.

Omega, my heart is ablaze,
my life is in an upward phase.
Come teach me now the secret phrase,
so that I can this planet raise.

**O Song of Life, you vitalize,
all hearts you truly synchronize.
O Sacred Sound, you alchemize,
turn earth into a paradise.**

3. I bless everything

1. The key to receiving what God gives me freely is to start giving. True giving means that the act of giving is separated from
any consideration of a return. I give because I know I am a sun
of God's light and it is my nature to give, to radiate light. It is my
nature to share who I am.

Beloved Alpha, God's great plan,
in Central Sun it all began,
what wondrous vision of a world,
the cosmic spheres were then unfurled.

Beloved Alpha, in your light,
I now see God with inner sight,
as man I will no longer live,
my life to God I fully give.

2. Pure giving carries its own reward. It is in the act of giving that I feel the reward of inner fulfillment. This is the inner sense of wholeness, of knowing I have more than enough to give. This is the abundant life.

Beloved Alpha, serve the All,
this is Creator's timeless call,
from out Creator's perfect whole,
sprang lifestreams with a sacred goal.

Beloved Alpha, in your light,
I now see God with inner sight,
as man I will no longer live,
my life to God I fully give.

3. Abundance is beyond lack. I am in a state of abundance, and I know I have more than I need for myself. The natural reaction is to give of my abundance to others. That is why God is giving of himself to me. I am the sun that always shines.

Beloved Alpha, all was one,
as we were sent from Central Sun,
to you we shall in time return,
for cosmic union we do yearn.

Beloved Alpha, in your light,
I now see God with inner sight,
as man I will no longer live,
my life to God I fully give.

4. In every situation I encounter, I seek to bless everyone involved and the outer conditions. No matter how challenging the situation might be, no matter what other people do *to* me or don't do *for* me, I always seek to bless them so that they can get to know better and thereby do better.

Beloved Alpha, I now see,
you with Omega form the key,
it was from your polarity,
that I received identity.

Beloved Alpha, in your light,
I now see God with inner sight,
as man I will no longer live,
my life to God I fully give.

5. I am centered in my heart and I focus on allowing the unconditional love of God to flow into any situation. I see the immaculate concept for how the situation could be transformed. I deliberately bless everything and everyone—with no desire for revenge or punishment but with a pure desire to see everything come closer to the perfect vision of the Christ mind.

Beloved Alpha, cosmic gate,
the nexus of your figure-eight,
I sprang from Cosmic Cube so bright,
I am at heart a spark of light.

Beloved Alpha, in your light,
I now see God with inner sight,
as man I will no longer live,
my life to God I fully give.

6. I am blessing everything and everyone I encounter. I am blessing every situation, every condition, every person. I am blessing myself. I always look beyond outer conditions and reach for the higher vision of the Christ mind.

Beloved Alpha, from your womb,
I did descend to matter's tomb,
but buried I will be no more,
my inner vision you restore.

Beloved Alpha, in your light,
I now see God with inner sight,
as man I will no longer live,
my life to God I fully give.

7. I am here to bless and magnify everything. I am here to raise up everything so that it can transcend imperfections. I do this by letting the light of God flow unconditionally. The light can do its work according to a higher vision, perhaps even a higher vision than I can grasp with my outer mind.

Beloved Alpha, I now know,
the love you did on me bestow,
a co-creator, I will bring,
the light to make all matter sing.

**Beloved Alpha, in your light,
I now see God with inner sight,
as man I will no longer live,
my life to God I fully give.**

8. I do not judge with the outer mind what the light and the love should be doing. I am letting the light flow and do its work. The love of God, the light of God, will magnify the situation and raise it higher according to the vision of Christ.

Beloved Alpha, on this earth,
a new age we are giving birth,
for we are here to bring the love,
that you are sending from Above.

**Beloved Alpha, in your light,
I now see God with inner sight,
as man I will no longer live,
my life to God I fully give.**

9. The true key to happiness, the true key to peace of mind, is to overcome the tendency to judge everything according to a dualistic standard. I am allowing my dualistic expectations to die one by one. I reach for the higher vision of the Christ mind.

Beloved Alpha, you and me,
we form a true polarity,
as up Above, so here below,
with life's own river I do flow.

Beloved Alpha, in your light,
I now see God with inner sight,
as man I will no longer live,
my life to God I fully give.

4. I find my true purpose

1. I know who I really am and I see the greater purpose for which I came into the material universe. The petty, self-centered expectations and desires of my mortal self are insignificant, and I am spontaneously letting them pass into the all-consuming fire of God's love.

Omega, I now meditate,
upon your throne in cosmic gate.
I'm born out of the figure-eight,
that Alpha and you co-create.

O Song of Life, you vitalize,
all hearts you truly synchronize.
O Sacred Sound, you alchemize,
turn earth into a paradise.

2. I am part of a large group of spiritual beings who volunteered to take embodiment at this time in order to help bring God's kingdom to earth. I am here for a purpose that is far grander than any of the desires of my mortal self. I am plunging myself into the River of Life and feeling that I am fulfilling my reason for being.

> Omega, in your sacred space,
> my cosmic parents I embrace.
> I see that it is such a grace,
> that I take part in cosmic race.
>
> **O Song of Life, you vitalize,**
> **all hearts you truly synchronize.**
> **O Sacred Sound, you alchemize,**
> **turn earth into a paradise.**

3. I am making the decision to step up to an entirely different approach to life, an approach that is not centered around the little self but around the greater Self that I am. It is time to start living like the spiritual being I AM.

> Omega in the Central Sun,
> you show me life is cosmic fun.
> And thus a victory is won,
> my homeward journey has begun.
>
> **O Song of Life, you vitalize,**
> **all hearts you truly synchronize.**
> **O Sacred Sound, you alchemize,**
> **turn earth into a paradise.**

4. I am allowing the River of Life to flow through me and take me where I need to go. I fully and unconditionally surrender to the higher will of my I AM Presence. I say with Jesus: "Nevertheless not as I will, but as thou wilt."

> Omega, femininity
> is doorway to infinity.
> With you I have affinity,
> to know my own divinity.

> **O Song of Life, you vitalize,**
> **all hearts you truly synchronize.**
> **O Sacred Sound, you alchemize,**
> **turn earth into a paradise.**

5. The higher will to which I surrender is not the will of an external being. It is the will of my own higher Being, the will that the Conscious You used when I created my divine plan. I surrender the dualistic, ego-crazed will of my mortal self that truly is alien to my own will.

> Omega, in your cosmic flow,
> my plan divine I clearly know.
> My heart is now a lamp aglow,
> as love on all I do bestow.

> **O Song of Life, you vitalize,**
> **all hearts you truly synchronize.**
> **O Sacred Sound, you alchemize,**
> **turn earth into a paradise.**

6. In experiencing the self-transcending River of Life, I am fully appreciating the nature of God. I am fully submerged in the River of Life, flowing with it and experiencing the abundant life that will forever become more in a cosmic dance of such beauty and joy that the mortal self can never comprehend it.

Omega, cosmic Mother Flame,
this is the light from which I came.
As I take part in cosmic game,
Christ victory I do proclaim.

O Song of Life, you vitalize,
all hearts you truly synchronize.
O Sacred Sound, you alchemize,
turn earth into a paradise.

7. I am leaving the desert of the mortal self and plunging myself into the Living Waters of the River of Life. I am letting my mortal self die so that the real me can be reborn into my true identity as an integral part of God's magnificent creation.

Omega, I now comprehend,
why I did to earth descend.
And thus I fully do intend,
to help this planet to ascend.

O Song of Life, you vitalize,
all hearts you truly synchronize.
O Sacred Sound, you alchemize,
turn earth into a paradise.

8. I am moving towards the infinite horizon of God's self-awareness that truly is becoming my self-awareness. God is All and in all. I am more than the mortal self and I too am All and in all.

Omega, I do now aspire,
to join the ranks of cosmic choir.
My heart burns with a Christic fire,
that is this planet's sanctifier.

**O Song of Life, you vitalize,
all hearts you truly synchronize.
O Sacred Sound, you alchemize,
turn earth into a paradise.**

9. I am letting my light so shine before men that they may see my good works and glorify God in all life. I have found my place in the tapestry of life, the fullness of God's creation, which is far beyond the vastness of the night sky. I am one with Mother Mary as I take my place as a spiritual star in the firmament of God's infinite Being.

Omega, my heart is ablaze,
my life is in an upward phase.
Come teach me now the secret phrase,
so that I can this planet raise.

**O Song of Life, you vitalize,
all hearts you truly synchronize.
O Sacred Sound, you alchemize,
turn earth into a paradise.**

Sealing

In the name of the Divine Mother, I call to Alpha, Omega and Mother Mary for the sealing of myself and all people in my circle of influence in the creative flow of the Divine Mother, the River of Life. I call for the multiplication of my calls by all representatives of the Divine Mother, so that we form the perfect figure-eight flow of "As Above, so below." Thus, I accept that this is fully manifest, because the mouth of the Lord, the Divine Mother that I AM, has spoken it. Amen.

AFTERWORD

My beloved, the purpose of this course is to give you the tools for transforming your consciousness by raising yourself out of the darkness of duality and into the light of the Christ consciousness. This can happen only when you understand and apply the Key of Knowledge. This course is meant to be an outer tool for stimulating intuitive insights from your Christ self and spiritual teachers. Such insights will be carefully adapted to your present level of consciousness and can therefore help you take the next step on your personal path. The teachings in this course are carefully designed to give you the insights you need at any level of the spiritual path. It would be naive to think that you can read this course once and extract everything you could possibly gain from it. This course is the gift that keeps on giving, in that it can serve as an inspiration at any level of the spiritual path. You can never outgrow this course for it truly has teachings that are given for and at many different levels of consciousness. I encourage you to not forget about this course but to use it over and over again, perhaps even read a small section daily, either before you give an invocation or before you go to sleep.

My goal for this course has been to provide you with an understanding of the basic dilemma of human existence, namely that people have become trapped in the duality consciousness. I have exposed to you the basic dynamics of the mortal self, but even a course as long as this one cannot explain every aspect of the mortal self or everything you need to know in order to walk the spiritual path. I encourage you to read others books about spirituality as you feel directed from within. Certainly, you might want to look at the many other books and teachings given through this messenger.

Be aware that the key to taking a step up the spiral staircase is to have an intuitive insight that replaces a particular dualistic illusion. Such an insight is beyond intellectual understanding. It can be triggered by an outer experience, but the purpose of any true spiritual teaching is to trigger such insights through words so that you can learn your lesson without experiencing the physical consequences of your former actions. Triggering an intuitive experience through words is a highly individual process. Two people might read the same words and one person understands the point intellectually whereas the other has an intuitive experience. The reason is that the words used did not trigger an intuitive experience for the first person.

I encourage you to read other books that talk about the same topics. How can one course use words that will work equally well for all people? Even though I attempt to explain the important points in different contexts and by using different words, there is no guarantee that this course will trigger an intuitive experience for you. Do not become discouraged or think that there is something wrong with you. Keep searching for other books and you will eventually find something that will help you rise higher. At some point in the future you might return to this course and find that you now understand it in a deeper way than before.

My final thought is to, once again, point out the importance of never stopping the process of self-transcendence. Keep taking the next step on the spiritual path until you know – with an inner knowing that is beyond the false security of your mortal self – that you are back in the River of Life. Then flow with that river as it takes you far beyond what you can imagine with your present state of consciousness. God's abundance is infinite and when you flow with the River of Life, you will go far beyond any limitation that might have been programmed into your mind in this world. The tapestry of life, the fullness of God's creation, is far beyond the vastness of the night sky. I look forward to greeting you as you take your place as a spiritual star in the firmament of God's infinite Being.

***

I want to comment on the use of my invocations. If you have followed this course as intended, you will have given an invocation a day for 216 days, and this vigil is designed to give you a significant shift to a higher level of consciousness.

Obviously, I cannot guarantee that giving an invocation a day for 216 days will reverse all imperfections created over many lifetimes. If you experience that you are in a positive spiral, I think you will be motivated to continue using my invocations. I have given a number of other invocations [See *www.transcendencetoolbox.com*] that each have a specific focus. I invite you to use them according to your individual situation and inner direction.

I will continue to release new invocations as the collective consciousness is raised, and I hope you will see the value of taking part in a planetary movement to use my invocations. When you join with people around the world to give a specific invocation once a day for a period of time, the power of the invocations will be multiplied exponentially with the number of people participating. This can be a very powerful force for world transformation, and doing something for the world will greatly increase your own spiritual growth. Giving an invocation is a powerful way to send an impulse into the cosmic mirror that will inevitably be reflected back to you in the form of a more abundant life.

As the representative of the Divine Mother for earth, my desire is for all people to have the abundant life that it is the Divine Father's good pleasure to give them. May you be more open to receiving it now than you were before starting this course.

About the Author

Kim Michaels is an accomplished writer and author. He has conducted spiritual conferences and workshops in 14 countries, has counseled hundreds of spiritual students and has done numerous radio shows on spiritual topics. Kim has been on the spiritual path since 1976. He has studied a wide variety of spiritual teachings and practiced many techniques for raising consciousness. Since 2002 he has served as a messenger for Jesus and other ascended masters. He has brought forth extensive teachings about the mystical path, many of them available for free on his websites: *www.askrealjesus.com, www.ascendedmasteranswers.com, www.ascendedmasterlight.com* and *www.transcendencetoolbox.com*. For personal information, visit Kim at *www.KimMichaels.info*.

CPSIA information can be obtained
at www.ICGtesting.com
Printed in the USA
BVHW01s1328010218
506848BV00034B/532/P